Jon Steele

THE THIRD MAN FACTOR

John Grigsby Geiger was born in Ithaca, New York,
and graduated in history from the University of Alberta.
The author of five non-fiction books, including the
international bestseller *Frozen in Time: The Fate of
the Franklin Expedition*, his work has been translated
into ten languages. He also authored, with Dr Peter
Suedfeld, the scholarly study 'The Sensed Presence
as a Coping Resource in Extreme Environments'. He
is editorial board editor at the *Globe and Mail* and
a senior fellow at Massey College, University of Toronto.
He is a governor of the Royal Canadian Geographical
Society and chair of the Society's Expeditions
Committee, a fellow of the Royal Geographical
Society and of the Explorers Club, and a member of
the Advisory Board of wings World Quest. He received
the Queen's Golden Jubilee Medal.

THE THIRD MAN FACTOR

SURVIVING THE IMPOSSIBLE

JOHN GEIGER

CANONGATE

Edinburgh · London · New York · Melbourne

This paperback edition published in 2010 by Canongate Books

1

Copyright © John Grigsby Geiger, 2009

The moral right of the author has been asserted

First published in Canada in 2009 by the Penguin Group (Canada),
90 Eglinton Avenue East, Suite 700, Toronto, Ontario, Canada M4P 2Y3
(a division of Pearson Canada Inc.)

First published in Great Britain in 2009 by
Canongate Books Ltd, 14 High Street, Edinburgh EH1 1TE

www.johngeiger.co.uk
www.thirdmanfactor.com
www.meetatthegate.com

Please see pages 257–258 for copyright acknowledgments

British Library Cataloguing-in-Publication Data
A catalogue record for this book is available on
request from the British Library

ISBN 978 1 84767 420 3

Printed and bound in Great Britain by
Clays Ltd, St Ives plc

FOR JAMES SUTHERLAND ANGUS GEIGER

JUNE 15–21, 2007

Who is the third who walks always beside you?
When I count, there are only you and I together
But when I look ahead up the white road
There is always another one walking beside you.
Gliding wrapt in a brown mantle, hooded
I do not know whether a man or woman
—But who is that on the other side of you?

—T.S. ELIOT, 'THE WASTE LAND'

CONTENTS

FOREWORD BY VINCENT LAM

John Geiger and I met and travelled together in the Arctic—the vast, icy, and beautiful landscape of the explorers. It is one of the places where men and women have sought to make lonely and difficult journeys to discover both the place and themselves. It is in such conditions that the Third Man has often appeared to comfort and assist lonely travellers. When John first told me about the Third Man phenomenon, and that he was writing a book to explore this subject, I recognized the topic immediately. I had experienced it myself.

My encounter with the Third Man occurred during my pre-medical studies. One winter, over a span of weeks, I faced a succession of daunting exams encompassing a huge range of material. I felt that I must perform flawlessly, and would otherwise ruin my chances of being admitted to medical school. During those weeks, I did nothing but study, eat, sleep, and write exams. Outside, it snowed steadily. Even when I slept, I dreamt of molecular biology and biochemistry, so that I never woke refreshed, only anxious to open the books again. I developed a sort of tunnel vision about my life because on these exams hinged my course grades, upon which rested my prospects for medical school, and that was a great part of my sense of self-worth and hope for my own future.

One evening, after a long day of intensive studying, I was completely exhausted by both the complexity of abstract information and the level of detail that I was trying to absorb. I decided to take a shower. In the shower, I sensed a presence. It did not alarm or frighten me because, like many in this book, I knew immediately that the presence, or Third Man, wished to help me. I felt that my guardian angel had been sent by God to guide me at a difficult time. The angel spoke to me and gave me advice. It offered practical suggestions about how to conduct my daily life, how to learn, and how to manage my emotions. The angel did not promise admission to medical school, but reassured me that things would work out as they should, that I should have faith.

I decided to record some of this valuable advice. I got out of the shower, sat down at the computer, and wrote several pages of guidance that was directly dictated by the angel's voice. I saved these words on both the hard drive and a floppy disk, went to bed, and had my first restful sleep in weeks.

Strangely, when I went to look for those pages of advice, to review what I had been told, I could not find them. I distinctly remember having saved the file in two separate locations because of its importance. My computer had not crashed. Nonetheless, I could find no trace of the dictation of my angel. As for others in this book, my angel departed when I was back on the right track. The rest of my exam period went smoothly. I continued to study

intensively, and felt more peaceful doing so. I scored high marks
and went on to medical school.

Humans are inclined to be connected to one another. We seek
the company of friends and family, we congregate in towns and
cities, and the groups we belong to—our communities of faith, our
co-workers, and our neighbourhoods—form part of our sense of self
and place. Yet, despite these social inclinations, there are journeys
that humans make that are difficult, and undertaken either alone or
in small groups. Some of these challenges are sought voluntarily, as
in the case of gruelling, long-distance voyages to remote parts of the
world, and in the practice of some traditional spiritual quests. Other
such journeys spring unexpectedly upon those involved, precipitated
by mishap in the outdoors, or by cataclysms such as the attack on the
World Trade Center on September 11, 2001. What happens to
people who are tired, afraid, alone, and have no choice but to address
their threatening situation? This fascinating book explores the ways
in which some are helped by a welcome presence.

My visit from a Third Man, whom I believe to be my guardian
angel, occurred within a personal moment of crisis, rather than in
the gruelling physical circumstances described by many of this
book's subjects. This sits well with John's argument that the Third
Man likely occurs more commonly than we recognize, and is not
limited to extreme travel and exploration.

As a physician, I am trained to understand and work with a
certain biological, empirical reality. In one sense, we are a collection of muscles, bone, neurons, and other bits and pieces that can
be measured and observed. Yet, in many ways, knowing the
mechanics of the human body reminds me of the reality that the

sum of the parts do not make the whole. Our experience as people may occur literally just beneath the surface of our skin, but a simple knowledge of anatomy is not sufficient to explain the everyday phenomena of consciousness or thought.

As a writer and as a person, I know that human experience is very real, and yet anyone would be hard-pressed to weigh or measure the dimensions of love, anger, fear, or pride in the way that the mass of an organ can be measured. Certain complex experiences—the quiet pleasure of watching a stunning expanse of sky, the excitement and satisfaction of reading a wonderful book, the strength of religious faith—are at once concrete and utterly ephemeral. They are part of the mystery of being human, the wispy territory in which we exist somewhere between our ambitious science and our daily frailties. In the mysterious gap between our knowledge of biological mechanisms and our everyday experience as people, we find that things occur that are not easily explainable, but are no less real for that.

The Third Man is one of these phenomena. It is something that happens when people are placed in difficult circumstances, often when their very survival is at stake. Amazingly, despite the harrowing situations in which it often arises, most judge the experience to be valuable and positive—for many, a life-affirming force. *The Third Man Factor* is an account both of physically amazing voyages and personal discovery at the extremes of human experience. The Third Man speaks to both the ways in which we are fundamentally alone, and to the ways that as humans we always contain the possibility of relationship with others. It reassures us that even in the worst of times, help may come.

CHAPTER ONE

The Third Man

RON DIFRANCESCO WAS AT HIS DESK at Euro Brokers, a financial trading firm, on the eighty-fourth floor of the south tower of the World Trade Center in New York when the plane struck the north tower opposite him. It was 8:46 A.M. on September 11, 2001. There was a loud boom, and the lights in the south tower flickered. Grey smoke poured from the north tower. At impact, all the stairwells in the north tower became impassable from the ninety-second floor up, trapping 1,356 people. Some waved desperately for help. Most of those who worked at Euro Brokers started to evacuate the building, but DiFrancesco stayed. A few minutes later, a terse announcement was broadcast over the building's public-address system. An incident had occurred in the other building, but, "Building Two is secure. There is no need to evacuate Building Two. If you are in the midst of evacuation, you may return to your office by using the re-entry doors on the re-entry floors and the elevators to return to your office. Repeat,

Building Two is secure ..."[1] DiFrancesco, a money-market broker originally from Hamilton, Ontario, telephoned his wife, Mary, to tell her that an airplane had hit the other tower, but that he was fine and intended to stay at work. "It was tower one that was hit, I'm in tower two," he told her.[2] He tried to focus his attention on the screens of financial data on his desk. Then a friend from Toronto called. "Get the hell out," he said.[3] They spoke briefly, then DiFrancesco agreed. He called a few major clients and his wife, Mary, again, to tell them of his change of plans. Then he began walking towards a bank of elevators.

At 9:03 A.M., seventeen minutes after the first impact, the second plane hit. United Airlines Flight 175, travelling at 950 kilometres an hour, sliced into the south tower, igniting an intense fire fed by 90,000 litres of jet fuel. The Boeing 767, carrying fifty-six passengers, two pilots, and seven flight attendants, had been commandeered by al Qaeda terrorists after taking off from Boston's Logan International Airport en route to Los Angeles. It struck the building's south face between floors seventy-seven and eighty-five. The plane banked just before it slammed into the building. The higher wing cut into the Euro Brokers offices, while the fuselage hit the Fuji Bank offices on the seventy-ninth through eighty-second floors.

DiFrancesco was hurled against the wall and showered with ceiling panels and other debris. Brackets, air ducts, and cables sprang from the ceiling. The building swayed. The trading floor he had just left no longer existed. DiFrancesco entered stairway A. The south tower had three emergency stairwells. Fortuitously, he had stumbled on the only one that offered hope of escape for people above the zone of impact. The stairwell was shielded from destruction by an enormous elevator machine-room on the eighty-first floor, where the nose of the 767 hit. The elevator equipment covered more than half the floor space, and had forced the tower's architects to route stairway A from the centre of the building towards the northwest corner—the farthest point from the impact zone.[4] DiFrancesco was joined by others in the stairwell and all began to descend. The stairwell was smoky, lit only by a flashlight carried by Brian Clark, an executive vice-president at Euro Brokers and a volunteer fire marshal on the eighty-fourth floor. Three flights down, they encountered a heavy woman and a male colleague who were coming up. "You've got to go up. You can't go down," the woman insisted. "There's too much smoke and flames below."[5]

They debated whether to ascend, and either wait for firefighters or a rooftop rescue by helicopter, or persist with their descent, risking the smoke and flames. Clark shone his flashlight into his colleagues' faces, asking each, "Up or down?" They heard someone call for help. Brian Clark grabbed DiFrancesco by the sleeve. "Come on, Ron. Let's get this fellow."[6] The two men left the stairwell and fought through debris on the eighty-first floor to locate the person. But DiFrancesco was soon overcome by smoke. He had a backpack, and held it over his face in an attempt to filter the air. But it wasn't helping, and he was forced to retreat. Gasping for air, he decided to ascend, hoping to escape the smoke. He climbed several flights but at each landing, when he tested the fire doors, he discovered they were locked. A mechanism designed to prevent smoke from flooding the building had malfunctioned after the impact, preventing any of the doors, even on designated re-entry floors, from being opened. He continued to climb, and eventually caught up with some colleagues from Euro Brokers, several of whom were helping the large woman. She had convinced all of them that the best escape route was up the south tower. But as DiFrancesco continued up, the stairwell became more crowded. All the fire doors were locked. He guessed he reached the ninety-first floor of the 110-storey building. Ron DiFrancesco is normally unflappable. He is a money-market broker in a high-stakes business that demands steel nerves. But he is slightly claustro-phobic, and with the intensifying smoke, he began to panic. He thought of his family, that he had to see his wife and children again at all costs. He determined that he was "gonna make it out."[7] DiFrancesco decided to turn around and start back down. This time, the situation was much worse. Thick smoke poured up the narrow stairwell.

He groped his way down, unable to see more than a few feet ahead. He stopped at a landing in the middle of the impact zone, on the seventy-ninth or eightieth floor. Overcome by the smoke, he joined others, about a dozen people in all, some stretched out, face-down on the concrete floor, others crouched in the corners, all gasping for air. They were blocked from descending further by a collapsed wall. He could see panic in their eyes, and fear. Some were crying. Several began to slip into unconsciousness. Then, something remarkable happened: "Someone told me to get up."[8] Someone, he said, "called me."[9] The voice—which was male, but did not belong to one of the people in the stairwell—was insistent: "Get up!" It addressed DiFrancesco by his first name, and gave him encouragement: "It was, 'Hey! You can do this.'"[10] But it was more than a voice; there was also a vivid sense of a physical presence.

A lot of people made split-second decisions that day that determined whether they lived or died. What is different about Ron DiFrancesco is that, at a critical moment, he received help from a seemingly external source. He had the sensation that "somebody lifted me up."[11] He felt that he was being guided: "I was led to the stairs. I don't think something grabbed my hand, but I was definitely led."[12] He resumed his descent, and soon saw a point of light. He followed it, fighting his way through drywall and other debris that had collapsed, obstructing the stairwell. Then he encountered flames. He recoiled from the fire. But still someone helped him. "An angel" urged him along. "There was still danger, so it led me to the stairwell, led me to break through, led me to run through the fire.... There was obviously somebody encouraging me. That's not where you go, you don't go toward the fire …"[13] He covered his head with his forearms and continued down, now running. He was singed by the fire. He believed the flames continued for three storeys. Finally, he reached a clear, lit stairwell below the fire, on the seventy-sixth floor. Only then did the sense of a benevolent helper, one who had been with him for five minutes, end. Said DiFrancesco: "I think at that point it let me go."

When he was making his way down, he passed three firefighters climbing up the stairs. "I'm having trouble breathing," he said.[14] He was told he would find help at the bottom. DiFrancesco continued down as fast as he could, finally reaching the plaza level. He headed for an exit, but was stopped by a security guard who told him it was too dangerous. He looked out in horror at the falling debris and victims. He was directed to another exit. He walked back through the concourse towards the northeast exit, near Church Street. He was still in extreme danger. Fifty-six minutes had passed since the plane hit. The impact had severed many of the south tower's vertical support columns. The heat from the explosion and fire had weakened the steel trusses. The floors of the crippled building began to "pancake down" in a floor-by-floor collapse. As he approached the Church Street exit, DiFrancesco heard an "ungodly roar." He saw a fireball as the building compressed. He doesn't know what happened next, and was unconscious for some time after his narrow escape, waking up much later at Saint Vincent's hospital in Manhattan.

Ron DiFrancesco was the last person out of the south tower of the World Trade Center before it came down at 9:59 A.M. The south tower collapsed in ten seconds, causing a ferocious windstorm and massive debris cloud. According to the official 9/11 Commission report, DiFrancesco was one of only four people to escape the building from above the eighty-first floor, the centre of impact for United Airlines Flight 175.[15] Moments before the tower collapsed, NYPD officers within the building informed dispatch that they had encountered a stream of people descending a stairwell at the twenties level. None of those people survived, but it is believed they were descending from above the impact zone, in which case they had followed DiFrancesco's lead, but not immediately, and even a few seconds later would have been too late. To this day, DiFrancesco cannot understand why he survived when so many others did not. But he has no doubt about the reason for his escape. A man of deep religious conviction, he attributes it to a divine intervention.

THE EARLY MORNING WAS PERFECTLY STILL and silent. James Sevigny, a twenty-eight-year-old university student originally from Hanover, New Hampshire, and his friend Richard Whitmire set out to climb Deltaform, a mountain in the Canadian Rockies near Lake Louise, Alberta. They ascended a couloir, an ice gully, in bright late-winter light on April 1, 1983, roped together and using ice screws in their climb. Whitmire, a thirty-three-year-old from Bellingham, Washington, was in the lead and at one point cut some ice loose. He yelled a warning—"Falling ice!"—to Sevigny below. The ice catapulted safely past Sevigny, but was suddenly followed by the collapse of a snowfield above the couloir on the north face. A tremendous roar broke the silence, and the bright light was consumed by instant darkness. An avalanche swept the two men more than six hundred metres to the base of Deltaform. Sevigny was unconscious almost from the moment the avalanche hit. Whitmire might have escaped had the pair not been roped together.

Sevigny regained consciousness, he guessed, an hour later. He was severely injured. His back was broken in two places. One arm was fractured, the other had severed nerves from a broken scapula and was hanging limply at his side. He had cracked ribs, torn ligaments on both knees, suffered internal bleeding, and his face— broken nose, broken teeth, and open wounds—was a mess. He had no idea where he was and what had happened to him. At first he thought he might be in Nepal, where he had spent six months trekking a few years earlier. Sevigny had finished his master's degree and at the time of the accident was basically a "climbing bum," living out of his Volkswagen. It took a while for him to recognize the mountain, but gradually Sevigny remembered the climb, and struggled to his feet to look for his friend. Whitmire lay nearby, and from his misshapen body, it was clear he was dead. Sevigny lay down beside him, certain he would soon follow. "I figured that if I fell asleep, it would be the easiest way to go." He lay there for about twenty minutes. Shivers were gradually replaced by the sensation of warmth brought about by shock and hypothermia, and he began to doze off. He realized there was no vast gulf separating life and death, but rather a fine line, and at that moment, Sevigny thought it would be easier to cross that line than to struggle on.

He then felt a sudden, strange sensation of an invisible being very close at hand. "It was something I couldn't see but it was a physical presence." The presence communicated mentally and its message was clear: "You can't give up, you have to try."

> It told me what to do. The only decision I had made at that point of time was to lay down next to Rick and to fall asleep and to accept death. That's the only decision I made. All decisions made subsequent to that were made by the presence. I was merely taking instructions.... I understood what it wanted me to do. It wanted me to live.[16]

The presence urged Sevigny to get up. It dispensed practical advice. It told him, for example, to follow the blood dripping from the tip of his nose as if it were an arrow pointing the way. As he walked, he kept breaking through the crust of the deep snow, and was almost unable to pull his feet back up because of his injuries. Part of the time he crawled. The presence, which stood behind his right shoulder, implored him to continue even when the struggle to survive seemed untenable. And when it fell silent, Sevigny still knew his companion was close at hand. Because of its enormous empathy, he thought of the presence as a woman. She accompanied Sevigny across the Valley of the Ten Peaks, to the camp he and Whitmire had started from earlier that day, a point where he hoped he could find food and warmth, and perhaps help. Such were his injuries that it took all day to make the crossing of about one and a half kilometres, and his companion was with him every step of the way.

When he reached the camp, Sevigny could not crawl into his sleeping bag because his injuries were too severe, and he could not eat because his teeth were broken and his face was swollen. He could not even light the stove. He sat down and, from the position of the sun, realized it was late afternoon. He believed that in a couple of hours he would be dead, after all. "I recall knowing I was about to die, pathetically, in a fetal position in the snow."[17] He had always felt that he might die while climbing, so it came as no real surprise, but he thought about how devastated his mother would be. Then, at once, he thought he heard some other voices, and called out for help. There was no response. It was at that moment that he felt the presence leave. "It was gone, there was nothing there, there was no presence. There was no one telling me to do anything and I could tell that it had left." For the first time since the avalanche, he was overwhelmed by a sense of loneliness:

What I thought then was I'm hallucinating, the presence knows I'm dead, and it has just given up on me. But as it turns out, those were people, and they did come up. One of them skied out and they flew me out that night in a helicopter. In fact, the presence had left because it knew I was safe.[18]

Allan Derbyshire, who was in a party with two other cross-country skiers, heard a faint cry: "Help! I've been in an avalanche." Had Derbyshire not heard him, Sevigny would have been left for the night, and would have almost certainly died, as there were no other skiers or climbers in the area. Derbyshire found him "staggering around in bad shape.... I got the impression that his condition was critical." Despite that, Sevigny was "quite lucid when I asked him what had happened, although he was obviously weak, soaked in blood, and in shock."[19] Sevigny, however, made no mention of his unseen companion. In a newspaper interview, Banff National Park rescue specialist Tim Auger later said Sevigny "was lucky both to survive the fall and then be discovered by cross-country skiers who happened to be in the area."[20] Sevigny understood there was more than luck involved.

THE OPENING TO THE UNDERWATER CAVE was barely wider than her shoulders. When she slipped through, Stephanie Schwabe entered a world few have ever seen, a world of absolute darkness now brilliantly illuminated by her lights. The crystalline walls of the cave glittered like jewels. Bone-white stalactites and stalagmites reached out towards her as she swam deeper and further into the Mermaid's Lair, on the south side of Grand Bahama Island, to her destination, nearly three hundred metres away, and thirty metres deep. For all its strangeness, it was a routine dive for the forty-year-old underwater explorer rated by *Diver International* magazine as one of the top divers in the world—except for the fact she was alone.

Usually, Schwabe had dived with her husband, British cave explorer Rob Palmer. He was an expert on the Blue Holes of the Bahamas, a system of spectacular submarine caves that includes the world's deepest known Blue Hole, a vertical cave given its name because the water of the cave is much darker than the blue of the shallow water around it. It is a world of skeletal calcite appendages and vast hidden cathedrals, inhabited only by small colourless species of sea life, many unknown to science.[21] Even today, most of the caves remain unexplored. The Mermaid's Lair, an extensive horizontal cave, was an exception. It had been explored previously by Palmer and Schwabe together, but not this day. Palmer was dead. He had failed to surface after a dive in the Red Sea earlier that year. Schwabe was left to continue alone their challenging and dangerous work, researching the water-filled Bahamian cave systems.

It was late August 1997, and Schwabe, a geomicrobiologist, was there to collect sediment samples for another scientist who was studying dust from the Sahara Desert that, centuries earlier, had been carried by winds across the Atlantic Ocean and deposited on the floor of the Mermaid's Lair. The day had already been unexpectedly eventful. When she was driving out to the dive site, Schwabe had been forced to stop by a poisonwood tree that had been blown down by a storm the day before, blocking the road. It took all her strength to push it aside, and in the process she suffered serious skin irritations from alkaloids in the sap. She decided to continue, however, and having reached her destination, climbed into scuba gear and began her dive, focused on collecting the samples and exiting quickly.

Once she reached the floor of the cave, she spent half an hour diligently gathering the red dust samples. When she was finished, Schwabe packed her equipment away and for the first time since she had reached the spot, lifted her eyes. She suddenly realized that she could not see her guide-line. She searched for it, at first calmly, but then with increasing anxiety, but could not find it. Cave diving is technically challenging. Unlike other forms of diving, in an emergency, the diver cannot ascend directly to the surface, but often must swim horizontally, sometimes through a maze of narrow passages. The guide-line is vital to get safely out of such complex submarine cave systems. It is literally a lifeline. Without it, a diver can quickly become disoriented, eventually run out of air, and be asphyxiated.

Schwabe experienced a growing sense of panic. She immediately realized her mistake. When she dived with Palmer, she often relied on him to serve as her guide. On this dive, she had inadvertently fallen into the same old pattern, and lost sight of the line. "I had based my dive on the unplanned assumption that he was there." But he was not there and had not been for months; she was alone. She checked her tank gauge, and realized that she had only twenty minutes left. Schwabe's panic turned to anger. She flew into a rage, furious at Palmer for his death, her sense of loss as palpable as the terror she felt. Angry, too, at herself for "being so stupid"—

making an elementary diving mistake that threatened now to claim her own life. "For all intents and purposes, at that moment, I had given up on life. I was ready to leave this world. I was so depressed and I missed Rob so much. I had had enough of the pain."[22]

Then, at the height of the rage and sadness, Schwabe said, "I suddenly felt flushed and it seemed like my field of vision had become brighter." She vividly felt the presence of another being with her. There was no doubt in her mind that someone was with her in the cave. She believed it to be her dead husband. She heard his voice, communicating mentally with her. "All right, Steffi, calm down. Remember, believe you can, believe you can't, either way you are right. Remember?" It is something Palmer used to say to her all the time, acting as an invocation to her inner strength. Schwabe was stunned by the intervention, but it was a help to her, and she did calm down. She sat there on the floor of the cave, "trying to get a handle on why my brain was going this route." About fifteen minutes had passed since she realized she had lost the line. Time was running out.

When she looked up again, she did so with renewed resolve and calm. She methodically scanned the cave. She thought she saw the flash of a white line. Simultaneously, she felt as if the presence had gone. Schwabe was alone again in the cave. She looked up once more to where she caught a glimpse of her guide-line, and she saw it again. Schwabe immediately swam up to the line, and followed it out. Eventually she saw the blue entrance, where light filtered into the cave. She thought to herself, "today was not a good day to die." She felt as if she had been saved by a presence she was sure was her deceased husband.

RON DIFRANCESCO'S ENCOUNTER IN THE SOUTH tower of the World Trade Center; James Sevigny's, at the foot of Deltaform; and Stephanie Schwabe's, in the Mermaid's Lair of Grand Bahama Island, may sound like a curiosity, an unusual delusion shared by a few overstressed minds. But the amazing thing is this: Over the years, the experience has occurred again and again, not only to 9/11 survivors, mountaineers, and divers, but also to polar explorers, prisoners of war, solo sailors, shipwreck survivors, aviators, and astronauts. All have escaped traumatic events, only to tell strikingly similar stories of having experienced the close presence of a companion and helper, and even "of a sort of mighty person." This presence offered them a sense of protection, relief, guidance, and hope, and left the person convinced he or she was not alone but there was some other being at his or her side, when by any normal calculation there was none.

There is, it seems, a common experience that happens to people who confront life at its extremes, and strange as it may sound, given the cruel hardship they endure to reach that place, it is something wonderful. This radical notion—that an unseen presence has played a role in the success or survival of people who have reached the limits of human endurance—is based on the extraordinary testimony of scores of people who have emerged alive from extreme environments. To a man or woman, they report that at a critical point they were joined by an additional, unexplained friend who lent them the power to overcome the most dire circumstances. There is a name for the phenomenon: It's called the Third Man Factor.

Stressed minds are capable of playing some interesting tricks. When I was seven I experienced something I have always wanted to experience again. I was on a field trip with my father, K.W. Geiger, a geologist who was working for the Research Council of Alberta, surveying the bedrock topography of southern Alberta. It was a sweltering summer day, and we were walking along a fringe of unbroken grassland near the top bank of the Oldman River. We climbed up a steep, dry embankment. There was a faint perfume of prairie rose bushes in the still air. I was following my father when I was stopped dead in my tracks by a rattlesnake, coiled and ready to strike.[23] The noise was not calming, like a baby's rattle, but had a buzz of urgency about it. The snake was under a protruding rock that might have been a den. Most alarmingly, it was between my father and me. My father had passed by it and was standing above me on the embankment.

I am unsure today exactly what happened next, and how much of my memory is real, and how much is a child's overactive imagination. But I do remember it all very clearly. There was a moment of sheer terror. Then suddenly there was a physiological shift of perspective. I felt detached from my immediate situation, and surveyed the scene from another, impossible angle. I was two people in two places at one time. I saw my father and I saw a child, a child who could only have been me. If not me, then who? Yet I was seeing it all unfold from a distance, as an observer. Time seemed to slow. And yet it was all over in an instant. My father grabbed the boy with one arm and, with what seemed like superhuman strength, pitched him over his shoulder and out of danger. It was an unforgettable experience—one that could not possibly have happened as I remember it. Or could it? All I know is that in my memory of the incident, when I count, there are not two, but three people there.

Then, years later, while reading Sir Ernest Shackleton's narrative *South*, I came across his strange report of an unseen presence that joined him during his escape from Antarctica after the expedition's ship, *Endurance*, had been crushed by the ice. This is the most famous of all these encounters. It was Shackleton's experience that gave the phenomenon its name: the Third Man. When I started looking, I soon found other, similar reports. They were different from my own experience. Wilfrid Noyce explained that difference in his book, *They Survived: A Study of the Will to Live*. Noyce, a brilliant and fearless climber, described how he was struggling over the Geneva Spur of Mount Everest without oxygen when he experienced a "sense of duality": "I was two people, the upper self remaining calm and quite unaffected by the efforts of the panting lower." My own childhood experience, obviously triggered at a much lower threshold, seemed like just such a sense of duality. However, in more fully developed instances, Noyce explained, the phenomenon strengthens and "the second self sometimes puts on the clothing of another human."[24] It has happened, again and again, high in the mountains, in the open sea, in the frozen wastelands of the poles. Noyce considered it a "second self." But there are many other theories. Some say the Third Man is proof of the existence of guardian angels. Some say he's an hallucination. Some say he's real. What was going on here?

It amazed me that these stories had never been collected in a single place, and so I began to assemble them. For five years I contacted survivors, read through old handwritten journals, combed through published exploration narratives and survival stories. Sometimes, all the conditions seemed right for such an experience, but there would be no mention of it in any published account. Then, when I would approach a survivor—such as the British climber Tony Streather, who narrowly escaped death on Haramosh in the Himalayas—I would discover that it had happened again. An unseen being had intervened to help.

The stories only grew more astonishing, and I began to realize that I had a kind of natural history of adventure in the making, a record of all the disasters that can befall man on ice, mountain, sea, land, air, and space, all linked by the mysterious appearance of a Third Man. I came to see not only that I possessed this inventory of human response to extreme peril, but also that I had a record of what it takes to survive. What follows, then, are some of the most remarkable survival stories ever told. We share a vicarious fascination with tales of those who cheat death, but here the stories all add up to something more. Only by reliving such exploits is it possible to answer the question, who, or what, is the Third Man?

Where possible, I have organized the accounts by the type of endeavour: polar explorers, mountaineers, solo sailors, shipwreck survivors, aviators, and astronauts. I should also say here that these represent only the best of the stories. I have collected many more than this, and have chosen to anthologize the additional stories online. The website, **www.thirdmanfactor.com**, is not only a repository for these stories, but also will serve as a place where anyone can post either their personal experiences or stories they themselves have read or heard about.

Drawn from all these examples are vital clues—the five basic rules that govern the Third Man's appearance and invest the experience with meaning. These rules are the pathology of boredom, the principle of multiple triggers, the widow effect, the muse factor, and the power of the saviour. Together, they help to explain the onset of the Third Man Factor. But they are causal in nature; they do not explain his origins or where the power comes from. Over the years, various theories have been proposed to explain the Third Man, and running concurrently with these, interspersed among the chapters of the book, are accounts of the search for an explanation. These attempts at understanding are themselves a record of man's changing conception of himself. They begin with the guardian angel, followed by the sensed presence, and the shadow person. As clerics and then psychologists, and finally neurologists, theorized about the phenomenon, the trend has been a gradual reduction from the outside in, from God, to the mind, to the brain.

Whether any of these explanations is, finally, enough to account for the Third Man mystery you will have to wait and see. But in compiling these stories, one thing, at least, became clear to me. The Third Man represents a real and potent force for survival, and the ability to access this power is a factor, perhaps the most important factor, in determining who will succeed against seemingly insurmountable odds, and who will not.

Biologists have a term for the boundaries that the physical world imposes on human beings: "limit physiology."[25] At some definable point, as conditions change, humans can no longer succeed, and at a more critical point, they can no longer survive. It is a formula based on a series of scientific measurements. For example, an increase of only five degrees Celsius to core body temperature causes fatal heatstroke, or at minus fifty degrees

Celsius bare skin freezes in a minute. "To state it plainly, rarely does one person survive under extreme conditions when another dies simply because the survivor has greater will to live," wrote Claude Piantadosi in his study *The Biology of Human Survival*.

And yet, in these stories—in situations where success appears to be impossible, or death imminent—something happens. There, amid the anxiety, fear, blood, sadness, exhaustion, torment, isolation, and fatigue, is an outstretched hand—another existence, proffering a "transfusion of energy, encouragement, and instinctual wisdom from a seemingly external source."[26] A presence appears, a Third Man who, in the words of legendary Italian climber Reinhold Messner, "leads you out of the impossible."[27]

CHAPTER TWO

Shackleton's Angel

Four members of the Transglobe Expedition, under the leadership of Sir Ranulph Fiennes, pitched their camp at the foot of Ryvingen mountain on the south polar ice cap and braced for the desolation of an Antarctic winter. They set up their prefabricated huts, insulated with nothing more than cardboard. They erected their radio hut fifty metres from the generator hut, which itself was twenty-five metres from the main hut that would serve as the expedition's winter home. They secured radio masts against the blasts of wind and by the following month, February 1980, were ready for the onset of the Antarctic winter, with its twenty-four-hour night and temperatures that plunged to minus forty-five degrees Celsius. Here, at the edge of the Antarctic plateau, some 480 kilometres inland, they would have to withstand winter's assaults for eight months before Fiennes could attempt what had been done only once before—by British polar explorer Sir Vivian Fuchs in 1957–58—and cross the continent of Antarctica, part of a longer journey around the world on its polar axis using surface transport only.

As base commander and radio operator, Fiennes' wife, Virginia, Lady Fiennes—called "Ginnie"—was the expedition's conduit to the outside world. She was slightly built, spirited, and resourceful, and had the ability to "make big men quake in their boots with a flash of her bright blue eyes."[1] When ice buildup on the antennas, coupled with the fierce winds, tore the sixty-centimetre-long metal screws from the ground, allowing the antennas to flap freely, Ginnie Fiennes was the team member responsible for the repair. She struggled tirelessly and without complaint in the blizzards, a flashlight in her mouth, untangling wires. With time, the constant demands caused her to get overtired, and the hours spent alone, outside in the darkness, and inside her cramped radio hut, contributed to a general feeling of unease. In the frequent blizzards, she often had to drag a sledge loaded with recharged batteries to the hut from their living quarters, while clipped to a safety line. The relentless cold and wind, and the uninterrupted polar night, either pitch black, or lit faintly by the aurora or by moonlight, over the many months, compounded the agitation and introversion that accompanied their profound geographic isolation.

In May, another team member, Oliver Shepard, mentioned casually to Ginnie that he had heard footsteps following him from the generator hut. He attributed this to his imagination, but he was not the only one who experienced a sensation of unseen company. At one point Fiennes herself came into the main hut and told her husband: "There's something there." He protested, but she insisted:

"I don't mean a danger but … a *strong* presence."[2] The sense abated, and the situation returned to its routine, but then, during a storm in June, she again felt something close at hand: "*It* came round behind the radio shack and followed me back down the tunnel." The entity was not menacing, but it was unsettling. Ranulph Fiennes believed his wife was "frightened that she might see it."[3] He started accompanying her, hauling the sledge, and would stay in the radio hut with her. He never encountered anything, and she never felt the presence when he was with her. However, the stresses were only compounded as the Antarctic winter wore on. In October, Fiennes described Ginnie as "dog-tired and hallucinating…. From time to time she heard crying in the darkness and someone whispering indistinguishable words from close behind her."

By October 29, the worst weather had passed, and Ranulph Fiennes' three-man team set off using snowmobiles on their Antarctic crossing. Ginnie Fiennes and Simon Grimes, who had flown in to the Ryvingen camp, remained behind temporarily to maintain the vital communication link until a planned relocation. The camp now also served as a base from which air support could haul fuel for the snowmobiles as the expedition neared the South Pole. At one point, Grimes went alone to visit the radio hut, which was then in the process of being closed up. He wrote in his journal: "No sign of Ginnie's ghost, a presence which she … felt during the winter…. A youngish man, I gather…. Not malevolent, just there. The long solo nights in the hut must have enhanced her perception." Grimes described it now as "an empty hut with an aura. I sealed it up as I knew I would not want to go back up there." Before he left, he noticed some graffiti that Ginnie had scratched on the wall, using three different pens—at different times, he presumed. He found the words "rather scaring in a way":

> As whistlers' and gibbons' cries
> Screech in the ears
> The ghost of Ryvingen
> Burst into tears.
>
> "Why have you come to disturb me
> after these many years
> I will haunt and will taunt you
> And drive you away."[4]

Ginnie Fiennes experienced a phenomenon not uncommon on the Antarctic continent. The first south polar expeditions described cases of sailors who, "working in the dark have incontinently flung down their picks and shovels and have refused to leave the ship again without companions," wrote Raymond Priestly in his pioneering examination of the psychology of exploration. Studies have shown that the extreme cold experienced in polar regions itself has a limited impact on the psychological state of those who winter over. Instead, the research shows it is monotony—coupled with isolation and solitude—that accounts for much of the stress encountered at Antarctic stations. This is not unexpected. Human beings are a social species; so social that solitary confinement is considered the cruellest punishment; so social also that even in solitude, "we address our thoughts and acts to some infinite Socius [companion] who will understand and approve."[5]

Antarctic winters are spent in conditions of being alone together, that is, in a small group in acute social isolation. Studies have revealed the existence of a "third-quarter phenomenon" experienced by people working in such environments. There is a quantifiable drop in mood and morale after the midway point of a prolonged stay in isolated places, such as high Arctic weather stations and Antarctic scientific stations.[6] This low ebb occurs during the third quarter of a stay, regardless of whether the stay is five months, a year, or some other period. While not generally severe enough to cause psychiatric disorders, some people do develop symptoms of what's called "winter-over syndrome." Typically, this includes mild to severe depression, avoidance, apathy, irritability developing sometimes into anger, chronic insomnia, difficulty concentrating, and in some cases the "Antarctic stare," a dissociative state not unlike that triggered in victims of disaster or war,[7] in which "thoughts drift from current reality into a vague absence that even the individual cannot always recollect."[8] Such conditions also invite experiences like that of Virginia Fiennes.

In May 1986, a young psychologist, Jane Mocellin, interviewed men living at the Argentine Antarctic base of Esperanza, as part of a study of human responses to living in polar and other extreme environments. Her research took an unusual turn when, through informal talks, she learned that some of the men had encountered a presence at the base, a fact subsequently confirmed by the resident medical officer.[9] These incidents had occurred over the four months immediately preceding her interviews. One after another, the men revealed how they had become convinced of the presence of an unseen being at the base. This always occurred in the building that housed the power plant, which they staffed on a rotating basis for twenty-four-hour shifts. The building was the most isolated of the structures on the base. The encounters usually occurred at night. One soldier described being overwhelmed by a "strong sensation of being observed by somebody," despite being alone in the building. Another, a twenty-seven-year-old mechanical technician, felt certain that he was being watched through a window. "I was alone, and this perception was so strong that I went outside of the building to check if somebody was there." No one was. On another occasion, however, he did actually see something, fleetingly, a "human form and he was male."[10] Another man had a similar experience. "I saw somebody watching me.... When I stood up myself to go there the image moved and disappeared out of my visual field." None described being afraid, just aware that they had company.

Mocellin collected similar accounts of "presence hallucinations" from members of a Chilean Antarctic crew, as well as Brazilian meteorological personnel stationed on a remote tropical island. Later, in collaboration with Peter Suedfeld, a professor of psychology at the University of British Columbia, she produced a landmark study of the Third Man phenomenon in the academic journal *Environment and Behavior*. In their paper, "The 'Sensed Presence' in Unusual Environments," Suedfeld and Mocellin observed an important distinction between reports like that of Ginnie Fiennes, of an aloof presence experienced at the Antarctic bases, and those reported by people in life-threatening situations: "in no case was there any communication between the observer and the entity, not any feeling of receiving help."[11]

In fact, what happened at the Antarctic stations is not all that unusual. The sense of a presence is far more commonly encountered than most people would care to admit. Graham Reed, a psychology professor at York University in Toronto, wrote that sensing an unseen presence is "frequently experienced by normal, healthy people under certain conditions."[12] Almost everyone has had the sensation that somebody is nearby, when they are alone. Reed noted that the occurrence is most common in unusual surroundings. Yet it can also happen in everyday situations where there is an absence of meaningful stimuli. When walking alone at night, people often develop a feeling that someone might be following them. They try to reassure themselves, and resist the idea, concluding that their imagination has gotten the better of them, but the sense is vivid enough that they almost invariably look around anyway, just to make sure. In one published account, a woman whose job required that she come home late in the evening, was walking up her quiet street when she "experienced a feeling of fear that she might be attacked by somebody. Then it seemed to her that somebody was really walking behind her. She walked quickly and didn't turn her head around for fear of slowing her pace and being caught by the pursuer."[13] This happened even though, all along, the woman "was convinced there was not anybody behind her." Silence and darkness often play a role. Both offer an "unstructured field which may act as a screen" upon which an individual can project his or her state of mind. Thus a mental state produced by such surroundings will infuse natural phenomena such as a draft, mist, cloud, shadows, or an echo, with meaning.

It happens even where faint stimuli have been removed. Scientists have suspended subjects in a tank of body-temperature water, and removed all sensory stimulation. After a relatively short period of time, usually about three-quarters of an hour, "quite normal persons, robbed in the tank of all sensory cues, begin to do a strange thing. With the screen of consciousness not filled with sensory images from the environment, the individual himself begins to fill the screen projectively with his own inner uncorrected fantasies."[14] Sensory deprivation research has often produced examples of subjects becoming convinced that "someone else was in the cubicle."[15]

There is little doubt that, as one writer put it, "strange and uninvited guests are likely to intrude on any protracted human solitude."[16] The result is that companionship, no matter the form, is often cultivated. Children are loath to go to bed without being able to hear their parents' voices, a television, or music player. They often request that a light remain on or a door be left ajar. The consequences of not doing so can be startling, as one girl recalled:

> … at a certain time after the evening meal she was sent to bed alone while the adults stayed in the dining room. To get to her room, she had to go through a dark corridor. Fear seized her and she had the impression that someone was behind her ready to reach out to touch her shoulder with his hand.[17]

Adults retain some of this behaviour in certain situations, such as when a spouse goes on a business trip. Suddenly dogs that are normally banished to the mud room are welcomed into the master bedroom. People who are alone at night seek to occupy the silence by humming, whistling, talking aloud, watching television, or playing music. These actions "mask slight stimuli that otherwise might be interpreted as signs of somebody's being present."[18]

In the wilderness, such effects can be compounded, "especially in areas where the stimulus environment is relatively unchanging and homogeneous: mountains, jungles, deserts, ice fields, and the ocean."[19] While in some cases travellers, such as climbers, trekkers, and explorers, are not truly alone, they are, like Antarctic workers, "alone together" in a small group in a remote location separated, often by great distances, from other people.[20] Here, as at polar outposts, the sense of presence does not involve any communication or assistance. It is simply a subtle, sometimes vaguely disquieting, awareness of someone nearby. What all these situations have in common is a low level of stimulation: monotony, isolation, and, often, what Graham Reed termed "loneliness in the face of Nature." Of the natural places on Earth, the polar regions are among the loneliest.

WHAT, EXACTLY, SIR ERNEST SHACKLETON and his men encountered on their harrowing crossing of the south polar island of South Georgia is a question that has confounded historians and inspired Sunday sermons ever since. The apparition impressed Shackleton as being not of this world, a manifestation of some greater power. It made its appearance near the end of the explorer's grandly named Imperial Trans-Antarctic Expedition of 1914–16, at the very point when Shackleton stood to ensure his survival and that of his men—or to lose everything in the attempt.

In August 1914, only days before the First World War unleashed its fury on Europe, Shackleton had set sail to claim for Britain a great polar prize by crossing on foot the Antarctic continent. The expedition came perilously close to ending in mass disaster; the fact that it did not is the foundation of Shackleton's legend. He was the right man for the job. A self-made explorer, Shackleton was possessed of resilience, will, and good humour. He was also an unabashed romantic, and said he had not thought of becoming an explorer until, as a twenty-two-year-old sailor in the merchant marine, it came to him in a dream: "I seemed to vow to myself that some day I would go to the region of ice and snow and go on and on 'til I came to one of the poles of the earth." But this, his third attempt at the South Pole, ended prematurely. The expedition's ship *Endurance* had threaded its way through the freezing Weddell Sea, becoming trapped by ice even before Shackleton could disembark for his attempt to traverse the Antarctic continent.

After being carried in the ice for nearly ten months, the ship was abandoned on October 27, 1915. Shackleton wrote: "She was doomed: no ship built by human hands could have withstood the strain. I ordered all hands out on the floe." The noise of the pressure against the hull sounded "like the cries of a living creature." With time, the ship was reduced to a wreck. The twenty-eight men stood a hundred metres off, provisions and supplies piled around them, the ice cracking beneath their feet. They were sixteen hundred kilometres and a vast ocean from the nearest human settlement. Shackleton gathered the crew together and said, quietly and without emotion: "Ship and stores have gone— so now we'll go home." It was a desperate situation. As the retreating crew picked their way for five months across the rotting ice, dragging the *Endurance*'s small boats, some were overwhelmed by their predicament: "The men were not normal; some of them wanted to commit suicide and [Shackleton] had to force them to live."[21]

On April 9, 1916, fifteen months after the ship first became trapped, the men made an escape from the ice, launching the small boats on the open sea. They were already greatly reduced in health and spirit. Huddled in the boats, they were now tormented by the surging seas. Salt from the sea spray reddened their eyes, bloodied their lips, and gave their faces the pallor of death. Some were suffering from dysentery from eating uncooked dog pemmican. At night, temperatures dipped well below freezing. They faced constant rain and snow squalls. Having spent three nights in the boats, Shackleton doubted all the men would survive a fourth. Then they saw the rugged cliffs of Elephant Island, a desolate outcrop off the Antarctic Peninsula, and landed, staggering to shore like a band of drunkards. However, their faces were sullen and haunted. Frank Hurley, the expedition photographer, wrote: "Many suffered from temporary aberration, walking aimlessly about; others shivering as with palsy."

Knowing there was no chance a relief expedition would find them, Shackleton decided to leave the majority of his crew behind on Elephant Island and take five men with him in one of the small boats, a whaler he named the *James Caird*, to risk the extreme perils of the ocean south of Cape Horn, "the most tempestuous area of water in the world." His goal was a whaling station on the British possession of South Georgia, more than eleven hundred kilometres away, yet still within the Antarctic Convergence, and so in the thrall of deep atmospheric depressions coming through the Drake

Passage, which produce extreme and unpredictable weather. He announced his decision on April 19. Shackleton wrote: "The conclusion was forced upon me, that a boat journey in search of relief was necessary…. The hazards … were obvious."

The six men endured gales, snow squalls, and heavy seas for seventeen days. Their existence was miserable. Most were seasick, soaked, and chilled to the marrow. After the third day, they were already showing signs of superficial frostbite; their feet and legs assumed a "dead-white colour and lost surface feeling." The only respite from the cold came when they crawled into their sleeping compartment, a "dungeon cell" roughly two metres long by one and a half metres wide, into which three men would cram at a time, bundled in damp reindeer-hide sleeping bags. They lay atop cases of supplies and bags of stone shingles used as ballast, sleeping fitfully, as their "unfortunate bodies" were "swung up and banged down on mountainous seas." Commander Frank Worsley, who had captained the *Endurance*, once awoke in the compartment gasping in fear that he had been buried alive.

To cap it all, one keg of drinking water was lost, and the absence of adequate fluid left them severely dehydrated. As their journey continued, they each were reduced to a small amount of brackish water per day. On the sixth day Worsley noted, "Our poor fellows lit their pipes—their only solace—for raging thirst prevented us from eating." Shackleton wrote: "Thirst took possession of us…. Lack of water is always the most severe privation that men can be condemned to endure." He was right; while people can survive for weeks without food, it is estimated that about four days is the maximum anyone can survive without water. "All very thirsty and badly in need of sleep," Worsley wrote in his navigation book. "Some of our people, in fact, seem just about played out."

Outside the conditions were even worse: The ice grew so thick on the boat that they were in danger of capsizing and had to take turns chopping it off with a carpenter's adze. Once, when it appeared there was a break in the weather, Shackleton shouted, "It's clearing, boys!" Then immediately after, "For God's sake, hold on! It's got us!" What Shackleton took to be a line of white sky, signalling improved weather, was, in fact, the foaming crest of an enormous wave, possibly caused by the overturning of an iceberg. They were very nearly swamped and had to bail for their lives.

They not only overcame the immediate crisis, but also, in an astounding feat of navigation by Worsley, succeeded in reaching South Georgia in the midst of a hurricane that threatened to drive them onto the rocks. They fought the storm for nine hours before finally making landfall. "We were about done," said Henry McNeish, the carpenter. Sleep deprived, their mouths dry and tongues swollen from thirst, they were also in a state approaching starvation. As soon as they beached the boat, they fell down into pools of fresh running water and lapped it up like wild beasts. They had to unload their sleeping bags and could barely even accomplish that task, having partly lost control of their extremities, which were numb from having been soaked in cold sea water for more than two weeks.

Their journey was still not over. They were on the opposite end of the island from their destination, the whaling station at Stromness. However, the severe weather and treacherous coastline made a further boat journey out of the question. So Shackleton opted to cross overland, a distance of thirty-eight kilometres as the crow flies, thereby attempting to become the first to penetrate South Georgia's mountainous interior. The island's backbone is formed by two ranges with more than a dozen peaks exceeding two thousand metres, all surrounded by ice fields and vast glaciers. For several days they did not move, however, the severe weather forcing them to sit and wait. They used the time to recover from the boat journey. They drank fresh water and ate the tender meat of albatross chicks.

Finally, at 3 A.M. on May 19, 1916, Shackleton, Worsley, and Tom Crean, second officer, left McNeish in charge of the others and the boat, and began their arduous crossing of the ranges and glaciers of the island. Duncan Carse, an explorer who retraced their crossing in the 1950s, was in awe of their courage: "They travelled under headlong duress, reduced by long privation to exhausted starvelings destitute of all but their own worn out clothing." They had virtually none of the equipment needed for climbing, except fifteen metres of rope and the carpenter's adze substituting for an ice axe. Said Carse: "Their only safety lay in speed and the short cut regardless of danger; they could not fail because '22 men were waiting for the relief that we alone could secure for them.'"[22]

They marched in moonlight and in fog. They ascended carefully, roped together, threading around crevasses and across snowfields. They had slender rations and went virtually without sleep. They confronted the Trident, a giant ridge, and twice were rebuffed when they found the descent impossible. Finally, they stood on an ice ridge, uncertain of what was over the other side because of a sharp incline. When a heavy bank of fog threatened to overtake them, they opted to jump into the unknown. As Shackleton wrote, "there could be no turning back now." Worsley later said: "I was never more scared in my life than for the first thirty seconds. The speed was terrific. I think we all gasped at that hair-raising shoot into darkness." At that point, only they knew the whereabouts of all the other expedition members. Had they dropped to their deaths, the entire expedition might have been doomed. Instead, they tested fate and survived, shooting down 275 metres in a couple of minutes. At the end, they dusted the snow off themselves and shook hands. Looking back, they saw grey fingers of fog appearing on the ridge, "as though reaching after the intruders into untrodden wilds. But we had escaped."

They had walked all day, and they continued through the night, for a time in near absolute darkness, until a full moon rose and a silver pathway lay before them. They reached Fortuna Bay, at first believing it to be their destination, Stromness, but soon realized their mistake. At five o'clock in the morning on May 20, exhausted and cold—one of the men now suffering from frostbite—they stopped to rest. They had no tent, and their clothes were in tatters, so they put their arms around each other for warmth. Within minutes, Worsley and Crean were asleep. Wrote Shackleton: "I realized that it would be disastrous if we all slumbered together, for sleep under such conditions merges into death." He waited five minutes then shook the others awake, telling them they had slept for half an hour. He then ordered a fresh start. As they trekked on, Shackleton later reflected: "We three fellows drew very close to each other, mostly in silence."[23]

At 6:30 A.M., Shackleton thought he heard the sound of a steam-whistle, and half an hour later, they all heard it. Wrote Shackleton: "Never had any one of us heard sweeter music." They marched on, eventually reaching a final ridge, before, at last, they had a view of Stromness Bay. A whaling boat hove into view in the distance, and tiny figures could be seen moving around the buildings. They stopped and shook each other's hands. They eventually shambled into the whaling station, barely recognizable as civilized men. Their beards were long and their hair was matted. Their faces were black and their clothes, filthy rags. The first three people they encountered recoiled in fear. Finally, a foreman took them to the house of the manager, whom Shackleton knew. "Well?" the manager said. "Don't you know me?" Shackleton asked. The manager replied doubtfully that he recognized the voice, but guessed wrongly at the identity of the hirsute and malodorous visitor standing on his doorstep. "I am Shackleton," the stranger said at last.

Rescuers were dispatched to collect the others across the island, and eventually to Elephant Island. All of the *Endurance*'s crew survived the ordeal. One of the men left behind on Elephant Island, Thomas Hans Orde-Lees, an experienced climber, later wrote: "Shackleton admitted frequently that he was no mountaineer. How later, he, Worsley, and Crean managed to cross South Georgia is an everlasting puzzle to me." They were not untouched by the experience. Shackleton, paraphrasing a passage from a poem by Robert Service,[24] wrote in his narrative *South*, published in 1919: "We had pierced the veneer of outside things. We had 'suffered, starved and triumphed, grovelled down yet grasped at glory, grown bigger in the bigness of the whole.' We had seen God in His splendours, heard the text that Nature renders. We had reached the naked soul of man."

Shackleton came to regard the desperate journey from Elephant Island to the whaling station on South Georgia as the supreme event of his life, surpassing even his greatest geographic achievement, the 1909 record for Furthest South. On that earlier expedition, he got to within 156 kilometres of the South Pole and earned a knighthood for his efforts. In the case of the Imperial Trans-Antarctic Expedition, Shackleton failed to achieve any polar prize, but he had attained something greater: He had led others to overcome seemingly insurmountable obstacles in order to survive. The crossing of South Georgia was the final act of the expedition's deliverance.

Shackleton took great pains to write his account of the journey, all the while cautioning: "There is much that can never be told."[25] In preparing his narrative, he struggled with something unspoken. In the house of Leonard Tripp, a friend and confidant, at Heretaunga, near Wellington, New Zealand, the explorer tried to come to terms with it. Tripp listened as Shackleton dictated his story to Edward Saunders, a journalist who acted as his amanuensis, and was amazed by what he heard. Shackleton paced up and down the room as he spoke, and he seldom hesitated, but every now and then he would tell Saunders to make a mark because he had not found the right word. Said Tripp of Shackleton: "I watched him, and his whole face seemed to swell—you know what a big face he had." With tears in his eyes, Shackleton then said: "Tripp you don't know what I've been through, and I am going through it all again, and I can't do it." He walked out of the room as if he intended to go away, and lit a cigarette, but then he returned. This happened on several occasions. Tripp recalled: "You could see that the man was suffering, and then he came to this mention of the fourth man."[26]

Shackleton, reciting Keats,[27] explained his struggle in *South*:

> One feels "the dearth of human words, the roughness of mortal speech," in trying to describe intangible things, but a record of our journeys would be incomplete without reference to a subject very near to our hearts.[28]

He revealed in the narrative that he had a pervasive sense, during that last and worst of his struggles, that something out of the ordinary had accompanied them:

> When I look back at those days I have no doubt that Providence guided us, not only across those snow-fields, but across the storm-white sea that separated Elephant Island from our landing-place on South Georgia. I know that during that long and racking march of thirty-six hours over the unnamed mountains and glaciers of South Georgia it seemed to me often that we were four, not three.[29]

He had said nothing to the others, but then, three weeks later, Worsley offered without prompting: "Boss, I had a curious feeling on the march that there was another person with us." Crean later confessed to the same strange sensation. Each of the three men had come to the same conclusion independently of the others: that they had been in company with another being.

Shackleton at first did not mention the fourth presence to anyone else, and the passage alluding to it, which Tripp heard

Shackleton dictate to Saunders, was omitted in the original draft of *South*, written in 1917. Because of this, and since it was not mentioned in any original document, the possibility has been raised that the encounter with the presence was a "fabrication in order to add a dash of spirituality to the story before it went to press."[30] Indeed, one Shackleton biography suggested the presence represented nothing more than "an attempt on Shackleton's part to court publicity, at a time of national emotion, by producing his own 'Angel of Mons.'"[31]

This is a reference to a First World War report that angels had appeared to safeguard the British army during its retreat from Mons in August 1914. The historian A.J.P. Taylor wrote of Mons being the only battlefield where "supernatural intervention was observed, more or less reliably, on the British side."[32] Lance-Corporal A. Johnstone, who had served with the Royal Engineers, wrote to the London *Evening News* on August 11, 1915, to affirm that angelic horsemen had appeared to the retreating troops:

> I remember turning to my chums in the ranks and saying: "Thank God! We are not far off Paris now. Look at the French cavalry." They, too, saw them quite plainly, but on getting closer, to our surprise the horsemen vanished and gave place to banks of white mist, with clumps of trees and bushes dimly showing through them …

Johnstone said that he and his fellow soldiers had marched all day and night with only a half-hour break. They were in extreme danger, imperilled by the enemy and exposed to hunger, sleep deprivation, and exhaustion. As Johnstone wrote, they were all "absolutely worn out with fatigue—both bodily and mental, marching quite mechanically along the road and babbling all sorts of nonsense in sheer delirium." On the basis of this, it has been argued that they were, consequently, "subject to a sensory illusion due to extreme fatigue."[33] The burden of stress and exhaustion suffered by the British soldiers at Mons bears a strong similarity to that endured by Shackleton's party, suggesting that far from being a fictional embellishment, *South* simply documents a similar response to extreme conditions.

In fact, the unseen companion does appear on a separate sheet of paper labelled "note" in another typescript of Shackleton's original manuscript. Apparently he initially withheld the passage, before deciding to include it in the final draft.[34] Shackleton said: "One couldn't write this sort of thing … about the mystery of that Fourth in our journey; but it was the heart of it, all the same."[35] He may have regretted that he ever allowed so deeply personal a feeling to be made public: "On occasions he would speak of it lightly, or with embarrassment."[36] He did, nevertheless, subsequently allude to it during some of his public lectures, and always with tremendous effect. One person who attended a banquet in Shackleton's honour recalled: "You could hear a pin drop when Sir Ernest spoke of his consciousness of a Divine Companion in his journeyings."[37] This caused a sensation on the pulpit at the time. Frank W. Boreham, a Baptist minister and popular writer, was one of many clergymen who linked Shackleton's fourth presence to a passage from the Bible, Daniel 3:24–5:

And Nebuchadnezzar the king was astonished, and rose up in haste, and spake, and said unto his counsellors, Did we not

cast three men bound into the midst of the fire? They
answered and said unto the king, True, O king.

He answered and said, Lo, I see four men loose,
walking in the midst of the fire, and they have no hurt; and
the form of the fourth is like the Son of God.

Boreham's views are unsurprising. "Flame or frost; it makes no
difference. A truth that, in one age, can hold its own in a burning
fiery furnace can, in another, vindicate itself just as readily amidst
fields of ice and snow," wrote Boreham,[38] adding: "the form of the
fourth is like the Son of God!"

Was the presence on South Georgia the guiding, protective
hand of the Divine Companion, or as Boreham declared, "the Son
of God"? Did the Almighty intervene to guide the ragged trio of
polar explorers to their rescue? Or was it something else?
Historians, in their accounts of Shackleton's expedition, have
surmised that it was some form of shared hallucination, as one put
it, that the "toil [was] enough to cloud their consciousness."[39] Or
that "this was probably a hallucination due to their common
dehydration."[40] Shackleton biographer Roland Huntford wrote:
"They were suffering from dehydration, and that was pushing
them over into the half world where physical and mental
phenomena meet…. Delusion hovered in the air. Shadows seemed
like ghosts. They imagined unseen companions by their side."[41]

A writer, Harold Begbie, recorded a conversation with
Shackleton in the London *Daily Telegraph*:

"In your book you speak of a Fourth Presence."
He nodded his head.

"Do you care to speak about that?"

At once he was restless and ill at ease. "No," he said, "None of us cares to speak about that. There are some things which never can be spoken of. Almost to hint about them comes perilously near to sacrilege. This experience was eminently one of those things."[42]

Shackleton returned to South Georgia on January 4, 1922, in the converted sealer *Quest*. The new expedition's goal was ill-defined but had the general objective of circumnavigating Antarctica in search of undiscovered islands. His crew included eight of the men from the *Endurance*, Worsley among them. As the *Quest* sailed along the coast of South Georgia, Shackleton and Worsley, "like a pair of excitable kids," pointed out geographic features from their trek over the mountains. The *Quest* finally came to anchor off King Edward Point, to the east of Stromness. "It is a strange and curious place," Shackleton wrote in his journal that night, adding: "In the darkening twilight I saw a lone star hover, gem-like above the bay." In the early hours of January 5, Shackleton, just forty-seven years old, suffered a fatal heart attack. He was laid to rest in the whalers' cemetery at Grytviken, on South Georgia, the place where he had been touched by Providence.

Strangely, history remembers Shackleton's visitor on South Georgia not as a fourth—Shackleton, Worsley, Crean, and one mysterious other—but as "the third man."[43] This is because T.S. Eliot referred to the phenomenon in "The Waste Land," written in 1922 and arguably the most famous English-language poem of the twentieth century, but used poetic licence to alter the number. In the poem, he wrote:

Who is the third who walks always beside you?
When I count, there are only you and I together
But when I look ahead up the white road
There is always another one walking beside you.

In his notes on "The Waste Land," Eliot said that the lines were inspired by an account of an Antarctic expedition, "I forget which, but I think one of Shackleton's."[44] The Anglo-American poet was impressed by the idea that a "party of explorers, at the extremity of their strength, had the constant delusion that there was one more member than could actually be counted." This, then, is the name that has become attached to the unseen being at the core of this book—the Third Man. Scientific researchers call it variously the "sensed presence," a "vivid physical awareness," or the "illusory shadow person." But manifestations of this benevolent force have become much more widely known as the Third Man. Climber Doug Scott, who partnered with Dougal Haston in 1975 to make the first ascent of Everest's southwest face, explained it this way: "It's the third man syndrome: imagining there is someone else walking beside you, a comforting presence telling you what to do next, and it can be as strong as a voice in your chest."[45]

Sir Ernest Shackleton felt an existence every bit as real and vivid as a flesh-and-blood person. And it was not just any person. At a point in their lives when he and his two colleagues were most in need of the help and encouragement of a friend, they were able to conjure one up apparently out of thin air. Just how they, and a great many others before them and since, have managed to do this is the mystery of the Third Man.

What was it, then, that transformed a sense of presence, like that reported at the Antarctic stations, into an instrument of hope embodied by the Third Man? Why is it that some encounters with a presence in polar regions, like that of Ginnie Fiennes and the Argentines, produced no sense of help or guidance, while in Shackleton's case, it did? The basic conditions—extreme isolation and monotonous polar surroundings—were similar, but Shackleton's situation was more complicated. For him, these factors were joined by acute stress. He was in a desperate situation, where the risk of death was obvious. This additional factor dramatically altered the nature of the experience, intensifying the effect.

Shackleton felt his encounter with a presence was infused with spiritual significance, that it was a manifestation of Divine Providence. When he referred to it, he did so with reverence. What he experienced was much more profound than the vague sensation of a presence that is common to so many of us, such as the fleeting anxiety we feel when we walk down a deserted street at night. It seems that the impression of a presence is much stronger when the background affective state itself is more powerful. The Third Man seems to grow in power in direct proportion to the intensity of the emotional state of the individual who experiences him. Why did Shackleton encounter a great and benevolent helper, when others have not? Because, unlike Ginnie Fiennes and the Argentines, he desperately needed one.

CHAPTER THREE

The Ghosts Walk in Public

IN THE DECADES IMMEDIATELY BEFORE and following Shackleton's mystical experience on South Georgia, there was an outbreak of Third Man reports. They occurred all over the world, under extreme—but also extremely different—conditions. Some of the cases described in this chapter were as famous and talked-about as Shackleton's in their day. Frank Smythe's offer to share his Kendal mint cake with his "companion" on Mount Everest is, for example, the single best-known case of the Third Man Factor involving a climber. Joshua Slocum's encounter with a phantom sailor during his attempt to complete the first solo circumnavigation of the world was published in newspapers at the time, and remains familiar to many yachtsmen to this day. Henry Hugh Gordon Dacre Stoker, a Royal Australian Navy submarine commander, published a popular book about his wartime adventures, at the heart of which was an elusive, unseen presence. Others, though, were unknown to the general public. The mysterious figure A.F.R. "Sandy" Wollaston followed out of the jungle of New Guinea to safety, or the unearthly presence William Laird McKinlay encountered in the Arctic ice, for example, were heard of only in the rarified circle of explorers who had experienced them.

Exploration itself had been going on for centuries, but suddenly people were popping up all over the place with Third Man stories. Something had changed. Perhaps it was the manner of exploration itself. Instead of large ships carrying a full complement of men, or vast columns of soldiers, the explorers had begun to travel solo, or in small groups "alone together." Or perhaps all that had changed was the willingness of explorers to own up publicly to their strange experiences, something unimaginable even a few decades earlier. The scrupulous reports written by nineteenth-century British explorers, for example, were narratives intended to impress the Admiralty with their authors' eminent good sense. The last thing they would want to reveal to their exalted superiors was a visit from a phantom companion. Whatever the cause, something had changed. At the end of the nineteenth century and in the first decades of the twentieth, the ghosts began to walk in public.

ON JUNE 1, 1933, FRANK SMYTHE and Eric Shipton emerged from their canvas tent at 8,351 metres on Mount Everest. A blinding blizzard had forced them to spend two nights at Camp Six, in the so-called high-altitude "death zone." Altitude above 8,000 metres is dangerous even for those who are acclimatized, and climbers have since learned to limit exposure by camping at lower altitudes before making a summit bid. But the era of high-altitude climbing was in its infancy in 1933. Smythe and Shipton's physical deterioration owing to altitude, lack of oxygen, sleep deprivation, and inadequate food had been rapid and serious. They began to worry about how long it would be possible for them to survive. After the second night, however, the weather eased and they made their attempt at the summit. So enfeebled were they that Smythe felt certain that anyone watching them leave the camp would have concluded they "ought to be in hospital."

They climbed slowly, and with frequent stops, diagonally up towards the Great Couloir on a gradual incline that reminded Shipton of a roof. Even so, he found himself "weak as a kitten," and when they reached a formation on Everest called the First Step at 8,500 metres, Smythe heard an exclamation behind him. Turning, he saw Shipton leaning heavily on his ice axe. A moment later Shipton slumped down, and announced he was unable to go on. The fourth British Everest expedition, which had begun as a large, meticulously planned military-style assault, had come down to just one man. Frank Smythe was an unlikely candidate for the job. He had been invalided out of the Royal Air Force in 1927, suffered a heart murmur, and was not obviously fit. Yet he was a skilled and resolute climber, and now he was on his own.

Some time after parting company with Shipton, Smythe encountered a fresh accumulation of deep powder snow. This new layer failed to support his weight, and with each step he sank deeply, greatly increasing the difficulty of the climb. He persisted, reaching the Great Couloir. The summit of Mount Everest was only three hundred metres higher, yet it might have been a thousand kilometres away. Smythe described being "overcome by a feeling of hopelessness and weariness." His limbs were trembling from the exertion. He gasped for air. His heart was pounding against his rib cage. In such a condition, the technical challenge of the climb began to appear insurmountable. Smythe felt like "a prisoner, struggling vainly to escape from a vast hollow enclosed by dungeon-like walls. Wherever I looked hostile rocks frowned down on my impotent strugglings."[1]

At one point he slipped, losing his footing so quickly that "my sluggish brain had no time to register a thrill of fear." Smythe was saved only because his ice axe was jammed in a crack and held his weight. Not until later did he fully comprehend the extreme danger of that moment. He was climbing now "in a curiously detached, impersonal frame of mind. It was almost as though one part of me stood aside and watched the other struggle on. Lack of oxygen and fatigue are responsible for this dulling of the mental faculties, but principally lack of oxygen."[2] He likened his condition to that of a drunken automobile driver. Smythe tried to continue, shovelling away floury snow with his gloves in order to gain each foothold. It was a laborious task, and it proved to be his undoing. Finally, Smythe determined: "It was the limit." He stood for some time alone at the "very boundaries of life and death," at an elevation as high as any man had ever reached. As he put it later: "The last 1,000 feet of Everest are not for mere flesh and blood."

Smythe then climbed down to a broad ledge and halted for a rest:

> When I reached the ledge I felt I ought to eat something in
> order to keep up my strength. All I had brought with me was

a slab of Kendal mint cake. This I took out of my pocket and, carefully dividing it into two halves, turned round with one half in my hand to offer to my "companion."[3]

After leaving Shipton, and throughout his subsequent struggles, Smythe had a "strange feeling ... that I was accompanied by another." He was embarrassed by the idea, and said it was only "with great diffidence" that he placed an account of the phenomenon on the official record, and then only at the request of Hugh Ruttledge, the expedition leader:

> All the time that I was climbing alone I had a strong feeling
> that I was accompanied by a second person. This feeling was
> so strong that it completely eliminated all loneliness I might
> otherwise have felt. It even seemed that I was tied to my
> "companion" by a rope, and that if I slipped "he" would hold
> me. I remember constantly glancing back over my shoulder.[4]

He emphasized the strength and sense of safety he gained from his unseen companion: "In its company I could not feel lonely, neither could I come to any harm. It was always there to sustain me on my solitary climb up the snow covered slabs." At the moment he held out the piece of mint cake, Smythe said the presence was "so near and so strong" that it was "almost a shock to find no one to whom to give it." He felt the intentions of his companion were clear:

> It seemed to me that this "presence" was a strong, helpful and
> friendly one, and it was not until Camp VI was sighted that
> the link connecting me, as it seemed at the time to the

beyond, was snapped, and although Shipton and the camp were but a few yards away, I suddenly felt alone.[5]

Smythe later wrote that his encounter with the presence was "by no means unique, and has been experienced in the past by solitary wanderers, not only on mountains but on desert wastes and in polar regions." He pointed to the Third Man that accompanied Shackleton and his companions as they crossed South Georgia. As Smythe put it, "there was an extra 'someone' in the party." He might also have mentioned Howard Somervell, who made a summit bid as part of the 1924 British Everest expedition. "I have often felt the presence of a Companion on the mountainside who is not in our earthly party of climbers," wrote Somervell, a surgeon.[6] Perhaps the best illustration of just how common the experience is was waiting for Smythe in the tent at Camp Six. In 1930—three years before Smythe's experience on Everest—Eric Shipton himself had encountered an unseen presence on Mount Kenya, Africa's second-highest peak. Shipton was with climber H.W. "Bill" Tilman, and on the descent Shipton "experienced that curious feeling ... that there was an additional member of the party—three of us instead of two."[7] He later admitted that he "had this experience regularly on arduous mountain journeys."[8] Shipton did not speculate as to the source of his unseen companion. Nor did Frank Smythe, who said only, "men under physical and mental stress have experienced curious things on mountains."

NOT ONLY ON MOUNTAINS. Joshua Slocum was sailing for Gibraltar after a brief stop at the Azores, on the first leg of his attempt to become the first person to circumnavigate the world alone, when his twelve-metre sloop *Spray* was struck by a violent squall. Objects on the deck were blown about by fierce winds "like bits of sea froth." To make matters worse, Slocum himself was taken suddenly and quite seriously ill, apparently from food poisoning. He threw himself on the floor in the cabin not far from the wheel. Slocum then was visited by a "strange guest" who he believed helped to steer the *Spray* for a forty-eight hour period through a dangerous storm as he lay incapacitated:

> I became delirious. When I came to, as I thought, from my swoon, I realized that the sloop was plunging into a heavy sea, and looking out of the companionway, to my amazement I saw a tall man at the helm. His rigid hand, grasping the spokes of the wheel, held them as in a vise.[9]

Before he fell ill, the fifty-one-year-old former merchant navy captain and naturalized U.S. citizen (he was born in Nova Scotia) had been overtaken by a pervasive loneliness, a "sense of solitude, which I could not shake off." He had adopted the practice of speaking out loud to himself, issuing orders as if there were a crew aboard. On one occasion, he yelled from his cabin to an imaginary man at the helm: "How does she head, there?" and again, "Is she on her course?" When he received no reply, "I was reminded the more palpably of my condition. My voice sounded hollow on the empty air, and I dropped the practice." Instead, Slocum spent idle time reading Washington Irving's *Life of Columbus*.

But in the midst of the severe storm, seriously ill, Slocum became convinced that there really was someone else aboard. He described the sailor as having "an ancient cast of visage," and thought it might be the pilot from Columbus' *Pinta*. Slocum's initial alarm at encountering the unexpected visitor was soon allayed by the man, who assured him: "I have come to do you no harm." In fact, he said, he had "come to aid you. Lie quiet ... and I will guide your ship to-night." Enormous waves were breaking over the *Spray*, and pounding on the ship's cabin, but Slocum was unworried.

When he recovered, and the storm abated, Slocum found the *Spray* "still heading as I had left her, and ... going like a racehorse." The sloop had made 145 kilometres in the night through rough seas, and was still on her planned course to Gibraltar. Slocum filed an account of his bizarre encounter to the *Boston Globe*. It was published on October 14, 1895, under the headline: "SPOOK ON SPRAY." Wrote Slocum: "If ever there was a man at a ship's wheel one stood at the wheel of the *Spray* through that livelong night. No thing could be clearer to me than that." Of the phantom sailor, Slocum said he had "the feeling that I had been in the presence of a friend and a seaman of vast experience." He felt, he added, "truly grateful to the strange sailor of the night."[10]

Slocum felt the presence of the "invisible helmsman" several times during the remainder of the voyage, and at one point was awakened by a shouted warning, allowing him to narrowly avert disaster during a storm off Cape Horn. Even during the last leg of his historic journey, as he sailed up the eastern seaboard of the United States towards his home port, the presence returned. It occurred last during a thunderstorm, in which "hailstones were pelting the *Spray*, and lightning was pouring down from the clouds, not in flashes alone, but in almost continuous streams."

Slocum described himself as "tired, tired, tired," but he succeeded in working the sloop towards the coast, and escaping the worst of it. Wrote Slocum: "After this storm I saw the pilot of the *Pinta* no more." He reached Newport, Rhode Island on June 27, 1898, marking the end of his remarkable passage.

IN 1913, WILLIAM LAIRD MCKINLAY experienced a presence while aboard a research ship in the Arctic Ocean. McKinlay described the occurrence in his narrative of the disaster that consumed the *Karluk*, the lead vessel in explorer and ethnographer Vilhjalmur Stefansson's Canadian Arctic Expedition of 1913–18. A veteran Arctic hand who had lived for years among the Inuit, Stefansson adopted their way of life, surviving on a diet of raw meat only. He was seeking to chart the region north of Alaska and the western Canadian mainland, when the research ship became trapped in ice in the Beaufort Sea, off the north coast of Alaska. Stefansson's behaviour from that point on has left a permanent stain on his reputation. He departed the ship to hunt caribou on the mainland, and told the crew he would return in ten days. In the meantime the ship was carried away by the ice drift and, instead of seeking help, Stefansson—as may have been his intention from the outset—simply resumed his explorations by sledge, leaving the *Karluk* and her crew to their fate.

McKinlay, a twenty-five-year-old schoolteacher from Glasgow who had signed on the expedition as magnetician and meteorologist, had no previous experience in the Arctic, and no one would have mistaken him for a polar explorer either. He had been a sickly child, and in adulthood was slight, pasty-faced, and bookish. His height was generously calculated at five feet, four inches (162 centimetres), earning him the nickname "Wee Mac." But appearances can be deceiving and McKinlay found a source of immense strength to assist him.

His first encounter with a presence came when full realization of their predicament swept over the *Karluk*'s crew of twenty-five. A fierce gale had been battering the ship, and ice held its hull fast. They experienced blinding whiteouts caused by drifting snow, and winter's darkness was strengthening its grip. The cold was extreme. McKinlay wrote: "The sense of insecurity, aggravated by the storm, was intensified by the eeriness of the dark." However, on October 5, 1913, the conditions briefly moderated, and McKinlay was able to go outside. He sat alone, watching a spectacular display of the northern lights:

> Then all at once I became aware of something new and strange, a consciousness of a "presence," a feeling that I was not alone. "Feeling" is not the word to describe it; there was nothing of the senses in it at all, only an awareness. H.G. Wells wrote that at times in the night and in rare lonely moments, "I experience a sort of communion of myself with something great that is not myself." Perhaps I was sharing a similar experience; I don't know. It passed.[11]

McKinlay was visited again in December. By then the situation aboard the *Karluk* was critical. The ship remained trapped, and it was increasingly clear that it would not escape the ice, which continued to build up pressure against the hull and which was producing a cacophony of grating, screeching, and rumbling noises. The strain of their situation was affecting the crew, some of whom were hatching plots against the ship's captain, Robert Bartlett. One man was behaving queerly, refusing to answer when spoken to, apparently deaf and dumb, yet singing loudly and talking to himself and to the sled dogs when alone. The food rations had been drastically reduced. They built snow houses on the ice floes, and began to frantically stitch together skins to complete garments to protect themselves from the cold when the inevitable happened, and they were forced onto the ice.

It was while experiencing such extreme duress that McKinlay, under a full moon, went for a walk on the ice, stopping about a hundred metres off:

> Once again I became aware of what I can only describe as a Presence, which filled me with an exaltation beyond all earthly feeling. As it passed, and I walked back to the ship, I felt wholly convinced that no agnostic, no skeptic, no atheist, no humanist, no doubter, would ever take from me the certainty of the existence of God. Whatever hardships the future might hold, whatever fate the North had in store for me, I felt supremely glad I had come.

His encounter with a presence had braced McKinlay for the ordeal that followed when, early in the morning on January 10, 1914, a severe shudder was felt through the ship. Water began pouring in through a large gash on the port side. The crew was forced to abandon ship. It was a terrifying moment, compounded by the conditions outside, the polar night where snow was being driven by an eighty-kilometre-per-hour wind. When the ship began to sink, Bartlett, who had remained inside during the *Karluk*'s last hours, put Chopin's "Funeral March" on the Victrola.

After the Canadian blue ensign finally disappeared into the water, they gathered in their ice houses and planned their retreat. Four men struck out across the ice to Wrangel Island to establish a shore camp. Those men were never seen again. The remainder of the ship's beaten company then also began to shamble across the heaving floes towards Wrangel Island. From there, Bartlett, with one man accompanying him, undertook a heroic eleven-hundred-kilometre journey by dog-sled, first south to Siberia, and then east across the Bering Strait to Alaska to summon help. For those left behind, the situation only worsened with the deepening hunger, the spread of disease, and a growing sense of despair. By the time help finally arrived, eleven members of the party had died—eight on the treacherous ice floes, two of starvation and disease, and one man had committed suicide. McKinlay, however, had help, and faced the disaster with courage, "erect and foursquare."

IN 1912–13, AN EXPEDITION PENETRATED eighty kilometres up New Guinea's Utakwa River, and then struck out through dense jungle to explore the island's uncharted Nassau range. Leading a party that included Dyak headhunters imported from Borneo to serve as porters was British explorer A.F.R. "Sandy" Wollaston, a Cambridge-educated physician, naturalist, and itinerant explorer who had previously travelled to remote corners of Sudan, Java, and the Ruwenzori mountains of Uganda, and had been a member of an earlier British expedition up New Guinea's Mimika River. Wollaston's discoveries were numerous and significant. He gave his name to a mountain in Africa, a Tibetan rabbit, a bat in New Guinea, and more than forty plants. His narratives of the expeditions, such as *From Ruwenzori to the Congo*, reveal an unusual sensitivity not only to natural wonders but to primitive cultures as well. He is credited with numerous exotic discoveries made along the border of Uganda and Congo, then a largely uncharted region, but perhaps the strangest of all was finding a pair of men's breeches, "unmistakably English," near the peak of Ruwenzori—a place no Englishman, indeed no European, had been known to visit.

During his first expedition to New Guinea, in 1910–11, which was commanded by C.G. Rawling, Wollaston had discovered villages of the Tapiro pygmies, a hitherto unknown tribe, but the expedition failed in its ultimate goal of reaching the Nassau mountains. It was defeated by torrential rains, dense undergrowth, meagre provisions, and tropical diseases including dysentery and beriberi. In all, twenty members of Rawling's expedition died. But Wollaston had glimpsed the distant snow-capped range and resolved to return.

In 1912, Wollaston was again deep in New Guinea's uncharted territory, and again he encountered remarkable hardships as the column of men, burdened by supplies, moved slowly towards their goal, the highest peak: Mount Carstensz, now known as Puncak Jaya, at 4,884 metres the tallest mountain in Oceania. They battled mud and the rain-swollen waters of the Utakwa. They were attacked by Papuans and by leeches. They encountered unknown

tribesmen who reached out to touch them and thrust curious offer-
ings at them. From the swampy lowlands they gradually ascended
to the foothills, and then finally into the mountainous country
that was the source of the Utakwa. From there, Wollaston felt his
way in fog through moss-forests towards the towering Carstensz.
He went on with only a small party of men, and at 4,300 metres
they reached the snowline. Then, within just 150 metres of the
summit, a wall of ice forced Wollaston to a halt. He decided that
to attempt the final stretch in fog and freezing rain would be to
court disaster: "I need not here dwell upon our feelings of disappointment as we slowly stumbled down to our camp again…. To
have the prize withheld when it was nearly within our grasp, was
almost more than Christian patience could bear."[12]

The retreat to the coast was plagued by mishaps. Wollaston
very nearly drowned when his canoe was overturned in the rain-
swollen river. He lost his notes, diaries, maps, and other valuables.
Then, he was horrified to find two bodies on the path, and soon
many more, all members of a tribe they had visited on their ascent.
What followed were, Wollaston wrote, "two days of the most
terrible I have ever experienced, we passed the dead bodies of
between thirty and forty people. All of them were on, or very close
to, the track; some had made shelters of sticks and leaves, and
others had crept, four or five together, into the shelter of rocks, and
had died beside the ashes of their fires." He thought at first they
might have been killed by a sudden epidemic, but there was no
sign of disease, so Wollaston speculated they may have died of
starvation: "Growing weaker daily, they just gave up and died, as
natives can."

Wollaston delivered an account of his journey to a meeting of the Royal Geographical Society in London, on January 26, 1914, within days of Sir Ernest Shackleton's speech seeking the Society's support for the *Endurance* expedition. One listener to Wollaston expressed admiration that an explorer "attired in immaculate evening costume, looking as if he had never been out of Piccadilly," could present so harrowing an account of "a river-road full of dangerous rapids and un-fordable pot-holes, hedged in by precipitous cliffs, bordered by pathless jungle full of mosquitoes, flies, leeches, and thorns; the night-hours passed in a freezing atmosphere in sodden clothes, short of rations, depressed by the all-obliterating mists; the boat-wrecks; the loss of irreplaceable records of an arduous adventure." It was indeed a remarkable story, but it was still more remarkable for that which Wollaston, a man of science, opted to withhold: a strange encounter with an unknown companion, a story Wollaston never wrote about, but instead confided to a Cambridge friend, the literary theorist I.A. Richards.[13]

Following his explorations of New Guinea, Wollaston was chosen for the first Everest expedition, a reconnaissance with George Mallory. He was later elected a fellow of King's College, Cambridge, where, in 1930, while working as a tutor, he was fatally shot, along with a policeman, by a deranged nineteen-year-old undergraduate. The murderer then turned the gun on himself. Fifty years later, Richards met Wollaston's son, Nicholas (who was four years old when his father was murdered) at a reception in London. Richards shared a fantastic story concerning that second expedition to the mountains of New Guinea, a story subsequently published by Nicholas Wollaston. Sandy, it seems, had help:

… mercifully, through tropical mists, heat haze, rainstorms, he was led on by another white man far ahead—the back view of a stranger travelling in the same direction towards the coast. Each time Sandy topped another ridge, the man was going over the further one. Each time Sandy turned another bend of a path or river, the man was disappearing round the next.

Yet was he really a stranger?[14]

Even though he was never able to make up ground on the man in the distance, Wollaston thought he looked familiar. He did get within earshot, but his shouts went unanswered. When the expedition finally reached the coast, the companion disappeared. Wollaston tried to establish the identity of the stranger, but no one knew anything about him. He had vanished as suddenly and mysteriously as he had appeared. "All Sandy knew was that another explorer, pressing on in front, kept him going and rescued the expedition."[15]

IN APRIL 1916, Henry Hugh Gordon Dacre "Harry" Stoker and two fellow prisoners of war escaped Turkish captivity, and made a dash for freedom. Born in Dublin, and a cousin of Bram Stoker, the author of *Dracula*, Stoker had joined the Royal Navy at the age of fifteen. At twenty-nine he was chosen to command *AE2*, a submarine built for the Royal Australian Navy. When the First World War broke out eight months later, Stoker set sail from Sydney to the Mediterranean. He was ordered to force a passage up the Dardanelles into the Sea of Marmora, and then to "generally run amok." He succeeded in harassing some Turkish warships before the submarine had to be scuttled, and Stoker and his crew were captured. Eventually, Stoker was moved to the fortress of Afion Kara Hissar, where he was held as a prisoner of war. It was, he later wrote, a "living death." Unwilling to endure it, on March 23, 1916, Stoker and two others made a daring escape while Turkish sentries were distracted by an accomplice. When they were finally missed, the camp commandant did not trouble to send guards in pursuit, because the prospects for the trio were so bleak. To reach the coast, they had to cross 480 kilometres of the rugged Taurus Mountains, without compass, maps, or adequate clothing.

They travelled under cloak of darkness, having to cover twenty-four kilometres a night if their food ration of raisins and powdered cocoa was to hold out. Wrote Stoker: "As we were often above or near the snowline the cold was intense, and sleep impossible when further progress was barred. Ever present was that ghastly hunted feeling; and hunger, thirst, footsoreness, and physical strain." They hid and rested during daylight hours. On the eleventh night, hungry and dispirited, they undertook a gruelling march through a mountain pass buffeted by heavy winds, their exhaustion compounded by nerves. At one point they thought they saw lights flashing, and feared that they had been sighted by their pursuers, who had then signalled to soldiers ahead. Wrote Stoker:

> In the midst of the night, I felt—not suddenly or surpris-edly—that we were not three men struggling along in line, but four. There was a fourth man, following at the end of our

line, in the correct position for a fourth man to be. When we stopped for a few moments' rest he did not join us but remained in the darkness, out of sight; yet as soon as we rose and resumed our march he dropped into his place forthwith. He never spoke, nor did he go ahead to lead us; his attitude seemed just that of the true and loyal friend who says: "I cannot help, but when danger is at hand remember always that I am here, to stand—or fall—with you."[16]

They trekked through the night and breached the pass before dawn. With the immediate danger past, Stoker turned back and saw that the figure was no longer accompanying them. He made no mention of the extra man to the other two. It was only after they reached a safe place to stop for the day, had made a fire, and sipped some hot cocoa, that the subject came up. One of Stoker's colleagues began by asking: "Did either of you see anything?" When no one answered, he continued: "I saw—I thought I saw a man ..." The other then said: "I saw him too."[17] Stoker later described the exchange:

They had both seen him. We had all three been sensible of his presence throughout the most trying part of the night; we all three agreed that the moment he left us was when we felt we had put the danger behind.

Again, I cannot exaggerate how real his presence was, how content one felt—despite the mystery of it—that he should be there, what a strength and comfort his presence seemed to be. It was a strange experience. We felt that his presence had brought us great luck.

Stoker elaborated slightly in a 1930s interview, saying that he and his companions were agreed on the presence's "general movements, the sense of friendliness and comfort he'd given us ..."[18] With the presence gone, their luck shortly ended. Wrote Stoker: "Our boots were in ribbons, food finished, strength ebbing fast. Food must be obtained at whatever the cost, or else we would only drop in our tracks and die." They came across a goatherd and threw themselves on his mercy. He provided food, but after they left, reported them to Turkish authorities. They reached the Mediterranean, as Stoker described it, "a wondrous, soul-inspiring, body-inspiriting sight to three worn and weary sailors." But on the eighteenth day of their flight they heard a crash in the bushes around their hiding place and found themselves staring down the barrels of rifles held by highly agitated Turkish soldiers. They were once again prisoners of war. Stoker would not be freed until February 1917.

After the war ended, Stoker wrote to Sir Arthur Conan Doyle, the author of the Sherlock Holmes stories, about his encounter with a fourth presence. Doyle, who had an acute interest in the supernatural, replied: "It is the same experience as Shackleton's sledge party, which had an extra man. One of you was probably mediumistic (without knowing it). Many are. Some friend took advantage of that fact ..."[19]

A world populated by unseen beings that can be summoned as required during times of great need bears little resemblance to the rational world we are supposed to inhabit. It seems like a throwback to an earlier age, when monks would disappear into the desert for years, only to emerge with accounts of religious epiphanies and encounters with divine beings, or when it was generally accepted that guardian angels watched over each one of us and would come, as needed, to our spiritual and physical aid. The first and most obvious explanation for the Third Man Factor, then, is that it is merely a contemporary twist on a very old idea, that of the guardian angel. The conditions encountered by explorers are, after all, not very different from the isolation and hardship that invited interventions from guardian angels, or God, in the past.

CHAPTER FOUR

The Guardian Angel

WHILE SERVING IN THE ROYAL NAVY during the Second World War, British neurologist Macdonald Critchley studied the cases of 279 sailors and airmen who had been cast adrift. In his 1943 study *Shipwreck-Survivors*, he described the ordeals that befell the men, including gruesome physical conditions like "immersion foot," but also harrowing psychological aberrations such as bioscopic fantasies, where past events from a person's life flash before them at incredible speed. It was during the course of one interview for his study that Critchley first came across a report of a very different experience, that of a "guardian angel."

The account came from a Royal Navy Fleet Air Arm pilot who, with his observer, was forced to ditch into the North Atlantic on May 25, 1941. They had been on a reconnaissance mission tracking the German battleship *Bismarck*, operating at night, in terrible weather, and without radar. They became lost over the sea, their aircraft eventually ran out of fuel, and was forced down. They were soon adrift in a rubber dinghy. The conditions were appalling, characterized by Critchley as "severe physical discomfort … going on to utter collapse. There had been exposure to bitter cold and wet; and intense thirst and lack of food…. Prospects of rescue were remote, and though from time to time hopes would soar in an extravagant and unwarranted fashion, they would soon be dashed again with realization of their tragic plight." Through it all, the pilot and observer both "kept imagining that there was a third person along with them."[1]

The two men had no doubt as to the identity of their visitor. They said an angel had helped to see them through their terrifying ordeal. Critchley found this "not surprising … especially in the case of distressed and exhausted shipwrecked seamen. The 'Guardian Angel' motif is inescapable to those with strong beliefs." He was aware of the weighty theological tradition behind the concept: "The notion of an *angelo custode* is a common teaching and is depicted in religious art as an angel with a wide wingspan standing as an unseen protector behind a little child." Not all who have encountered an unseen presence attribute it to a divine origin. But for those with strong beliefs, like Ron DiFrancesco in the World Trade Center, or the Fleet Air Arm pilot and his observer, help came in the form of an angel. For others of faith, the Third Man came cloaked in different religious garb, as with Shackleton's "Divine Companion" and McKinlay's overtly spiritual encounter with a presence. It was, then, not in scientific journals that Critchley turned to look for further accounts of the Third Man. Instead, he wrote, "in theological literature we find the most explicit references." Critchley examined works of purely religious character, and found examples he thought more likely to have been presence experiences than religious visions. He identified one in the autobiography of the Spanish nun Saint Teresa of Avila (1515–82):

> I was in prayer ... when I saw Christ at my side—or, to put it better, I was conscious of Him, for neither with the eyes of the body nor with those of the soul did I see anything.... I could not help realizing that He was beside me.... It is not a suitable comparison to say that it is as if a person were in the dark, so that he cannot see someone who is beside him, or as if he were blind. There is some similarity here, but not a great deal, because the person in the dark can detect the other with his remaining senses, can hear him speak or move, or can touch him. In this case there is nothing like that.[2]

IT HAS BEEN ESTIMATED that during the early years of Christianity, as many as five thousand Christian hermits retreated to the desert where they sought spiritual renewal and communion with God through solitude, fasting, self-inflicted pain, meditation, and prolonged prayer.[3] The fourth-century monks of the Thebaid felt the near proximity of God in the deserts of Egypt, where they lived in an isolated environment of reduced sensory input. Wrote social critic and novelist Aldous Huxley about the role of sensory deprivation in religious traditions: "If you read the life of Milarepa, the great Tibetan hermit, or if you read the lives of St. Anthony and St. Paul, hermits in the Christian tradition, you can see that this isolation did in fact produce visionary experiences."[4] Milarepa, after living for many months in a cave, was visited by his sister who was terrified at the sight of him. She felt as if she had seen a ghost. Little wonder. In his *Life* Milarepa described his appearance:

> My body was wasted by asceticism. My eyes were sunk in
> their sockets. All my bones protruded. My fleshes were dried
> out and green. The skin covering my fleshless bones looked
> like wax. The hair on my body had become coarse and grey.
> From my head it streamed down in a frightening flood. My
> limbs were about to fall apart.[5]

Milarepa, however, is credited with having attained a state of complete enlightenment, and a Tibetan Buddhist monastery now stands at what is purported to be the entrance to his cave.

Similarly, among tribal people in Africa, Asia, and commonly in aboriginal groups in North America, a solitary period in the wilderness, with attendant hardship and deprivation, marks a rite of passage from childhood to adulthood through the acquisition of a guardian spirit. In particular, the vision or spirit quest of North American Indians represents a "sought vision induced by hunger, thirst, purgatives, and self-laceration."[6] A young man would be sent to an isolated place to fast and pray. The result: "He may be visited by what, he thinks, are supernatural beings."[7] A similar rite is practised by the Inuit, where monotony, through long walks on the tundra, or confinement to an igloo, is used to evoke a spirit.

A Jesuit account from 1642 described a North American Indian spirit quest. A young man, "when but fifteen or sixteen years of age, retired to the woods to prepare himself by fasting for the appearance of some Demon." After living in isolation and going without food for sixteen days, "he saw an aged man of rare beauty who came down from the Sky, approached him, and looking kindly at him said: 'Have courage. I will take care of thy life.'" In another recorded case, a Plains Indian named Medicine Crow "fasted for four days. He cut off a finger and offered it to the Sun.... The blood poured down." He collapsed, but near dawn, "he saw a young man and a young woman coming from the west." The benevolent beings "talked with him [and] gave him medicine."[8] These rare surviving aboriginal accounts are remarkably similar to those given by Western explorers and climbers, and also by survivors of man-made disasters.

The devout always find God, or angels, in situations of extremity. John Brown, a sixty-five-year-old collier, trapped for twenty-three days in a British coal-pit without food in 1835, was near death when finally rescued: "A more ghastly figure could hardly be pictured. His face had not the pallor of a fainting fit or of death, but wore a strange sallow hue like that of a mummy. His flesh seemed entirely gone, nothing left but the bones, under a thin covering of leather-like skin." Most grotesquely, a white fungus, usually found in the rotting logs of the mine shafts, had crept over his entire body, as he had lain still—too weak to move—for much of his entombment. A newspaper quoted Brown saying afterwards, "In the darkness I was not alone; I had company the earth could not exclude, for God was with me." A commentator later argued: "It is at least probable ... that he had that feeling, common to others in extreme ordeals, of the company of another person, and that, since he was a devout Presbyterian, that other person was for him God."[9]

An August 1967 article in the *American Journal of Psychiatry* gave an account of a mine disaster in Pennsylvania in which two men survived entombed more than ninety metres below the surface for fourteen days. For the first six days of their entrapment they had no contact with the outside world, neither light nor food. After that point, rescuers were able to lower lights, microphones, and food to them. When they were finally rescued, the miners "both claimed to have seen things while in the cavern."[10] They were examined by psychiatrists on the second and third day after their ordeal ended. Both reported having overtly religious encounters with a presence, experiences that were focused on the first six days of their ordeal, when they were out of contact with the outside world. They were interviewed alone, and together, and in several instances both "claimed to have seen the same things at the same time." In particular, both miners, one a twenty-eight-year-old Lutheran man, the other a fifty-eight-year-old Roman Catholic, described having "seen" Pope John XXIII dressed in his papal regalia. After the pope's appearance, the younger miner said: "I knew we were going to be saved." He said he was not especially religious, but nevertheless had the feeling that the "Lord was with him all the time." The second man said they had looked at the Pope often—"about 5,000 times." The younger man also said that he had seen a woman with long hair kneeling at prayer, and that her presence had persisted for several days, even after rescuers had made contact with them.

Building collapses can lead to similar accounts. Park Seung-hyung, a nineteen-year-old clerk who worked in the children's clothing section of the Sampoong department store in Seoul, Korea, was trapped after the store collapsed in July 1995, killing more than three hundred people. Park went without food and with little water for sixteen days, surviving in a pocket beneath a crushed elevator shaft, a space that was too small for her even to sit up in. All around her were the decomposing bodies of other victims. The young woman, who was suffering from severe dehydration when she was finally pulled from the debris, reported that a monk had appeared to her a number of times during her ordeal. "He gave me an apple, and this kept my hope alive," she said.[11] Her mother called the monk's visit a miracle.

Another account of an overtly religious experience involved Will Jimeno, a New York Port Authority police officer who rushed to the World Trade Center on 9/11. Jimeno's story was made famous by Oliver Stone's 2006 film, *World Trade Center*. That morning, Sergeant John McLoughlin asked for police volunteers to assist in mounting a rescue in the north tower. He needed men trained to use a breathing apparatus, and Jimeno, who had graduated from the police academy that January, volunteered. The five-member team was in a concourse that connected the south and north towers, pushing carts with the heavy air packs, when there was a loud noise, and a shudder. Suddenly they saw a "wall of destruction" bearing down on them. McLoughlin yelled: "Run toward the freight elevator!"[12] Dominick Pezzulo was in front, Jimeno followed, McLoughlin was third, and two other officers followed when they were all buried in the debris from the collapse of the south tower. As soon as the noise subsided McLoughlin called out: "Sound off." Of the four, only Pezzulo and Jimeno answered.

Jimeno was pinned in a sitting position, with a slab of concrete on his lap. Pezzulo, who was close by, was able to free himself from the debris and he worked to free Jimeno, but the concrete was too heavy for him to shift. McLoughlin was trapped in a tiny air pocket about six metres from the others. At one point Pezzulo drew his sidearm and fired it into a hole through which light from above filtered. He hoped to attract the attention of rescuers, but soon the ground began to shake for a second time and a loud noise built into a violent crescendo. Twenty-nine minutes after they had been trapped, the north tower was also collapsing. "Dominick, something big is coming," Jimeno said. The crush of concrete compacted the open space into something the size of a small tent. Pezzulo was hit with terrible force. He cried out at the impact, then moments later said in a calm voice: "I'm hurt. I'm hurt bad." The two men spoke to each other for a few minutes, before Pezzulo died facing the pale natural light that still filtered into their prison.

Jimeno's situation was deteriorating. He was in acute pain from his leg injuries and was desperately thirsty. Time passed slowly. It seemed hopeless. He was in a small space, buried under concrete slabs, broken pipes, and steel beams. Dust and smoke hung in the air. Even after he and McLoughlin had been buried for close to ten hours, there was no sign of any rescue attempt. McLoughlin would groan every so often. Jimeno closed his eyes. Then all at once, he was aware of a powerful presence with him: "I saw Jesus coming toward me. I was really thirsty. When I saw Jesus, I knew."[13] There was no face, but Jimeno knew it was Christ. "I remember asking Jesus, 'If I get to Heaven, can I have some water?'"[14] The vision did not stay with him for long, but it infused him with hope. He felt it was telling him something: "We're going to make it out." Of the 2,800 people buried by the collapse of the World Trade Center, only twenty emerged alive from "the pile,"

as rescue workers called the enormous mound of debris—
1,360 metric tons of steel girders, concrete, and other wreckage.
Among them were Will Jimeno and John McLoughlin.

THE WORD *ANGEL* APPEARS SEVERAL HUNDRED TIMES in the
Bible, where they are portrayed as mighty messengers and soldiers
with frightening powers, the executors of God's will, as in Genesis,
where they guard the east gates of Eden with flashing swords, or in
Revelation, where they battle a dragon. But they also act as
guardians, like the angel who delivered St. Peter from prison. In
the Old Testament, God says to Moses: "My angel shall go before
thee." In Psalm 90:11 we are told: "He hath given his angels
charge over thee; to keep thee in all thy ways." In the New
Testament, the idea appears in Hebrews 1:14: "Are they not all
ministering spirits, sent forth to minister for them who shall be
heirs of salvation?" The Roman Catholic Church maintains a Feast
of Guardian Angels, which has for centuries been held each year on
October 2. In his "Meditation for the Feast of the Guardian
Angels," Pope John XXIII wrote: "We must remember how
admirable was the intention of divine Providence in entrusting to
the angels the mission of watching over all mankind, and over
individual human beings, lest they should fall victims to the grave
dangers which they encounter."[15] Nowhere is this idea more fully
developed than the appearance of the archangel Raphael in the
Book of Tobit.

The Book of Tobit was written in the second century BC, and
describes a time about six hundred years before the birth of Christ.

The setting is Nineveh, a great city of Assyria, located on the banks of the Tigris (modern-day Mosul, Iraq). Tobit and other Jews lived there as exiles following the deportation of the northern tribes of Israel to Assyria in 721 BC. A wealthy man, Tobit was a model of his faith, practising prayer, charity, and "continually blessing God and acknowledging God's majesty." His devotion landed him in trouble however, when he defied an Assyrian law that required those executed for crimes against the state to have their bodies dumped outside the city walls where they were left for scavenging animals. Whenever a Jew was put to death, Tobit would carry the body away secretly for burial. When he was found out, his property was seized, and he was forced into hiding. A series of further misfortunes culminated in Tobit's sudden blindness. He became despondent, and prayed that the Lord would "command my life breath to be taken from me." At the same time, in Ecbatana, in the realm of Media (in present-day Iran), a young woman, Sarah, also prayed to die. A distant relative of Tobit, she had tried to marry seven times, but on each occasion, on her wedding night, her husband was slain by the demon Asmodeus. According to the Book of Tobit, God heard the prayers of Tobit and Sarah, and dispatched the archangel Raphael to aid them.

The book's major narrative involves Tobit's son, Tobias, who was sent by his father to Media to collect some money Tobit had deposited there before his troubles began. During an adventurous journey, Tobias was in the constant company of a traveller who claimed to be "Azarias," a cousin of the family, but who was, in fact, Raphael in disguise. The angel guarded and guided Tobias on his arduous journey. When Tobias was attacked by a large fish (a symbol of death) while bathing in the Tigris, Raphael intervened. He ordered Tobias to seize the fish and to remove its gall, heart, and liver because they make "useful medicines." Later, at Raphael's urging, Tobias married Sarah, and used the fish's heart and liver to drive Asmodeus from the bridal chamber. The demon fled "to the remotest parts of Egypt. But Raphael followed him, and at once bound him there hand and foot," rendering him harmless.

What is striking about this story is that Raphael in the Book of Tobit is not only a guardian to Tobias, but also, more specifically, he is a fellow-traveller and a guide to someone who takes a journey in lands he does not know.

God sends Raphael down to Earth in answer to the separate prayers for help of Tobit and of Sarah. Neither Tobit nor Sarah specifically asks for a guide on the roads of western Asia, but Tobit does urge Tobias to find someone as a companion on his journey, and Raphael providentially shows up when Tobias goes out to look for such a person. Raphael says he knows the region well. When introduced to Tobit, Raphael amusingly tells a not-so-angelic white lie by claiming to be Azarias. More to the point, he repeats that he knows the roads in the region, which does seem to be true. Tobit then says something that implies a pre-existing belief in angels who serve as guardian travel companions. He hopes, or perhaps prays, that an angel will accompany Tobias (and Azarias) on the journey. Again, when his wife expresses her fear about the journey, Tobit asserts confidently that a good angel will accompany Tobias—more truly than he realizes.

When Tobias and Raphael return to Nineveh successfully, Tobias follows Raphael's instructions and rubs the fish's gall into his father's eyes, restoring Tobit's sight. The angel then says to Tobit: "When you did not hesitate … to go and lay out the dead, your good deed was not hidden from me, but I was with you. So now, God sent me to heal you and your daughter-in-law Sarah." Raphael then reveals his true identity, saying that his apparent human body was a vision—evidently an angelic operation on the senses of human beings: "I am Raphael, one of the seven holy angels who present the prayers of the saints and enter into the presence of the glory of the Holy One." He points out that he never ate on the journey, as he would have done if his body had been real: "All these days I merely appeared to you and did not eat or drink, but you were seeing a vision."[16] Then, stricken with fear and humbled by this intervention by an emissary of God, Tobit falls to the ground as Raphael ascends to Heaven.

THOMAS AQUINAS, A THIRTEENTH-CENTURY Dominican friar, philosopher, and "angelic doctor," showed interest in the study of angels, largely basing his discussion on Biblical references and a few well-established authorities such as Saint Jerome. In particular, he looked to the Book of Tobit for evidence.

In his great theological statement, *Summa Theologiae*, Aquinas speculated on the nature of angels, taking a clear position that angels are incorporeal, meaning that they do not merely have bodies unlike ours, being made of light or air or some other subtler material than flesh and bone. Rather, they are spirit. They can nonetheless assume, or take on bodies, and they have power to move matter, though they are immaterial themselves. When speculating on whether angels in assumed bodies exercise "works of life," Aquinas directly quotes a conversation between Raphael and Tobias about whether he knows the roads in Media, and Raphael says he has often journeyed there. The argument is advanced that travel is one of the "works of life," to which Aquinas himself replies that the assumed body moves, but that is incidental to the angel's incorporeal substance.

Angels, he says, cannot alter the will of human beings, that is, they cannot make our basic desires and inclinations different from what they are; only God has the power to do that. They can, however, persuade or influence us, by presenting specific desirable objects and images that help call us to God and virtue, and to resist the opposing persuasions of the fallen angels, or devils.[17] He goes on, accordingly, to argue that angels can affect our imagination and our senses in various ways, both inwardly (in mental images and in dreams) and outwardly. They can affect our temperament by influencing our chemistry, that is, the balance and motion of our "humours." Outwardly, they can present themselves to us by way of their assumed bodies (which are no more their own substance than our clothes are ours).

When he turned to the help that angels give us, as "ministering angels" (to minister in this sense connotes the supply of services or goods), and in particular to the ministering role of some of them as our guardians, he concludes that there are indeed guardian angels and each of us (not just Christians) has one.

Mostly, this guardianship has to do with guiding or "instigating" us towards goodness and God, rather than extricating us from particular physical or psychological difficulties. That explains why Aquinas was concerned with persuasion and enlightenment ("illumination") rather than rescue. Angels are not primarily security guards or safety experts.

"Sometimes, however," he writes, "beyond the general law, they appear visibly to human beings, by an exceptional favour (or grace) of God, similarly to how miracles happen beyond the order of nature." We can speculate on why these exceptions might occur. Moral and physical challenges can often overlap; the angels may want to save people from death before they have done their work in life, and they may want to save them from despair or death while in a bad state of mind. In emergencies, guardian angels may want to show up visibly, tangibly, in order to give clear, unmistakable directions, going beyond inner promptings and dreams.

The familiar expression, "How many angels can dance on the head of a pin?" is associated with medieval theology and particularly with Aquinas. The expression is usually used pejoratively, to draw attention to unreal abstraction or excessive subtlety, which, indeed, Aquinas often is accused of. The line seems to go back to friendly jokes among medieval university students, but Aquinas really does come close to counting angels dancing on the heads of pins. He held that angels, although incorporeal, can physically act upon the material world, but he raised the question whether more than one angel can act at one place—and the head of a pin is certainly a place. Aquinas concluded that only one angel can act at one place (and that an angel, not being the infinite God, can only act at one place at one time).

So Aquinas does suggest one possible answer to the question about how many angels can dance on the head of a pin: One.

However that may be, the one-angel-at-one-time-at-one-place theory is consistent with many of the experiences in this book. The presences—call them angels—do not show up as whole search-and-rescue teams, but as lone individuals. One angel, it seems, is quite sufficient for the task at hand.

IT HAS BEEN MORE THAN SEVEN HUNDRED YEARS since Aquinas took up the problem of angels. What is remarkable is that polls show that most people still believe in their existence. One survey, conducted in 1993 for *Time* magazine, revealed that 69 percent of Americans accepted angels as a fact, and that 46 percent said they have their own guardian angel.[18] Such beliefs do not arise from reading ancient writings like the Book of Tobit. If anything, many people today are aware only of the sentimental-ized angels that serve as garden cherubs, or the putti which appear on everything from greeting cards to tote bags. There are also the angelic guides of New Age spirituality.

Michael Murphy, in his 1992 book *The Future of the Body*, which is regarded as holy writ among New Agers, argued that some visions of angels can be readily dismissed as the "fancies of super-stitious folk." But some, he said, "defy easy explanation. For example, apprehensions of phantom figures have been reported by ultra-distance runners, sailors, explorers, and adventurers not given to occult experience." Murphy argued this is evidence "that humans can indeed perceive disembodied entities." He said that these entities provide guidance at moments of extreme hardship, and "sometimes lend comfort, challenge comfortable assumptions, convey information, suggest that life has dimensions beyond the range of the ordinary senses, or bring ecstasy to their percipient."[19] Murphy further suggested that the presence was manifest when each individual struggled at the point of exhaustion to maintain vigilance: "Conceivably, this stress-induced vigilance focused their perception to an extraordinary degree while their ordinary perceptual barriers were lowered through fatigue so that they were open to psychic visitations."[20]

Contemporary angels are, however, often stripped of their great powers, even their powers to "challenge comfortable assumptions," and are instead portrayed either as adorable, chubby children in nappies, or beautiful, golden-haired youths. While angels remain of interest to the devout, the belief also proliferates among people who have only a generalized sense of spirituality. "One of the things God created angels to do was to be our friends," said Eileen Elias Freeman, author of the bestseller *Touched by Angels*. But for many people, God would seem to have very little to do with it, and the concept of friendship is often an entirely selfish one. People are likely to treat angels like domestic workers, available to assist with menial tasks such as helping them to find convenient street parking, or lose weight. Harold Bloom, in his book *Omens of Millennium*, likened angels to "household pets," there to provide companionship and unconditional love. "Whatever original purpose the angels served, their prime enterprise now seems to be reassuring Americans," Bloom wrote.[21]

The angel encountered by Ron DiFrancesco at the World Trade Center was different. So too was that which aided the two Fleet Air Arm servicemen. They had all the appearances of a true angelic revelation, and seemed to be, like the angel who bound the demon Asmodeus in Egypt, or the angel who protected Daniel in the lion's den, beyond the order of nature.

WILLIAM JAMES, IN HIS INFLUENTIAL 1902 study, *The Varieties of Religious Experience*, described the phenomenon this way: "It is as if there were in the human consciousness a sense of reality, a feeling of objective presence, a perception of what we may call 'something there,' more deep and more general than any of the more special and particular 'senses.'"[22] In his study, James did not rely on examples of presences derived from life-and-death adventures, but from everyday experience in common surroundings.

James, a professor at Harvard University and the brother of novelist Henry James, was a philosopher and psychologist. He considered his study of religion essentially "a study in human nature," but his intent was to fashion a defence of the religious impulse. The book was written when James was in Europe convalescing from acute heart pain that had left him severely debilitated. He was not yet sixty, but was confronting his own mortality. The book is a descriptive survey that addresses aspects of human nature that involve religious experience. He was less interested in religious institutions or doctrines of faith, than in "the feelings, acts, and experiences of individual men in their solitude, so far as they apprehend themselves to stand in relation to whatever they may consider the divine." He resisted proselytizing, but he did write that through religious experience it is possible to access a greater, alternative reality: "The further limits of our being plunge, it seems to me, into an altogether other dimension of existence from the sensible and merely 'understandable' world." Among the cognitive experiences of religion he collected were reports of an unseen presence. Wrote James:

> It often happens that an hallucination is imperfectly developed: the person affected will feel a "presence" in the room, definitely localized, facing in one particular way, real in the most emphatic sense of the word, often coming suddenly, and as suddenly gone; and yet neither seen, heard, touched or cognized in any of the usual "sensible" ways.[23]

He quoted a friend who had encountered a presence, a perception that "was indescribably *stronger* than the ordinary certainty of companionship when we are in the close presence of ordinary living people. The something seemed close to me, and intensely more real than any ordinary perception." On another occasion, the friend described an abrupt sense of a presence developing with urgent intensity, but this time it went beyond

> a mere consciousness of something there, but fused in the general happiness of it, a startling awareness of some ineffable good. Not vague either, not like the emotional effect of some poem, or scene, or blossom, of music, but the sure knowledge of the close presence of a sort of mighty person, and after it went, the memory persisted as the one perception of reality.

James also cited an 1895 published account: "Suddenly without a moment's warning my whole being seemed roused to the highest state of tension or aliveness, and I was aware, with an

intenseness not easily imagined by those who had never experienced it, that another being or presence was … quite close to me."
In *The Varieties of Religious Experience*, William James placed such
experiences squarely in the realm of religious, if not specifically
angelic, experience.

This same intensity and sense of aliveness is sometimes
reported in cases described by explorers. Pioneer American
naturalist John Muir, in October 1872, found himself stranded
halfway up a cliff face on Mount Ritter in the Sierra Nevada. His
arms were spread out and he was unable to move up or down: "My
doom appeared fixed. I must fall. There would be a moment of
bewilderment, and then a lifeless tumble down the one general
precipice to the glacier below." Then, very suddenly, he was
possessed of a new power. Whatever it was, it "came forward and
assumed control…. Had I been borne aloft upon wings, my deliverance could not have been more complete." That day Muir, who
later was to help found the Sierra Club, became the first person to
reach the summit of Mount Ritter. He had no idea what happened
to him, but offered as one possible explanation, a guardian angel.

For people of faith, this is the most obvious explanation for the
Third Man phenomenon. What is striking, however, is that many
of those who have experienced a sensed presence, particularly in
more recent years, consider it not an intervention from an external,
supernatural agency but something from within, the product of
physiological or psychological mechanisms. It is not, for them, a
religious experience at all.

CHAPTER FIVE

The Pathology of Boredom

ENCOUNTERS WITH THE THIRD MAN are more prevalent today than at any point in history for the simple reason that far more people are engaged in journeys of endurance in extreme and unusual environments (EUEs) than ever before. Psychologists coined the term *EUE* to describe environments that are extreme, in the sense that they pose danger or cause discomfort, and unusual, because they're novel. A large number of factors determine if an environment achieves the EUE standard. They have been generally lumped into three broad categories: environments in which survival depends on advanced technology (space, deep ocean); environments that require special equipment and techniques but can be a natural habitat for some human groups (the Arctic, mountains, deserts); and environments transformed by disaster (earthquake, hurricane, war, terrorist attack).[1] Other EUEs include traumatic environments, such as those experienced by shipwreck survivors adrift in the ocean. Antarctica certainly fits the bill. So do sky and space. One frequent characteristic of EUEs is monotony.

THE AVIATOR CHARLES LINDBERGH found he was not alone during his attempt to make the first solo, non-stop transatlantic flight from New York to Paris, when the twenty-five-year-old was taxed to the point where he felt that he was "crossing the bridge which one sees only in last, departing moments." Lindbergh had taken off from Roosevelt Field near New York City early on May 20, 1927. Using only a magnetic compass and an air-speed indicator, he flew his monoplane, the *Spirit of St. Louis*, northeast along the coast, and was spotted over Nova Scotia and Newfoundland, before turning out over the Atlantic Ocean towards Ireland. The flight was gruelling. Ice collected on the wings as he passed through a thunderhead, and a magnetic storm upset his bearings. He then flew blind through banks of fog. After he had been airborne for seventeen hours, Lindbergh felt he could not go on without sleep. Sleep meant certain death, however, and Lindbergh was grateful for the structural instability of the *Spirit of St. Louis*, which, when he drifted into the borderlands of sleep, would veer in such a way as to jolt him awake. At other times he braced himself with icy rainwater. He gradually became aware that, while his body demanded sleep, and his mind made decisions his body failed to heed, he had ceded control to a "separate mind," a force that he recognized as being something of himself, and yet not.

At the nineteenth hour, Lindbergh reached the halfway point of the flight. He had planned to celebrate the achievement, but found it singularly unimportant when the time came. He was no longer hungry or thirsty. He abandoned writing in his log. Still the plane droned on. It was during the twenty-second hour that Lindbergh suddenly encountered a presence in the fuselage of the *Spirit of St. Louis*. Struggling to stay awake, and at times flying so low to avoid thunderheads that he could feel the spray from the surging Atlantic, Lindbergh became aware that he had company. In fact, he thought there was more than one being travelling with him. He recalled staring at the instrument panel, and then,

> the fuselage behind me becomes filled with ghostly presences—vaguely outlined forms, transparent, moving, riding weightless with me in the plane. I feel no surprise at their coming. There's no suddenness to their appearance. Without turning my head, I see them as clearly as though in my normal field of vision.[2]

Lindbergh felt the "phantoms" were speaking to him, and he judged them to be friendly. He was in no way startled by these beings. He felt he knew them; they were familiar, and he felt also that they were there to help, "conversing and advising on my flight, discussing problems of my navigation, reassuring me, giving me messages of importance unattainable in ordinary life."

Later the same day Lindbergh saw a speck on the sea. As he flew closer he realized it was a fishing boat, and then he saw many others. He soon reached a green headland, which he established was the southwestern coast of Ireland. He spiralled down towards a village, and saw people run out of their houses into the streets, look up, and wave. Lindbergh found: "The wish to sleep has left, and with it the ghostly presences which began to ride with me this morning."[3]

He had expected to be eighty kilometres off course, even with perfect flying weather, but now calculated that he was in fact only about five kilometres from his intended path. Word of the success of his flight was telegraphed around the world. Lindbergh continued on his way, flying over Plymouth, England, but intent on reaching Paris in order to complete the historic non-stop flight between the two continents. When he was approaching the French coastline, the *Spirit of St. Louis'* engine began to shake violently. Lindbergh thought he might have to make an emergency landing, but then realized that one of his fuel tanks was empty, and with the turn of a valve the engine's comforting drone returned. He had already broken the world's distance record for a non-stop airplane flight. Now he was readying to make history. He made a triumphant circle around the Eiffel Tower, then found the landing field, Le Bourget Aerodrome. His arrival, ending a flight of thirty-three hours and thirty minutes, was witnessed by a crowd of 150,000 people. Lindbergh was mobbed as he emerged shakily from his cockpit. As the news of his safe arrival travelled, he became a hero in the United States and world-famous.

In a book published shortly after his historic flight, Lindbergh made no mention of his encounter with the ghostly presences. It was a factual account that sought to preserve something of the privacy the shy young man came to covet. But with time he gradually let his secret out. He first recorded the "disembodied beings"[4] in a fragmentary, unpublished memoir written in 1939. He later added detail to what was obviously a highly personal experience, but it would still be years, nearly three decades from the date of the flight, before he finally revealed publicly his unusual encounter. It was the most talked-about revelation in his book, *The Spirit of St. Louis*, which became a bestseller and won him a Pulitzer Prize. However, the news first appeared in the *Saturday Evening Post*, on June 6, 1953. Lindbergh wrote:

> I've never believed in apparitions, but how can I explain the forms I carried with me through so many hours of this day? Transparent forms in human outline—voices that spoke with authority and clearness—that told me—that told me—but what did they tell me? I can't remember a single word they said.

Lindbergh never dismissed the presences as hallucinations, but embraced them as "emanations from the experience of ages." He had the sense of having, through his long flight, touched a greater reality. Despite being unable to remember the details of his communications with his phantom companions, he did remember enough to have described them as "friendly advice" and reassurance.

THE PSYCHOLOGIST WOODBURN HERON theorized that Charles Lindbergh's encounter with ghostly presences was a product not of sleep deprivation, the most obvious explanation, but of monotony, and argued "it is not improbable that some unexplained airplane and railroad accidents have been occasioned by effects of prolonged monotonous stimulation."[5] He pointed out that the brain depends on continuing arousal from sensory bombardment, and that "a changing sensory environment seems essential for human beings." Said Heron: "Monotony is an important and enduring human problem." High signal pressure—that is a constant barrage of signals received by the sense organs—is needed to maintain not only vigilance but also wakefulness. People have evolved for, and are accustomed to, a "normal" range of stimulus input and variety. They are little prepared for its absence.

Monotony is not confined to wild places on Earth. Monotony, together with isolation, can also be found in "capsule environments." These artificial environments make it possible for human beings to survive in places where it would be difficult, if not impossible, to sustain life, such as in the sky, at great ocean depths, or most significantly, in space.[6] Capsule environments are slowly transforming human existence, as ever greater numbers of people enter capsules for work or play. Monotony had a place in humanity's past, and it has a place in humanity's future.

It is a curious fact that explorers are driven into rigidly monotonous environments in an effort to escape from … monotony. In his study of the psychology of space travel, British neurologist W. Grey Walter argued: "The urge to explore is a part of our nervous equipment…. The human species is unstable in stable environments."[7] Walter studied societies during periods in history when there was an explosion of geographic exploration and adventure, and found the theory of some historians that exploration was a response to economic and military necessity to be largely untrue. In fact, Walter noted that the home countries during such periods were often "hospitable, prosperous and plagued only by familiar woes." Instead, he argued, an "interaction of mental forces" was a more powerful and more persistent factor. This is more true today than it ever has been. Large and growing numbers of people are involved in extreme sports and adventure travel, willingly placing themselves in extreme and unusual environments, as the first space tourists illustrate. Walter explained this as an attempt to escape monotony. Some contempt for bodily comfort, and a need for stimuli derived from risky activities, are part of everybody's makeup.

In research published in the journal *Neuron*, scientists even identified a primitive part of the brain that has a role in making people adventurous. By measuring blood flow, the British researchers found "novel stimuli" made the ventral striatum more active in subjects during controlled tests. The ventral striatum is involved in processing rewards, suggesting that seeking new and unfamiliar experiences is rewarded with what the authors called a "novelty bonus," through the release of neurotransmitters such as dopamine. (They further argued that this human tendency is exploited by companies that remarket "identical, or near-identical, products" with new packaging.)[8] The desire to be adventurous is not a characteristic only of humans. Even laboratory rats in a maze choose different routes to food, when the option is available, and avoid areas that are familiar. In other words, rats too seek "to explore."

The irony is that in seeking to escape monotony, people place themselves in monotonous conditions, and there are no more monotonous conditions than those found in artificial environments, such as an aircraft cockpit under certain conditions, but especially in space travel. Heron coined a term for the consequences of the absence of sensory input, calling it the "pathology

of boredom." As an example of the effects of monotony, he
pointed to long-distance truckers, who sometimes report bizarre
hallucinations. But of particular interest is Heron's reference to the
"break-off" phenomenon encountered among solitary pilots in
high-altitude flights, when the aircraft is flying straight and level,
when nothing else is near, and the horizon is no longer visible. The
pilot is secured to his seat, often in heavy clothing, with a limited
view, and subjected to background white noise from the engines.
Consequently he or she is exposed to a reduction in patterning and
organization of sensory input, while at the same time confronted
with "greater than usual stresses," because of the nature of the job.
Pilots in such circumstances break off the flight and descend.
Preceding these incidents, pilots have reported they were "keenly
aware of intense loneliness, isolation, and a sense of 'being out of
reach.'"[9] In one case, a pilot on a routine high-altitude test "had the
impression of being detached from the aircraft, of looking at
himself and the machine from outside."[10] Many fail to report the
experience, "feeling that it represents a mental aberration."[11] The
reports were not, after all, "from mystics but from practical men,
reluctantly given." Other pilots have described a feeling of "close-
ness to God." It is the tradition of many religions to use isolation,
monotony, and boredom to "achieve creative religious insights,
divine revelation, or spiritual rebirth. Such experiences are often
accompanied by visions of divine figures."[12] Piloting an aircraft
may appear "radically different from meditating in a cave," yet it
can also be an isolated and monotonous environment.

Heron, working with the psychologist Donald O. Hebb, used
funding from the Defence Research Board of Canada to make a

systematic study of "the effects of exposure for prolonged periods to a rigidly monotonous environment." Heron conducted sensory-deprivation experiments by isolating subjects in a chamber where, as much as possible, patterned or perceptual stimulation was cut off. The subjects, for example, wore translucent visors, and had their hands and lower arms insulated against the sensation of touch. After long periods of isolation, many experienced "stimulus-hunger." They would "talk to themselves, whistle, sing or recite poetry." The need for stimulation became so intense that even stroking one finger with another could evoke intense pleasure. Some "reported that they felt as if another body were lying beside them in the cubicle; in one case the two bodies overlapped, partly occupying the same space."[13]

Hebb related this to a "disturbance of the body image." The body image is, as he put it, a "mental construct," that can be overlooked by normal people since it is supported by other cues: "Your awareness of yourself, at this moment, is a hallucination that happens to agree with reality." However, the sensation of the phantom limb experienced by people after an amputation illustrates that our awareness of the body is "not a direct perception." So did Lindbergh's encounter derive from a disturbance of body image? Hebb supported Heron's suggestion that Lindbergh's phantom passengers were a product of monotony. In his *Essay on Mind*, Hebb argued that at high altitude, "the ground below may take on a monotonous sameness. The ocean does the same from lower altitudes, and Charles Lindbergh in his solitary flight across the Atlantic was aware of 'ghostly presences.'"[14] Others have been, too.

EDITH FOLTZ STEARNS BELONGED to the generation of pioneer
women aviators of whom Amelia Earhart is the best known. She
earned her pilot's licence in 1928, and started barnstorming in the
northwestern United States. In 1929, she flew in the first-ever
all-female air race dubbed the "Powder Puff Derby," which started
in Santa Monica, California, and ended in Cleveland, Ohio,
4,300 kilometres and eight days later. Entrants had to navigate
using only dead reckoning and road maps. A quarter of the twenty
competitors failed to finish the race, and one died. Stearns finished
second in her class of light aircraft.

In a 1932 competition, Stearns found herself off course and low
on fuel. She felt her only chance to avoid crashing was to attempt a
landing on a railroad track she had been following. She began her
descent and was preparing to risk a landing when a voice cried out:
"No! No, Edie, don't!" She recognized it as belonging to an old
classmate, a girl who had died in an automobile accident as a
teenager. Startled, she climbed quickly, levelled off, and continued
dead ahead. Within a few minutes, the Phoenix runway came into
view, and she was able to land safely. Said Stearns: "I never fly alone.
Some 'presence' sits beside me, my 'copilot' as I have come to think
of it. In times of great danger some unseen hand actually takes the
controls and guides me to safety."[15]

The phenomenon of an intervention by a "guiding spirit"
occurred again in dramatic fashion during the Second World War,
when Stearns was serving with the Air Transport Auxiliary in the
United Kingdom, flying new or refurbished aircraft from factories
to air force bases. On one occasion she was ordered to fly a
Mosquito bomber from Hamble to Hawarden, a Royal Air Force

base in Scotland, despite limited visibility. She was reluctant to take off, and sat for some time in the cockpit until an officer asked her what she was doing. She didn't want to reveal that she was waiting for her unseen co-pilot. Stearns then took off without incident, but as she approached what she calculated to be her destination, she became disoriented in thick fog with zero visibility. She circled the area and dropped down, several times, but the appalling conditions forced her to pull up, a pattern that was repeated again and again. Night was descending, and as slim as her chances seemed for a daylight landing, they would be made worse at night. Said Stearns: "I've had some close calls in my time but never have I felt so lost and alone, so utterly doomed." She began to pray for guidance.

Suddenly, a voice barked out, "Edie! Look out!" This time, it was, she felt, her father, who had died only recently. Without hesitation she shot upwards, and narrowly missed a hill. "From that moment I was no longer alone." She realized that she was well off course, but now felt strangely calm. With time and despite the darkness she found a highway, and followed it until she found a runway, nosed the plane safely down, and taxied up to the control tower. An irritated officer came running out and demanded to know why she disobeyed his orders and landed: "This field is closed." She replied that she had no radio, and that it was an emergency landing. In an account of her exploits published a decade later, Stearns said: "I never doubted I would make it—with the help of my copilot."

BRIAN H. SHOEMAKER IS ONE OF THOSE PILOTS whose ability to fly in difficult, sometimes extremely hazardous, conditions allowed for the true scientific "discovery" of Antarctica. Stationed at the United States Navy base at Quonset Point, Rhode Island, his squadron, VX-6, was deployed to McMurdo Station for four months during the Antarctic summer, when the extreme cold abated and allowed scientific parties to establish temporary encampments on the continent. Shoemaker Glacier, a tributary in the Southern Cross Mountains, in Victoria Land, is named for him. His contribution to what was technically called Naval Support Force Antarctica, but what most people called Operation Deep Freeze, eventually resulted in his appointment as commander during the 1980s. But in 1967, Lieutenant (later Captain) Shoemaker was on the frontlines of the quest for knowledge about the white continent as pilot of an H-34 helicopter.

In December of that year, he departed McMurdo, itself located on the southern-most tip of Ross Island in Antarctica, 3,500 kilometres south of New Zealand, with a co-pilot and another crewman, to fly a research team to a campsite on the Antarctic Plateau, the highlands that surround the South Pole for hundreds of kilometres in every direction. The altitude of the plateau, averaging close to three thousand metres, and its latitude, make it one of the most inhospitable places on Earth, raked by constant winds, and registering some of the coldest temperatures ever recorded. Shoemaker flew the helicopter to the west, crossing McMurdo Sound, and then up through the Trans-Antarctic Mountains, finally reaching the plateau and the site where the team of four glaciologists wanted to set up. Procedure called for the

H-34, its engine idling because of the cold, to remain with the science party until they had erected their tent, and demonstrated that their radio worked. The process took longer than anticipated. The scientists could not get the radio beacon to work. However, the radio itself was working, and Shoemaker made the decision that it was safe to leave them.

The helicopter started back, and about half an hour later, McMurdo lost all radio contact with it, likely because of a magnetic storm. With the loss of contact, the helicopter crew also lost their line back to the base. They had no navigator aboard. With twenty-four hours of daylight, and the landscape below a virtually unchanging field of white, they could not get a fix on their position. Shoemaker grew concerned that they were off course. He and his co-pilot could not see the mountains, and there was no way to maintain their heading. Shoemaker asked: "Are we drifting? Are we flying in a circle?" Their predicament remained unchanged for some time. Then Shoemaker felt that a "guiding presence" had joined them in the cockpit. It spoke, assuring him: "You're doing alright." Shoemaker asked himself, "Who was that? What was that?"[16] but he was not startled, and did not let on to his co-pilot what had happened. The presence then advised him to "turn to a heading about 20 degrees to the right." The co-pilot evidently sensed nothing wrong, but Shoemaker felt the presence of a Third Man strongly, standing immediately behind him. He turned the H-34 twenty degrees to the right as instructed. "I had nothing else to go by…. It was eerie. It wasn't frightening. It was a solace. That was the decision I had to make; follow it, or follow my own, and I had no idea which way to go."[17]

He never discussed the experience with his co-pilot, thinking perhaps "he might question my decision as to the bearing." The sense of presence lasted for at least half an hour, and persisted even after the helicopter reached the mountains that marked their correct route. But eventually, Shoemaker felt he could "brush this thing aside." They made it back to base within the normal margin of safety in terms of fuel.

Nor did Shoemaker discuss what had happened in the wardroom with any of the pilots; he was concerned about what they would think. But he later mentioned it to Father Gerry Creagh, a New Zealander who served as honorary U.S. Navy chaplain for over twenty-five summer seasons at the Chapel of the Snows, at McMurdo Station, becoming known unofficially as the Chaplain of Antarctica. Creagh told him "what had happened was not as uncommon as might be supposed. He said that it was one of those mysteries that is unexplainable in practical terms, but one that can be identified in terms of one's faith."[18]

AFTER A NIGHT LAUNCH OF THE SPACE SHUTTLE *Atlantis* on January 12, 1997, the shuttle docked with the Russian space station *Mir*. Along with a mountain of supplies, it deposited NASA astronaut Jerry M. Linenger, a medical doctor and Ph.D. in epidemiology who had served in the U.S. Navy before joining NASA in 1992. Linenger had previously flown in the space shuttle *Discovery* on an eleven-day mission in 1994, but was now to remain on *Mir* for an historic 132 days, logging 80 million kilometres in more than two thousand Earth orbits. The psychological effects of prolonged isolation, estrangement from the familiar, reduced sensory input, and unrelieved monotony—coupled with a need for high alertness—would be a source of significant stress. Together with other pressures, including physical changes, such as bone weakening, and what's called "space-adaptation syndrome" (a series of strange physiological shifts caused by weightlessness and space travel), this might have been stress enough. *Mir*, however, was operating well beyond its design life and consequently was plagued by a "domino-like progression" of mechanical failures. The mission was beset by chronic malfunctions, a dreary routine interrupted only by life-threatening emergencies.

There were frequent primary oxygen-system failures, and for several months the three crewmen—two Russian cosmonauts and Linenger—were inhaling ethylene glycol fumes and enduring thirty-two-degree Celsius temperatures, resulting from leaks in *Mir*'s corroded cooling lines. But these were the least of their worries. Early in Linenger's mission, during a crew changeover when six crewmembers were on *Mir* instead of the usual complement of three, a fire broke out on the space station. When the master alarm sounded, it was initially treated by the crew with relative indifference, because they had become so accustomed to its sound. Linenger was moving through the station, when he almost collided with Vasily Tsibliev, the incoming commander, who was floating frantically in the weightless environment from the module to which Linenger was headed. Linenger asked if it was serious, but before the Russian could answer, Linenger saw "a tentacle of smoke snaking its way behind him." He then saw the source: a roaring fire, the flames thirty centimetres in diameter at its base and jumping a metre high, spitting sparks. The fire was so hot it began melting metal. It threatened to swiftly cut its way through the aluminum hull. This would result in decompression and suffocation of the crew.

The smoke filling the modules was so thick that, Linenger said, "we could not count the fingers in front of our faces for nearly an hour." The crew appeared like wraiths through the haze, working frantically to suppress the fire. One passed close to Linenger clutching a dirty rag over his face. Warm air and smoke do not rise in space, so there was no escaping the smoke that burned their eyes and filled their lungs. Linenger struggled to put on an oxygen respirator, holding his breath while trying to untangle the head straps. Once on, he tried to draw a breath, but the device failed. Linenger thought he was going to die. He didn't panic: His training and character would not allow that. Instead he faced the situation with sober awareness. He began feeling along the bulkhead for another respirator. His head hurt, he was enveloped by darkness, time passed, each millisecond seeming like an eternity, and then he felt another respirator. This time, it worked.

Without oxygen respirators, Linenger said, "we would all have suffocated. Any more life-threatening, even a smidgeon, and we would have been six dead space explorers. Period."[19] Three of the Russian crewmen were dispatched to prepare one of the two *Soyuz* capsules docked on the *Mir* for evacuation. The second *Soyuz* capsule, however, was inaccessible because of the flames. The one spacecraft that was available could carry only three men. This meant three would die unless they could put out the fire. Three fire extinguishers were used to try to end the emergency, but they seemed to have no effect. In the end, after fourteen minutes, the fire burned itself out and they were spared. Three of the Russians then left, and those remaining did not dwell on what had happened—there were too many emerging demands of a routine nature—but they were not unaffected by it. Wrote Linenger: "We all reflected on how tenuous our existence was here on the frontier, how our lives could be snuffed out in an instant."

Later on, *Mir* barely escaped a "near-death" collision with an unmanned Progress cargo ship. The Progress resupply vessel had recently disgorged its cargo, and then had been loaded full of broken equipment and garbage. After it left, the spaceship, now effectively a garbage scow, would normally be directed into the upper atmosphere and burn up on re-entry, its mission complete. However, to the surprise of the *Mir* crew, a week after the disposable Progress had departed, they were informed by Russian ground control that the spaceship had in fact not been ordered back to Earth, and was to re-dock. The reason given was to test a new docking procedure that required the use of a manually controlled backup system on *Mir*.

This did not seem like a very good idea to Linenger: "It was designed to be a close-proximity backup system and was never intended to be used to drive the Progress in from great distance." What is more, there was no backup to the manually controlled system, since it *was* the backup system. If something failed, they would be in serious trouble, and this being *Mir*, failure was a reasonable probability. As it turned out, they did soon find themselves in trouble. A video screen that was to provide crucial visual cues filled with static, making it impossible to direct the approaching spacecraft. Suddenly the garbage scow took on all the characteristics of an incoming missile.

The Russian commander, Vasily Tsibliev, was forced to fly back and forth from his control station to the nearest porthole, to try to gauge the spacecraft's trajectory. At one point the other cosmonaut, Sasha Lazutkin, shouted: "It looks like it is coming right at us! It's coming way too fast." Tsibliev's face was covered in sweat as he blindly started firing the braking thrusters of the Progress. It was such a close call that at one point Tsibliev screamed to Linenger: "Prepare to abandon ship and get into the *Soyuz*!" All three men expected the Progress to hit *Mir*, but it somehow avoided impact. This time they found themselves thanking God for their survival.

The trouble continued. At another point, the failure of an altitude control computer sent *Mir* tumbling out of control. As a result, *Mir*'s solar panels could not track the sun, and the station lost power, going dark, and resulting in an "unnerving silence." It was a critical situation. Once again the crew faced the possibility that the power-dead station would have to be abandoned, and they might be forced to escape on their life raft, the *Soyuz* spacecraft. They turned off all the operating systems and waited in the dark until their orbit carried them back to the lighted side of the Earth, where the solar panels captured enough light to partially recharge the batteries. Then they had to wait again for the next orbit to bring them back into the sunlight. It took them two days to gather enough power to right *Mir*.

With such emergencies, and the routine breakdowns of critical systems causing the station's master alarm to blast on an almost daily basis, the burden of the mission began to take a serious toll on the crew. As a medical doctor, Linenger began to observe pathologies in the behaviour of his crewmates, caused by the combination of isolation and the nearly constant stress of life aboard the aging *Mir*. He was surprised that men psychologically screened for such conditions could be pushed, in his words, to "the edge of losing it." Even Linenger, who had experienced isolation while serving in the U.S. Navy, and who had studied the psychological impact that prolonged isolation can produce, "was astounded at how much I had underestimated the strain of living cut off from the world in an unworldly environment. The isolation was extreme in every way."

Notably, it was not the terrifying events that occurred on *Mir*, and the numerous brushes with death, but the isolation, and the monotony, that seem to have had the most profound impact. Linenger took measures to ensure he did not get to the same point of vulnerability as some of his crewmates. He maintained a vigorous work schedule, but always also made sure he had an hour a day on the treadmill, the effect of which seemed to relieve much of the mental burden. It was near the end of his mission, three and a half months in, that he had an experience quite unlike any he had ever had before.

When he was on the treadmill, Jerry Linenger would try to escape from the "painfulness" of his situation by visualizing places back on the green Earth. He would follow in his mind the same running routes he had taken before his mission. He would be transported in his mind back to California, where he would be running on the beach, seeing the homes, the Hotel Del Coronado, and the people, smiling, laughing, waving. He would be winking at the girls.

This process was described by Woodburn Heron, as early as 1957, as a necessary and understandable response by people to "rigidly monotonous environments…. [Some people] thought about traveling from one familiar place to another and would try to imagine all the events of the journey."[20] For Linenger, the visualization process would get him through a half-hour of the workout, which was important, because exercise in space is extremely difficult, and when he was on the treadmill he always felt as if he was carrying a man on his shoulders. He appreciated the escape.

Then one time, when not engaged in the process of visualization, Linenger suddenly became aware of the presence of another person, just at the periphery of his vision. He continued looking straight ahead. There was no need to turn and verify it. He knew the presence was there, and he knew also that it was not one of the cosmonauts. The presence was that of his father, Don Linenger, who had been dead for seven years. "I felt his presence strongly, perhaps because I was up there in the heavens, nearer to him. I would hold a silent conversation with him, and tell him that I missed him."[21] Jerry Linenger also understood his father's message, which was as strong as if it were spoken and it was encouraging. His father said, "I'm proud of you. You always wanted to be an astronaut, you made it, way to go."[22]

The presence did not relate to the misery of the conditions Jerry had been encountering, but had the effect of lifting him out of that situation. It afforded an opportunity to "escape." The astronaut found it a profoundly moving experience. He had been close to his dad. He'd had a happy, normal childhood, and they had always maintained a good relationship. At one point Linenger became concerned that a cosmonaut would come into the module and find him in this emotional state, and he tried to blink the presence away, but it remained with him for twenty minutes. After the experience ended, he felt mentally 100 percent better: "All that stress and strain just drained away."

Over the next few weeks, as his mission wound down, the experience was repeated. In all, he had a vivid encounter with the presence on three separate occasions, and perhaps had another seven episodes where he was just aware that his father was nearby, but there was no communication. Said Linenger: "It wasn't a religious experience, and I understood it as a physician as a psychological defence mechanism. But I didn't want to disbelieve it and I didn't rationalize it."[23]

THESE OCCURRENCES SUGGEST A RADICAL IDEA—that we are never, really, truly *alone*, that we can summon someone—some other—in certain situations, most commonly in extreme and unusual environments, where monotonous conditions prevail. The Third Man can be explained in part as an attempt by the brain to maintain a sufficient level of stimulation in a monotonous environment. There is no doubt that the pathology of boredom is an underlying factor in many EUEs, and that the Third Man feeds on monotony. But as we've seen, there's more to it than that.

CHAPTER SIX

The Principle of Multiple Triggers

ANOTHER KEY TO UNLOCKING THE THIRD MAN mystery is found in the experiences of three recent explorers in Antarctica: Briton Robert Swan, New Zealander Peter Hillary, and American Ann Bancroft. Each, at different times, experienced the Third Man during a struggle to the South Pole, across the cruel and monotonous landscape that Hillary termed "the great white everywhere." They each confronted an inventory of obstacles, including extreme fatigue, pain, and deprivation, often in combination with additional factors—a system of multiple triggers—with dramatic consequences. Each came to the same recognition: that there are unseen beings out there walking at the elbow of those in need. But the timing of the appearance of the Third Man is telling, as it is tied directly to specific incidents on their south polar journey. Wrote Hillary at the end of his own: "Oh, yes. They're still out there. I see them come and go…. And I still don't know what to do with them. Isn't that how it is for everybody?"[1]

ON DECEMBER 4, 1985, ROBERT SWAN was five hundred kilometres into a seventy-day march to the South Pole. The journey was intended to be a tribute to Captain Robert Falcon Scott, the doomed British explorer who was beaten in the race to the South Pole by Roald Amundsen, and died in 1912 with members of his sledge party on the return journey. Swan, along with Roger Mear and Gareth Wood, had been dragging sledges for nine hours a day, seven days a week, in an atmosphere largely devoid of sensory input. There was a predominant colour: white. There were no sounds save for the howl of the wind, those generated by the exertion of the men, and the sledge runners on the ice. Except for the numbing cold, Swan felt he might have been incarcerated in a sensory deprivation chamber.

They were closing in on the Beardmore Glacier, a vast river of ice more than fifty kilometres wide that made for treacherous travelling, its shattered surface mimicking the turbulent waters of a surging mountain stream, concealing dangerous crevasses. Things had not been going well. Swan wrote in his diary: "It's almost too awful to recount, but my sledge has become nearly impossible.... I just wanted out for the first time in my life, and that has hurt me very much indeed." It was the last three-hour session of the day, and Swan was struggling to pull his sledge. He was exhausted and reached the point where he concluded he could not continue for another kilometre, least of all the nine hundred kilometres remaining to the South Pole. It was a terrible realization, "a monumental kick in the stomach," to think that the Pole, which had been his goal for fifteen years, would prove to be out of reach. He had conceived the idea for the expedition and was its leader. He had done the most training. He was supposed to have been the toughest of the three. And he watched impotently as the other two men moved farther and farther away, until they were mere dots on the horizon. To make matters worse, a blizzard was gathering. Roger Mear wrote that "Robert was a distant black point, so minute that he was, at first, scarcely discernible. He was farther behind than any of us had ever been."[2] With the "weather continuing to deteriorate, the contrast poor and our tracks drifting over," Mear decided to go back to help Swan, who was now fully one and a half kilometres behind.

During his struggle, Swan had developed an odd idea: He became convinced that there were three men ahead of him, instead of two. In fact, he had experienced the sense so many times that, "it became quite normal." Still, he kept asking himself: "Am I the last? There are meant to be two … I am definitely number three at the moment, but I have just seen three ahead. How can that be?"[3] Swan finally arrived at the point where he could not continue, and sat down on his sled. He had reached the end. Then he immediately felt, though the others were still a great distance away, that he was not alone. He realized that the Third Man he had seen up ahead was now sitting there beside him. He thought it might be Robert Falcon Scott. Whoever it was, the sensation was vivid, so real, that he realized this other being was … laughing. Laughter is contagious, and Swan too began to laugh. He was soon "crying with laughter, at the futility of it and at the extraordinarily strange moment." He understood, however, that he was responding to the presence of another: "This laughter did not come from me, it came from whatever was there. And it was comforting."[4]

When Mear reached him, he was concerned about Swan's condition. He told him not to worry, and said he'd pull the sledge. Swan, still grinning, shrugged, and said: "Well, this is really quite bizarre." Mear is a tough guy, and Swan wondered whether he thought that he was losing his mind. Mear instructed Swan to ski ahead to the rest stop, and started to haul the sledge the remaining distance: "It took no more than four or five steps to realize that what Robert had been pulling for days felt heavier than the sledge at the beginning of the journey. It was more like hauling a great pine log through soft sand." They inspected Swan's sledge, and discovered that the runners had been mounted incorrectly, vastly increasing the burden on Swan. It was remarkable that he had made it as far as he had. They repaired the runners and resumed the trek. Swan never mentioned his encounter with the Third Man, saying it was a "personal thing. I felt it was keeping me sane, therefore I did not want to make it common, and talk about it."[5]

On January 11, 1986, Swan, Mear, and Wood reached the South Pole after travelling 1,421 kilometres, setting a record for the longest unassisted Antarctic march. Three years later, on May 14, 1989, Robert Swan reached the North Pole, and the British explorer claimed the last of the great polar prizes, becoming the first man in history to walk unsupported to both the North and South Poles.

IT WAS AN EXCRUCIATING ORDEAL FROM THE OUTSET. Peter Hillary, the adventurous son of Everest conqueror Sir Edmund, whose joint summit of Everest made them the first father-and-son team to accomplish the feat, set off from Scott Base on November 4, 1998, for the long haul, pulling two hundred kilograms. Hillary, a New Zealander, with Australians Jon Muir and Eric Philips, intended to complete Scott's final journey. Their goal was to get to the South Pole on foot, first crossing the Ross Ice Shelf, then dragging their sledges up the Shackleton Glacier to the Polar Plateau. Rather than fly out, they planned to turn around at the Pole and return by roughly the same route, the round trip totalling 2,900 kilometres. But the cold already bit at their fingers and toes. Storms pinned the men in their tiny tent. Winds pounded on them relentlessly. They were slowly starving, as the brutal march, and the weight of their heavily laden sledges, burned more calories each day than they could replenish.

The loads were heavy, but so was the company. Early in the trek, Hillary overheard Philips complaining about him into a satellite phone, and he suspected that both were talking about him as a problem. The burden of these suspicions weighed heavily on their subsequent endeavour. Hillary felt that they began to exclude him from their social interaction. Hillary's response was to pull back, allowing the others to go ahead as he sought solitude. The unchanging nature of the landscape only aggravated the situation. At one point he described life on the Ross Ice Shelf as a "monochrome of misery." "Everything was white, and my mind had nothing to read: nothing was coming in, because everything was white … with nothing coming in, I believe now everything comes out of you, everything is leached out of you like salt is leached from soil by fresh water." In such an environment, he wrote in his diary, "your sustenance is all from the thoughts in your head."[6]

Then, on day eighteen, November 21, he became aware of a presence close by him and recognized her immediately: It was his mother, who had died with his sister in an airplane crash near Kathmandu in 1975. In his rich account of the South Pole expedition, *In the Ghost Country* (written with John Elder), Hillary described the phenomenon, which went beyond simply living a memory: "It was like she'd come out there to keep me company. It was like she was really there. Right there. In a way that was almost scary. Yet it seemed natural as anything to walk along talking to her."[7] He told me that his expedition was, in a sense, a twenty-first-century equivalent of

> what the monks of old had done. They had gone off, lived in isolation under an overhanging rock; they had vows not to speak or not to interact with people. Perhaps they had those sorts of experiences. I believe it is like that…. You are isolated, very often with varying degrees of sensory deprivation.[8]

The presence left Hillary in the early afternoon. Late in the afternoon she returned, and remained through that evening. He felt it possible the other two members of the expedition had seen him smiling.

The tension among the men only seemed to deepen in subsequent days. Hillary felt the implication was always that he was slowing them down. He had been struggling for days with one of his boots, which kept coming apart. Philips at one point insisted that he would carry some of Hillary's load, but Hillary refused. He recognized that he was slower, but not significantly so. The difference would not affect their chances of success. On November 24, the presence returned. There was no conversation, only "a long walk taken in the most comfortable silence." Then, days later, in a tent, when he was half awake, he again felt the sense of the presence, sitting close by.

On December 1, there was a break in the tension. Philips apologized to Hillary for complaining about him, and they shook hands. Muir mumbled: "Thank you, fellows." Hillary wrote in his diary that things should get better now. But he later thought that he would have been less lonely had he made the journey solo. On day thirty-six he was joined by other visitors. Presences were "peopling the tent" with him and he recognized them as two dead climbing friends. Then, late in the afternoon on day thirty-nine, as he fought his way through a blizzard, the winds like a freight train and clouds sweeping his face, he felt the presence of his mother again. He noticed that "the clouds passed through her where she stood." He described the Polar Plateau as "a high, cold ice plain of raging winds, spindrift that flows like sand from one side of Antarctica to the other." There was no sky, no landscape, only cloud and snow merged, an environment without definition.

The blizzard left them tent-bound, the fumes from the stove burned their eyes, their food supply dwindled. Hillary, a tough man who had overcome many physical and psychological challenges in his adventurous career, was humbled by the power of the natural world. He felt frail. He remembered Scott's words: "Great God. This is an awful place." It was at that point that they decided to abandon the return portion of their journey. Wrote

Hillary: "If we'd done the trip in the Captain's day, there would have been another tent out there with three people lying [dead] in it." As they were approaching the South Pole, Hillary experienced one last visit: "Just as the smudges of my two companions drifted in and out of focus, so too did my mother's image with the wavering of my thoughts." This time he said goodbye to her. Soon, he saw the buildings of the station at the South Pole. He was approaching the last place on Earth, but there were flesh-and-blood people there. There would be no return journey by land. His ordeal was over.

FOR AMERICAN EXPLORER ANN BANCROFT, it happened very early on, in November 2000, only weeks into a three-month journey in which she would attempt to cover more than 3,200 kilometres, traversing the continent from Queen Maud Land to the American McMurdo Station. The crossing of Antarctica by Bancroft and fellow explorer, Norwegian Liv Arnesen, if successful, would make them the first women to accomplish the feat, and would also set a distance record. But for Bancroft, it produced something utterly unexpected.

The terrain was particularly difficult. Both women were hauling heavily laden supply sledges of 120 kilograms (more than double Bancroft's body weight), struggling over sastrugi—waves of ice—and forced to do switchbacks in order to ascend steep inclines to reach the Polar Plateau. It was also snowing heavily. To succeed, they needed to travel at the rate of thirty-two kilometres an hour, on skis, aided by sails. Yet from the outset they were well off the required pace, and were consequently experiencing not only arduous physical demands, but enormous psychological pressure created by the prospect of failure. As Bancroft later wrote: "Doubt was to become our new companion, the unwelcome third guest on this expedition."[9] The temperature was fairly constant at minus thirty-four degrees Celsius, and the winds were gusty, but with periods of unusual calm, which threatened to sabotage their plan to use the sails and turn the Antarctic winds to their favour. As if these were not obstacles enough, Bancroft suffered an excruciatingly painful muscle strain when one blast of wind tore her arm outward as she struggled to untangle a tow line.

With four pulling hours left on a particular day, Bancroft encountered an abrupt sense of being in very close company with another person. Arnesen, who was stronger to begin with, and was not labouring with an injury, was well out in front. Bancroft felt the presence just behind her right shoulder. Almost immediately she was infused with a sense of comfort, warmth, and strength. Said Bancroft:

> It startled me, because there was a flood of emotion with it, because it was so strong, and almost unmistakable, and it was good medicine, it was what I needed. It worked, whatever it was…. I was accepting of the feeling and the sense of presence.[10]

Like Hillary before her, she understood that the Third Man was actually a woman, and unusually, felt Bancroft, "there was no mistaking who the presence was." She wrote in her journal on day twelve, November 25, 2000:

> A strong feeling of my mentor (who had passed away not too
> long ago), filled the area. It was a presence of egging me or
> encouraging me along. This feeling gave me not only a sense
> of strength but of great comfort.[11]

It was her deceased grandmother, whom she called Rannie, and she was surprised not only by the very strong sense that she was nearby, but also because it was not the grandmother she would have predicted if she could have imagined such a situation. It was her paternal grandmother, a woman who had died six years earlier, and with whom Bancroft was not as close as with her maternal grandmother.

The sense of her presence persisted for some time. Recalled Bancroft: "It hung around for a while to the point where—it feels a little bit silly to say—to the point of actually saying something, speaking out loud to this presence."[12] In response, Bancroft received a message of encouragement, and an assurance that she would prevail: "You're going to get through this, it's just going to be bloody hard." The initial sense of a presence was very strong, then it receded. Yet the sensation, at a lower, background level, lingered for the rest of that day and night. Her situation improved the following day, and Bancroft persevered, and with Arnesen ultimately triumphed. For Bancroft, the episode offered critical relief when she most needed it, and proved to be a "significant motivator as well as a coping mechanism."[13]

IN EACH OF THESE THREE CASES—Swan, Hillary, and Bancroft—the critical change in the nature of the experience occurred when the baseline of monotony and isolation was joined by some other stress, or combination of stresses. Several studies have been made of polar explorers and the phenomenon of the Third Man and several different conclusions drawn. For Evan Llewelyn Lloyd, it was the addition of cold stress that played a pivotal role. An anaesthesiologist at Princess Margaret Rose Orthopaedic Hospital in Edinburgh, Lloyd studied reports of presence experiences including Shackleton's, and in 1981 delivered a paper at the Fifth International Symposium on Circumpolar Health in Copenhagen, arguing that: "Cold stress, sometimes alone but often accompanied by fatigue, are common factors in all these case reports."[14] Cold-stress–induced hallucinations are not uncommon once the core body temperature drops, "and are occasionally reported by individuals exercising in the cold as well."[15] Lloyd argued that the hallucinations occur before hypothermia has developed sufficiently to incapacitate an individual, who remains from outward appearances normal. Lloyd speculated that cold stress caused "neurochemical changes," and that the hallucinations "may also occur as a form of self-hypnosis in response to a situation involving extreme discomfort."[16] Such situations, after all, created "a deep-seated desire for another person to provide company and assistance."[17]

Fiona Godlee, writing in the *British Medical Journal* in 1993, advanced another theory, that the experiences of Shackleton's party crossing South Georgia had a medical cause, one that might apply to other South Pole expeditions, being symptomatic of "blood glucose concentrations almost incompatible with life."[18] Godlee based her conclusions on a study of the physical effects of the extreme hardship confronted by Sir Ranulph Fiennes (on one of his later expeditions) and physician Mike Stroud who, during a 1992–93 unsupported walk across Antarctica, endured a starvation diet because they burned off more calories than they were able to replace. During one stretch, as they climbed up towards the Antarctic Plateau hauling their heavy sledges, the explorers worked off more than 11,000 calories (46,000 joules) each day—twice what they were able to replace through their food intake. This was, wrote Stroud, "a deficit equivalent to total starvation while running a couple of marathons a day."[19] Inadequate nutrition is the source of low blood glucose, and Stroud reported "dreadfully low glucose levels" and radical weight loss: Fiennes lost twenty-five kilograms (fifty-five pounds) and Stroud, twenty-two kilograms (forty-eight pounds), during the ninety-five-day journey.

Similarly, researchers have calculated that Robert Falcon Scott and his men would have lost almost 40 percent of their body weight by the time of their deaths in March 1912. Scott's party was similarly burning up far more calories than they were able to replace, and they became seriously emaciated: "These men lacked adequate rations and continually suffered from hunger. The failure of such experienced explorers to survive is no mystery when the provisioning is assessed by modern nutritional standards."[20] As Godlee argues, there are symptoms other than weight loss. During his own trek with Fiennes, Stroud described how he would be "often drifting through a haze of unreality." Godlee wrote, "such low blood glucose may have contributed to the mixing of reality and imagination experienced by many polar explorers … Shackleton and his team were aware of a so called 'third man,' a comforting presence seen by some of them, who they looked on as their guardian."[21]

Peter Suedfeld and Jane Mocellin, in their 1987 study published in the journal *Environment and Behavior*, agreed it was more than monotony, which alone does not necessarily produce physiological signs of stress. Instead, they argued, stress is produced when boredom or monotony are combined with a need to maintain a high level of alertness.[22] But, they pointed out, stress comes in many other forms, and it is stress that always changes the nature of the experience. "Stress," Suedfeld and Mocellin argued, "is involved in the communication or assistance component of the sensed presence effect."[23] It might be that "ambient cold" was a relevant environmental factor, or it might be something else—hypoxia, thirst or starvation, disease or injury, exhaustion, sleep deprivation, putative fear—or some combination thereof.[24] Or it might be the highly specific challenges each faced. In Bancroft's case it was an injury; for Hillary, a sense of being ostracized; for Swan, an equipment malfunction related to his sledge. If an explorer is going to experience the Third Man, it will take at least some of these factors, or all. Not a single trigger, but a burden of stresses. This is the principle of multiple triggers.

CHAPTER SEVEN

Sensed Presence (I)

NEUROLOGIST MACDONALD CRITCHLEY'S main areas of research involved headache, disorders of higher nervous activity, and developmental dyslexia. He made important contributions to his specialties. His book on the parietal lobes is considered a classic; he formally recognized and named "musicogenic" epilepsy (seizures caused by music); and he lent his own name to several neurological disorders, including one involving involuntary grasping and groping. His contributions didn't end there. His interest in human behaviour extended to such widely divergent topics as the medical aspects of boxing, man's attitude to his nose, the supposed telepathic properties of the hallucinogenic drug ayahuasca, and Miss Havisham Syndrome—a condition of arrested living named for a character in Charles Dickens' novel *Great Expectations*.

Critchley cut a striking figure. While his peers preferred public transportation, he drove to the hospital in a vintage black Rolls-

Royce. He was shy with strangers, with whom he'd proffer a languid handshake, look at the ground nervously, and say "how do you do?" his voice trailing off. Yet he gave bravura demonstrations of neurological cases in the lecture theatre and had, in fact, once considered a career as an actor.[1] Critchley was fastidious in dress, impeccably mannered, and possessed of an uncommon erudition. With such attributes, he handily became the toast of the international neurological set, serving as president of the World Federation of Neurology.[2] Unusually, he was also a collector of Oscar Wilde memorabilia and ceramic paste pots.

As a member of the Royal Naval Reserve during the Second World War, he had come across instances of Third Man factor among wartime shipwreck survivors. This led him to make enquiries among explorers and survivors, and to pore over accounts of their adventures. He read Shackleton's memoir *South*, among others. The Third Man phenomenon seemed to him to be not uncommon:

> It has been described to me in mountaineers immobilized by bad weather at great height, as well as in prisoners on a cruel march from one German concentration camp to another. An explorer scaling Mount Everest developed this same trick of the imagination, probably from anoxia rather than exhaustion. During his solitary voyage around the world in a tiny sailing vessel, [Joshua] Slocum at times had the fancy that he had a companion with him.[3]

Critchley was the first scientist to seriously study accounts of the Third Man among the normal population, and he was certain that its origins lay not outside the body, but within. These cases were not, as far as Critchley was concerned, proof of the existence of guardian angels. He published an essay in 1955, "Idea of a Presence," the purpose of which was to describe what he termed "a rather unusual mental experience." In that paper, Critchley presented the classic description of the phenomenon:

> A feeling, or an impression—sometimes amounting to a veritable delusion—that the person concerned is not alone. Or, if it should be that he is actually in the company of others, that there is also some other being present, when really this is not so....[4]

While there have been cases where the Third Man was a "clearly perceived, seemingly flesh and blood entity,"[5] Critchley observed that the presence generally remains elusive and intangible, existing only in the hinterlands of vision:

> Sometimes the idea is vivid; sometimes it is subtle and ephemeral. In duration it may be either sustained or transient. Or, yet again, it may repeatedly come and go, wax and wane. The identity of the visitant or "presence" is but rarely established. Usually the feeling merely entails the belief that there is "someone" in the vicinity. Or, the impression may not amount to anything more than an intangible feeling "as if" one were not alone. [6]

Critchley noted there are cases where the "someone" is encountered without any accompanying emotion, and that "the visitant in these cases is neutral, colourless and devoid of personal significance."

Something similar happens to epileptics, narcoleptics, schizo-phrenics, and people with brain injuries, he added. Critchley himself reported the case of a woman with biparietal atrophy, a clinical syndrome linked to Alzheimer's disease, who would "often wake in the night with a trenchant feeling that someone was in the room." So compelling was the feeling that she would at times get out of bed, "and go on tiptoe from room to room with the object of surprising this interloper." In some of these cases involving organic brain disease or other conditions, "the unseen presence seems to threaten rather than sustain."

Critchley lamented the fact that "scarcely any clear-cut account of this phenomenon exists in neuro-psychiatric writings." He found only a brief discussion among the work of German philosopher and psychiatrist Karl Jaspers. In 1913, while working in a hospital psychiatric ward in Heidelberg, Jaspers came across a curious experience shared by six schizophrenics, each of whom reported encountering an unseen presence nearby. One described feeling as if she was being watched. Another felt as if "his fiancée was standing behind him, back to back, making synchronous movements." And another said: "I felt as if someone constantly walked at my side."[7]

Jaspers argued that this awareness is different from that of a person who enters a dark room where there really is another person. In that case, the awareness is based on factors such as faint sounds, slight movements, or changes in air pressure. In this case the awareness appeared innate. Something else set the experience apart. Jaspers said the sense of an unseen being had "the character of urgency, certainty and vividness." He cited one case in which a person felt there was someone shadowing his movements: "The patient had never seen or heard him and had never felt him nor touched him and yet he experienced with an extraordinary certainty the feeling that somebody was there."[8]

Jaspers gave the condition the name *leibhaftige bewusstheit*, which according to one clumsy English translation means a "deception based on the nonsensory/nonperceptional awareness of a proximate presence." It has also been called a "vivid physical awareness." Jaspers' observations were restricted to psychiatric patients, but he still offered the first scientific definition of the experience:

> There are patients who have a certain feeling (in the mental sense) or awareness that someone is close by, behind them or above them, someone that they can in no way actually perceive with the external senses, yet whose actual/concrete presence is directly/clearly experienced.[9]

Nearly three decades after Jaspers' work on the subject, a Swiss physician, Ferdinand Morel, also described the impression of a presence among psychiatric patients and situated it within the framework of visual hallucinations. He gave the phenomenon a different name, referring to the unseen being as "the accompanier." He described the case of a sick woman who "felt more than she saw" a mysterious invisible presence, a few metres away from her, sometimes a little behind her, who accompanied her when she walked. This being "had its eye on her," she observed. But like Jaspers, Morel had no explanation, stating only that, "in the presence of a symptom like this, we do not know yet how to detect precisely the system … that is disturbed."[10] However, Morel argued, it is "well defined and relatively frequent" in various brain disorders.

What Critchley had over these pioneering researchers was not only the fact that the sense of a presence could involve "normal persons exposed to severe peril, privation, or exhaustion." But he also began to realize that in such cases the presence often had a "beneficent quality." Critchley considered it some sort of hallucination, yet he could not explain the obvious differences between this and the other, conventional hallucinations, with their attendant sense of unreality. Explanations based on psychotic or feverish hallucinations did not seem to apply. Critchley instead made an extraordinary observation: that the Third Man appeared in the absence of delirium, and, indeed, when the person involved has his or her senses comparatively intact: "At times the idea of a presence can be looked upon as being almost the opposite phenomenon to the more common illusory states."[11] But Critchley could produce no theory for its origin. He could not organize the seemingly irrational nature of the Third Man phenomenon in the same orderly fashion he arranged his collection of paste pots.

CHAPTER EIGHT

The Widow Effect

In July 1953, twenty-eight-year-old Austrian mountaineer Hermann Buhl attempted the solitary conquest of Nanga Parbat, a Himalayan peak and the ninth tallest mountain in the world. Its name means "naked mountain," but it is also known to be a killer mountain. Climbers have died there in numbers disproportionately higher than on any of the other 8,000-metre peaks, and to date the mortality rate on its slopes is three times that of Everest. Thirty-one lives were claimed before Buhl's attempt, among them the British climber Alfred Mummery, who disappeared there in 1895, and ten climbers killed on a German expedition led by Willy Merkl in 1934.

Buhl, and a second climber named Otto Kempter, were camped at 6,900 metres and had defied repeated recall orders from base camp because of concern over worsening weather. It was, Buhl knew, a tremendous risk: "Nothing like it had ever been done at such an altitude in the Himalaya and it was wildly beyond reasonable

124   JOHN GEIGER

practice. But what could we do? The porters wouldn't go any higher, and we had to make an effort without them." At one o'clock in the morning on July 3, 1953, Buhl began to prepare for the ascent. Kempter was groggy and told Buhl he would follow later. Knowing he needed every minute in order to complete the summit in one day, Buhl set off on his own.

He was, in some respects, singularly ill-prepared. His provisions were inadequate, he was without supplementary oxygen, and was thus "fighting a desperate battle for that essential commodity—air." He was also alone, because Kempter never did rejoin him. Buhl ascended rapidly, despite the extreme difficulties involved in a climb that required seventeen hours of nearly superhuman effort, "every step ... a battle, an indescribable effort of will-power." Buhl realized he was "obeying the dictates of my subconscious which had only one idea—to get up higher; my body had long since given up. I moved forward in a kind of self-induced hypnosis." The hours passed and his physical condition deteriorated. Presently, he could no longer stand upright: He was, he said, a "wreck of a human being." He ended up crawling slowly on all fours.

Then something changed: Buhl noticed the ground was no longer rising. When he reached the summit, it was without a sense of victorious exultation, only relief. Utterly worn out, he collapsed, in the process driving his ice axe into the snow. Buhl then took photographs and built a small cairn near the axe. Only then did he look around. On every side, the stone faces of Nanga Parbat dropped precipitously from the small summit platform: "I felt as if I were floating high above everything, out of all relationship with the Earth, severed from the world and all humanity." At 7:10 P.M.,

Buhl started his descent. The sun was disappearing, and very suddenly it became intensely cold.

What followed was a decision that verged on suicidal: a bivouac—a temporary encampment—within a few hundred metres of the summit. He risked death by exposure, but Buhl had little choice. Barely 130 metres into his descent, night enveloped him. Some distance away, he could see the outline of a large rock and made his way towards it. Since it was too steep to sit on, he was forced to spend the night standing against the rock face. As Buhl had neither emergency bivouac gear nor sleeping bag, he put on all the extra clothing he had with him, pulled a balaclava down over his head, and put on two pairs of gloves. Still, the cold was nearly unbearable. He was tortured by hunger and thirst. Overcome by exhaustion, he could barely stay upright. His head kept lolling forward. He began to doze, but then woke with a start. He was not immediately sure where he was, and then remembered he was still high on Nanga Parbat. With his boots frozen stiff, his feet gradually lost all feeling. He felt as if time itself had slowed, and feared the night would become an eternity. The moon emerged at 2 A.M., but since he was out of its bright light, he had to wait until morning to continue. With the dawn—he called it the "light of salvation"—his body was gradually warmed, and he was able to go on with his descent. It was a painstaking process. The slightest miscalculation could prove fatal. Whenever he slipped even slightly in the snow, it took so much out of him that he required minutes to compose himself, before he could take the next small step. Danger was heightened because he had left his ice axe as his triumphal monument at the summit.

But Buhl had begun to draw upon support from a wholly unexpected source: "During those hours of extreme tension I had an extraordinary feeling that I was not alone. I had a partner with me, looking after me, taking care of me, belaying me. I knew it was imagination; but the feeling persisted …"[1] Not only did he sense that a being was aiding him, but he also felt responsible for his unseen companion's safety, which in turn increased his own caution. When he was edging over fragmented rocks,

> everything I touched came away. It seemed too great a risk, for one small slide or fall would be the finish of me, and I should certainly drag with me my companion and friend, non-existent though he be.… I had to exert extreme care every foot of the way down.[2]

At midday, Buhl had removed his two pairs of gloves in order to grip a rock. But when he went to put his gloves on again, one pair was missing. He asked his companion if he had seen them. Buhl heard the answer clearly: "You've lost them." He thought the voice was familiar, but could not identify it, other than as the voice of a friend. "Many times I found myself in the act of turning around to address my companion," he later said.[3] Yet at no point did he feel his ability to reason had been in any way impaired.

Buhl's descent was a sustained and arduous ordeal. His thirst was searing. His tongue was virtually welded to his gums. He began to foam at the mouth. He moved slowly, taking twenty breaths for each step. Finally he rested and began to doze, but dusk was again approaching, and he knew he could not survive a second night exposed on the mountain. This realization seemed to bring a new surge of energy, and using his final reserves, he continued:

> The whole of this time my companion was with me, that staunch companion whom I never saw, and whose presence was more definite at danger spots. The feeling calmed me, lulled me into security: I knew that if I slipped or fell, this "other man" would hold me on the rope. But there was no rope; there was no other man.[4]

Finally, Buhl sighted the camp he had left forty-one hours earlier. He could see dots that were definitely people: "Then I knew I was safe." Buhl staggered and swayed before he collapsed into the arms of another member of the team, Hans Ertl, who had rushed to meet him. Buhl's appearance was shocking: "He looked aged by twenty years. His face, desiccated and deeply lined, bore the imprint of intolerable suffering."[5] Buhl said only: "Yesterday was the finest day of my life."

When he learned of Buhl's encounter with an unseen companion, another Austrian climber, Herbert Tichy, speculated about the source of the experience. "It may have been a sixth sense, his subconscious, his guardian angel, or the help of dead friends," Tichy wrote.[6] Buhl felt only that "a kindly Providence" had permitted his conquest of the great mountain. Although he had survived this triumphal climb, he was not through with mountaineering. Within four years, Hermann Buhl was dead, having plunged off a cornice on Chogolisa in the Karakoram region of Pakistan. His body was never recovered.

DR. GRIFFITH PUGH, THE PHYSIOLOGIST on the 1953 British
Everest expedition (on which Sir Edmund Hillary and Tenzing
Norgay made the first successful ascent to the summit), and an
expert on the physiology of cold and altitude, acknowledged many
climbers have encountered the Third Man, but dismissed it as a
"decay of the brain functions." Pugh agued that "all these ghostly
sightings were no more than hallucinations caused by extreme
cold, exhaustion, and lack of oxygen, even when breathing equipment was being used."[7] Said Pugh: "Exhausted men pitting their
strength against a mountain may well see anything. A meeting with
dead relatives or friends is typical."[8]

Certainly, climbers have seen just about anything on
mountains. Edward Whymper, on his descent after conquering the
Matterhorn in 1865, and hours after three of his companions had
plummeted to their deaths, saw crosses floating in the air. At one
point on Everest, Frank Smythe saw "pulsating teapots." And,
according to one account, "dancing horses have been observed
high on Aconcagua in Argentina."[9] It is into this category of bizarre
imaginings that Pugh lumped encounters with the Third Man.

Charles S. Houston, medical doctor, mountaineer, and expert
on the physiology of altitude, likewise noted the frequency of these
reports. "The most common hallucination is of a companion
nearby, walking, talking, sharing the experience."[10] Houston attributed the phenomenon to a serious manifestation of altitude
sickness, cerebral edema, which occurs when the body, struggling
to get enough oxygen, compensates by increasing blood circulation, which in some instances causes swelling of the brain. Wrote
Houston: "Most persons with brain edema hear voices, many see

bizarre objects. Disorientation in time and space is common. By the time these extreme signs have appeared, the diagnosis is obvious and treatment essential to save life."[11]

In their book, *Man at High Altitude*, Donald Heath and David Reid Williams also agreed, "the most characteristic phenomena … is the phantom companion." They too viewed encounters with a presence as a symptom of extreme altitude, arguing "hypoxia [a deficiency in the amount of oxygen reaching body tissues] exerts an increasingly severe effect on higher cerebral functions." But Heath and Williams made an important additional observation. They acknowledged the experience is a help: "the phantom companion at extreme altitudes is probably fabricated in the mind to bring some psychological support in a very insecure situation."[12] Charles Clarke, a British neurologist who has participated in many climbs, agreed the extra companion is comforting and suggested a number of relevant factors, including sleep deprivation and anxiety, but broke with the pattern by expressing doubt that "metabolic disturbance such as hypoxia" is responsible.[13]

Pugh failed to answer Macdonald Critchley's question. If the Third Man is caused by "decay of brain functions" as Pugh argued, why then would it offer such support, so different from conventional hallucinations with their attendant sense of unreality? We have seen it in Antarctica, on and under the oceans, and we see the same phenomenon also on mountains: Appearances of the Third Man are in no way characteristic of delirium. When failure—even death—seems inevitable, an unseen being joins those at risk. What changes? What turns the virtual certainty of death into the miracle of survival? It begins with belief, a belief that a companion stands with them. And for those who experience the Third Man, there is never any thought given to the possibility that it is a symptom of a breakdown.[14] Just the opposite! Many climbers ascribe to the Third Man powers that compensate for altitude-related mental impairment. Wrote the climber Greg Child: "Those who have experienced the other presence make a distinction between it and hallucinations, which often misguide and disorient. The presence seems much more real, assisting by either guiding or allaying fears with companionship."[15]

If the cause were "brain decay" brought on by high altitude, how is it, for example, that Stephanie Schwabe had such an experience while diving in The Bahamas? Or Joshua Slocum, while crossing the Atlantic? In fact, Critchley points out that helpful, friendly, unseen companions are an accepted and perfectly normal part of the lives of many young people. Healthy children report with startling regularity having had just such an encounter. The imaginary playmate of childhood is one example of a benevolent unseen being that most people have heard about and many have experienced. As Critchley wrote: "In states of putative danger, or illness, or in uneasy solitude, the idea of a presence may be particularly vivid, and may be confidently associated by the child with its belief in a celestial protecting agency or companion."[16]

Children will give this unseen being a name, describe its appearance, refer to it in conversations, and play with it. In other words, it will have, "an air of reality for the child, but no apparent objective basis."[17] The playmates can come in any imaginable form. They can be "old and young, dour and joyous, elaborate and simple." They appear to about 30 percent of children between ages three and six, and last for six months on average. Some researchers who have studied the phenomenon are convinced that it is not make-believe, but involves real hallucinations. They say the children are not pretending, but are actually seeing their playmate, and hearing him or her speak, and so are, in fact, conversing. As evidence of this, children have been shown to adopt strange voices in order to imitate their playmates. One study of female U.S. college students found that half of them "had had such halluci-nated playmates, and half of those clearly remembered the pitch and quality of the voices."[18] The vividness of these friendships can frighten parents, although many are kept in the dark by children who seem to anticipate that their parents will not understand.

Child-care books formerly advised against allowing children to play with imaginary playmates, but since the 1960s, they have been viewed as "positive and a sign of good, creative health."[19] Usually, invisible playmates are associated with children who are lonely, or are under stress. Their first appearance, for example, might be timed with the birth of a sibling, or often as a result of the stress of loss, during a parent's extended absence, for example, or following a divorce, or the death of a parent. It also occurs disproportionately among only children. Psychologists, conse-quently, believe they may serve a protective function in alleviating loneliness and stress. Certainly, this is how children view them.

In some instances, the imaginary playmate survives beyond the preschool years, in which case "it too grows up with the child and begins telling him or her what to do in times of stress."[20] A recent study revealed that the phenomenon also occurs during adolescence, particularly around ages fourteen and fifteen. Adolescents don't resort to an imaginary friend simply for lack of a close real friend, and those who experience them are, to the contrary, "socially competent and creative."[21] Rarely, even normal adults in routine situations report them. One woman who had experienced multiple playmates as a child, found as an adult that, when under stress, "all her imaginary playmates come back, and they are all grown up like her."

How different, really, are the imaginary playmates of children, from the Third Man who intervened to help Frank Smythe survive on Everest, or Hermann Buhl on Nanga Parbat? Do the circumstances of an individual's needs dictate the form in which the angel appears, and so for lonesome children, the presence appears as another little child to play with or a parent-surrogate, while for those in crisis situations on mountains, he appears as an authority figure?[22]

The stresses of climbing are both numerous and extreme. Little wonder, then, that the Third Man is nearly as much a part of high altitude climbing as supplementary oxygen. Not all have experienced the phenomenon, but few have not heard of it, or do not know of someone who has. One study of thirty-three Spanish climbers at extreme altitude (over 7,500 metres) found one-third had experienced "hallucinatory episodes," the most common of which involved "the sensation of an imaginary accompanying presence behind one's own body."[23] Certainly, isolation, monotony, and solitude are a factor. So, too, is the cold. Pugh felt, and it is accepted wisdom among climbers, that altitude is the predominant factor. There are also any number of other psychological and physiological stresses. But in the case of Hermann Buhl, and each of the following accounts, there was one other dynamic at play—the stress of loss. This factor is called the widow effect.

OF ALL THE CIRCUMSTANCES TO HAVE EVOKED the Third Man at great altitude, perhaps none was as incredible as the disaster that befell members of the Oxford University Mountaineering Club in 1957, during their ascent of Haramosh, which, like Nanga Parbat, is a peak in the Karakoram of northwest Pakistan. The expedition was conceived and organized by twenty-three-year-old Bernard Jillott, an impulsive man, but a fine rock climber, who was joined by another Briton, medical student John Emery; Rae Culbert, a New Zealander who had been studying botany; and Scott Hamilton, an American. Since none of the men had sufficient high-altitude experience, they sought out Tony Streather, a British soldier who had served in the Indian army immediately before Partition, and in the Pakistani army for several years after. He later became an instructor at Sandhurst, the British military academy. Streather began climbing almost by accident, when he enlisted as a transport officer on a 1950 climb of Tirich Mir in northwestern Pakistan. He took to it immediately and, with his aptitude and discipline, proved himself an indispensable member of the team, making it to the summit on his very first climb. In 1953, he distinguished himself for his mental toughness during an American climb of K2, and two years later he reached the summit of Kangchenjunga, then the world's highest unclimbed peak. It was on the basis of these accomplishments that Jillott approached Streather to lead a climb of the 7,409-metre Haramosh.

The expedition, aided by Hunza porters on the approach, was intended to be nothing more than a reconnaissance expedition, but the single-mindedness of Jillott was infectious, and it was clear they would push the climb as far as they could. They had to battle heavy snow on their ascent, and established their Camp Four on the northeast ridge of what was, in fact, Haramosh II, a secondary summit of 6,684 metres. They realized by then that the main summit was out of reach. The party, except for Hamilton, who remained at Camp Three, elected to scale the final three hundred metres to a crest that would afford them the best vantage point, before beginning their descent. They reached the prospect on September 15, 1957. It was a brilliant, clear day, and the four men were rewarded with splendid views of the main summit. Jillott believed that a slightly better view could be had if they traversed a slope farther along nicknamed the Cardinal's Hat. While Streather and Culbert remained behind, Emery agreed to accompany him.

Jillott and Emery picked their way up the slope, but just as Jillott neared the top, there was a "muffled explosion, a crunching and grinding sound." The slope gave way under their feet. Their path marked the cut, the point at which the avalanche began. Below them, everything began to move at once with gathering speed. The two men were carried down the slope by the avalanche. They looked like marionettes, jerking awkwardly, as if manipulated by strings. Streather and Culbert watched in impotent horror as Jillott and Emery were swept over a ridge into a vast snow basin below.

While recovering from the immediate shock of what they had just witnessed, and anticipating the worst, Streather and Culbert traversed to the bare ground, scoured clean by the avalanche. Streather, secured at the end of a rope by Culbert, was able to reach the edge of the slope and gaze into the basin. Plumes of powder still reached into the sky, but through them he could see a tiny figure in a green coat. It was Jillott and he was moving. Soon,

Jillott appeared to begin to dig through the snow with his hands. Another figure then emerged. Miraculously, Jillott and Emery had survived the fall, although vast ice cliffs stood between them and the others. "I can't see how we're going to get them out," Streather said to Culbert.[24]

It was early in the evening. Jillott and Emery made one abortive attempt to find an escape route, then returned to the track of the avalanche so the others would be able to locate them, and prepared to bivouac. They had no food, drink, or shelter, and the cold was deepening. All they could do was wait. Streather and Culbert, meanwhile, returned to Camp Four to rest, eat, and prepare a bundle of clothes and food for the stranded climbers. Streather later dropped the pack down towards Jillott and Emery, but it slid away and disappeared into a crevasse, intensifying the need for an immediate rescue.

Streather and Culbert began to climb down the steep, sixty-degree slope into the basin. Streather, secured to Culbert by a thirty-metre length of rope, went first, kicking steps into the ice. They moved deliberately, and the long night gradually stretched into day. At the top of the ice cliffs they were forced to traverse to the right. The ice was rock-hard. Each step had to be hacked out, a gruelling procedure requiring all of their strength. During this tortuous traverse, Culbert lost a crampon, a set of metal spikes strapped on to each climber's moulded, rubber-soled boot to improve traction. Crampons are vital for such a climb, and the loss was a further blow to their prospects. Culbert was forced to kick off his canvas overboot because it was too slippery to allow for adequate footing.

When Streather thought they were within earshot, he yelled out to Jillott and Emery: "Start climbing, however difficult it is. It's a matter of life and death." He couldn't hear their disheartening response: "We can't … we've lost our ice axes."[25] Streather and Culbert were forced to continue their descent, until the four men were reunited at the bottom of the basin. Few words were exchanged. Jillott and Emery were given a Thermos of soup, the first food or drink either had had in twenty-four hours.

It was by then late in the day. They decided their only course was to attempt an immediate climb out of the basin. They roped up. Culbert led, followed in order by Streather, Jillott, and Emery. They had climbed about sixty metres, and the starting point for the traverse was in sight, when Culbert, who had struggled to maintain his footing without the crampon, slipped and fell backwards, knocking Streather off. All four men then tumbled like dominoes back into the snow basin. While none was hurt, Streather lost his ice axe in the fall. They immediately tried again, this time with Streather in the lead, using the last ice axe, the one belonging to Culbert. As they neared the same point, Jillott fell asleep in his tracks, and again the whole party was dragged down sixty metres, back to where they had started. In the process, they lost the last ice axe. Exhausted, the climbers found a ledge where they huddled together for warmth. By now Culbert was suffering from frostbite on his left foot. They passed a fitful night, interrupted by shouts from Jillott who was hallucinating, likely the result of a concussion. He was given an injection of morphine and they all managed to get a little sleep.

With daylight came their last chance of survival. It was

September 17, two days after the original fall. Without shelter, food, or water, it seemed unlikely all would survive another night. Ralph Barker, in his harrowing official account of the expedition, wrote that at this point, "They had all lost the power of reasoning, and their actions were instinctive."[26] Of the four, Streather, because of his experience and mental discipline, was perhaps the best equipped for the struggle ahead. This time they did not use the climbing-rope. Each man was on his own. After they climbed ninety metres, they discovered one of the lost ice axes. Streather used this to cut better steps to improve their chances on the traverse. They reached the platform that marked the start of the traverse and began the most difficult and perilous part of the climb. Somehow they got through it.

Then, as they began the final push, Jillott shouted: "Rae's in trouble!" Culbert's foot, swollen from frostbite, made it impossible for him to go farther. He asked Streather for a belay (to secure him by a length of rope) over the last part. Streather climbed to the place where the slope began to taper off, near the top and at a point of safety, then planted his ice axe as firmly as he could. The rope was meant to steady Culbert, but it would be difficult to hold him if he came off the mountain, which, after a few steps, he did. The jerk was sudden and hard. Streather, who was out of eyesight and earshot, had no warning, and lost his balance. Both men then plunged once again into the snow basin, their fall retracing the original track of the avalanche. They landed hard, but survived. The horrible irony of the situation was obvious. Emery and Jillott were on the upper slope, and had escaped. Their erstwhile rescuers, Streather and Culbert, were trapped in the basin.

Emery and Jillott were determined to reach Camp Four, where they hoped to eat, rest, and recover some strength before returning. It was now dark, and Emery suggested they sit and await the moonrise, but Jillott insisted they go on, and Emery reluctantly consented. Jillott marched ahead, and Emery quickly lost sight of him, but managed to follow his track in the deep snow. At one point, Emery lost his footing and slipped into a small crevasse. His slide was halted at a place where the crevasse narrowed. He was able to extract himself and "chimney" up the ice fissure. As he struggled out, he had the feeling that he "had two minds or ... was two people."[27] One mind was consumed by the drudgery of the effort to extricate himself; the other was entirely detached, watching. "At times the observer was the only one in possession, and I would do nothing at all," he later said. Once clear, he decided it was too risky to continue and waited for the morning.

At dawn, Emery resumed the trek, reaching a ridge above Camp Four. To his right was a deep crevasse that emptied into the Stak valley. He gave the lip of this ridge a wide berth. He saw the old track left by the four men on their ascent, and then noticed a set of fresh tracks left by Jillott. But instead of joining the old track, Jillott's footprints crossed them at a right angle. He must have missed the track in the darkness. His footprints continued for two metres before they ended. At that point the ground fell away and there was a sheer drop to an ice or rock ledge ninety metres down, and below that, an eighteen-hundred-metre drop into the valley. Jillott, Emery realized, was dead. Emery was stunned. He continued on his way to Camp Four. His toes and fingers were frozen. He could not feel to grip. It took him a long time just to light the Primus stove and to open a tin of juice. The outer layers of skin were peeling off his fingers like the skin off a grape, leaving only raw claws. He slipped into a half-sleep.

Back in the snow basin, Streather regained consciousness at daylight. Culbert was nearby, disoriented, and almost entirely without the use of his left foot. They immediately began to climb. About halfway to the start of the traverse, Streather looked back and saw that Culbert had once again fallen into the basin. He yelled down and Culbert replied that he was all right and would try again. Streather reached the point where the traverse began and noticed that Culbert was making steady progress, but when he looked again, Culbert was back in the basin. This time, Culbert did not get up, but sat motionless. "What shall we do?" he called out. Streather urged him to stay put and said the other two men would soon return to assist them.

Streather made up his mind to continue, to try to reach Camp Four and organize a rescue if the others did not come first. Snow had almost completely obscured the steps cut the day before, and he was virtually snow-blind, but he climbed deliberately, mechanically, scratching the steps clear with his elbows. His situation was, Streather felt, "quite appalling."[28] He was only barely conscious, but was encouraged by the thought of the wife he had left in England, and his young child, and by the idea that if he failed he would be letting them down.

He then became aware of something else, an "abstract presence,"[29] assisting him. It was as if he was trapped deep in a well, and there was somebody—or as he put it, "a being of some sort"— at the top, encouraging him to keep going in order to get out.[30]

The presence at times seemed to step beyond encouragement to actively help pull him up, "as if from a black pit." The feeling persisted, on and off, for several hours. He later described the sensation to another climber, Wilfrid Noyce, who wrote: "With this somebody or something he must co-operate by doing his own part. If he climbed he would be helped."[31] The presence did not depart until Streather was safely out of the snow basin.

He continued on to Camp Four and was reunited with Emery, who told him Jillott was dead. This steeled the resolve of the two men to return the next morning in an effort to save Culbert. They were too seriously affected by exposure to eat, but they drank soup and Ovaltine. They dozed on and off but, by dawn, Streather was weaker than the day before, barely able to crawl out of the tent, and Emery was a virtual invalid. At first Emery could not stand up, and then he was able only to hobble, supported by ski poles. They came to accept that they could not help Culbert, who may have been dead already. The decision was dictated by necessity, but it would haunt them, as Culbert never did emerge from the snow basin. Their own survival was still very much in question as they made their way tentatively down the steep slope towards Camp Three, but they reached Hamilton, and with his help, finally, the Hunza porters and safety.

Emery, whose frozen digits were amputated once they escaped from Haramosh, and who underwent painful surgery using skin grafted from his chest to reconstruct his hands, completed his university training, and then began to climb again. He died a few years later in another climbing accident. Streather returned to lecture at the military academy at Sandhurst, and it was during one of those lessons on teamwork and leadership that he first spoke of his encounter with the presence. A student had asked him: "What was it that kept you going? How did you get out?" Streather mentioned the presence—"to provoke discussion on team work and survival"—but had no theory as to what it was that had aided him. As Noyce wrote: "The feeling he had then of having for a time been 'over the other side' remains with him … wedged for ever in the spirit, unforgotten if unexplained." It came down, simply, to this: "There was some being which helped me survive."[32] Streather later elaborated, telling me: "The 'companion' I encountered while climbing out of the basin was almost certainly a spiritual encounter."[33]

REINHOLD MESSNER, FROM SOUTH TYROL in Italy, is widely considered history's greatest climber. He is the first man to have conquered Mount Everest solo and without supplementary oxygen. He is also the first to reach the summit of all fourteen of the world's 8,000-metre peaks. But when Messner began his solo attempt on Nanga Parbat, crawling out of his tent beneath Merkl Couloir shortly after 2 A.M. on June 27, 1970, he was a little-known twenty-five-year-old. His goal was to move as quickly as possible to reach the top before an anticipated deterioration in weather conditions. This strategy, which had been the basis of Hermann Buhl's success, had been developed in consultation with other members of the team, two of whom—his younger brother Günther, and Gerhard Baur—stayed at Camp Five, as Messner began his ascent of Nanga Parbat's Rupal face.

He headed straight up Merkl Couloir, a deep, ice-filled chute. He was without the burden of extra equipment so at first moved quickly, reaching a ramp between the South Shoulder and Southeast Ridge. He crossed the ramp, but found the going hard as the heat from the late-morning sun beat down on him and, combined with the thin air, sapped him of his strength. Stopping often to rest, he looked back to register the route he would need to follow for his descent. During one of these pauses, he noticed a figure approaching rapidly, and realized it was Günther. At sunrise, the younger Messner had been working with Baur to install fixed ropes to aid Reinhold's return, when he impulsively bolted after Reinhold. This had not been the plan, and Reinhold later admitted to being irritated. His aggressive climb required that he move swiftly and lightly. Another climber would inevitably upset his calculations. But he waited for Günther and the brothers began the final ascent together.

The day drew on as they moved up the last, sharp peak, and soon they stood together at the summit. For Reinhold it was anticlimactic. He was exhausted and felt there was not much to see. It bore little resemblance to the place he had often dreamed of. But Günther took off a mitten and the brothers shook hands. The climb had taken much of the day, and they could remain at the summit only a short time before daylight seeped away. Günther was extremely tired, and on the descent he began to show symptoms of altitude sickness. He seemed to be paying a price for his earlier rapid pursuit of Reinhold. He announced that he could not return by the technically challenging route they had followed up; he was too tired. He wanted to descend by the Diamir face, insisting it would be easier. Reinhold, believing the single most important consideration was to lose altitude, consented. This decision, to leave the known route on the Rupal face, with fixed ropes, camps, and fellow climbers below, set a sequence of events in motion, events that would claim the life of one brother.

With darkness came a bivouac at extreme altitude. The brothers found a hollow below some crags and readied for the night. It was extremely cold. Günther and Reinhold huddled together under a space blanket (a plastic-and-aluminum-foil blanket used to restore body heat in people affected by exposure or exhaustion) and waited for the dawn. When light returned, they continued down the Diamir face. It was a terrible risk: The ice-clad, four-thousand-metre precipice was known to them only from maps and photographs. Compounding the difficulty was Günther's condition, which if anything, had worsened. Reinhold was in front, sometimes so far that they almost lost sight of one another, as he tried to spare Günther the agony of false leads. Once a route had been established, Reinhold would wave and shout for Günther to follow, which he did with excruciating slowness. In *The Naked Mountain*, Reinhold Messner described what happened next:

> Suddenly there was a third climber next to me. He was descending with us, keeping a regular distance a little to my right and a few steps away from me, just out of my field of vision. I could not see the figure and still maintain my concentration but I was certain there was someone there. I could sense his presence; I needed no proof.[34]

The figure was silent. No words were exchanged. None were necessary: The figure moved with Messner, climbing when he did and stopping when he did, always keeping a certain distance. Reinhold had no fear, no sense that what was happening was anything out of the ordinary. "It is not that I was sitting there and saying, 'Oh! This is something special,'" he told me. "I had a feeling it was normal."[35] Nevertheless, he tried to shake the conviction, rationalizing that it could not be another climber, that there were only two of them, not three. But the sensation persisted, and it was a comfort: "The mere presence somehow helped me regain my composure."[36]

Evening returned. The smooth ice face was now pocked with rocky outcrops. Even with the fading light, they could not risk a stop because of a threat that one of a series of seracs—towering blocks of ice formed where the glacier surface had fractured— would collapse and they would be crushed by an avalanche. They continued their descent by starlight. At midnight they made their second bivouac, and waited through the deepest part of the night. When the moon cast its pale light, they resumed their descent.

The rest, and the loss of altitude, seemed to have restored some of Günther's strength. They were moving nicely down the slope, each choosing a path that offered for him the least resistance. Reinhold kept waiting for Günther, shouting exhortations for him to hurry, because he feared an avalanche once the midday sun reached the slope. The brothers discussed a final route that would take them out of harm's way. They were exhausted from their gruelling climb, but Reinhold concluded they had succeeded in escaping from Nanga Parbat. He stopped waiting for Günther to catch up, feeling he would be fine. They would meet at the head of the Diamir valley. But Günther didn't appear. Reinhold waited for a while, drinking glacial runoff, then continued into the valley, wondering where his brother was, but as yet unworried.

Messner sat by a stream. He thought he heard voices, one calling his name and others uttering whole sentences, but he could take in only fragments. He felt light-headed, and closed his eyes. He sat there for some time. He thought he recognized one of the voices as his mother's. Then he again heard his name: "Reinhold!" Messner knew it was the "strange presence" calling: "Bewildered, I got to my feet and there he was again, the lone climber. But no, it wasn't Günther."[37] He then confronted the possibility that his brother was in trouble. It was late in the day, but he had regained enough strength, and decided he would start back. He first retraced his steps to the base of the Diamir glacier, but he could see no sign of Günther, so Messner worked his way up towards the Diamir face. If his brother had failed to follow his route—and he had not, or he would have seen him by now—then this was the only other way down. Messner came across debris from a fresh avalanche: huge blocks of ice, interspersed among powdered snow. He stood and stared at the jumble, suddenly overcome by a sense of horror, but not acceptance, that Günther might be somewhere in that mass.

Frantically he began to search, and as he clambered amidst the debris, he realized, "My ghostly third man was there, too."[38] Messner spent the night wandering around, shouting, collapsing into brief fits of sleep, and then, awoken by the cold, resuming his desperate search. Hungry, weak, his toes frostbitten, he felt that his own situation was becoming critical. He was now far gone, exhausted, and alone, yet not alone: "Somewhere in my subconscious the third climber was still present." He tried to come to grips with what it all meant, wondering if the Third Man was not actually himself, viewed from "a different plane of existence."

Messner eventually staggered down the valley. He was half-starved, badly frostbitten, and in despair. He was, he felt, "more dead than alive."[39] He found some woodcutters who took him to a village. He was carried on a stretcher by four young men until they reached a road where a soldier took over his care. Reinhold Messner survived, but was forced to come to terms with the death of his younger brother. Later, he wrote that whenever he climbed, he felt as if Günther was with him. On Nanga Parbat in June 1970, there was another climber with him as well, and the Third Man helped him through the greatest ordeal of his life.[40]

ON JUNE 3, 1981, PARASH MONI DAS, an experienced Himalayan climber and officer in the Indian Police Service, was caught up in a disaster following an ascent of Bhagirathi II, at 6,150 metres, one of four peaks making up the Bhagirathi massif in the Garhwal Himalaya of India. Das, twenty-eight, was climbing with two other men, Pratiman Singh, who served as an officer in the Indo-Tibetan Border Police, and a mushroom farmer named Nirmal Sah, both also with Himalayan experience.

Bhagirathi II was considered technically simple, except for a forty-metre pitch of mixed rock and ice just below the summit. They roped up for the final push, with Singh leading, Sah in the middle, and Das roped to the end. Singh was climbing with such confidence up the incline that he often placed his left hand into his pocket. They reached the summit at 6 P.M., and after handshakes and a photograph, Das noticed a storm approaching from the south. They immediately began their descent. This time, Das was in the lead, with Sah the middleman, and Singh in the rear. The first two moved cautiously, but Das worried that Singh, overly pleased with himself for having broken trail on the ascent, was distracted: "His whole being seemed to betray his feeling and this was dangerous." Das stopped to remind the others that they needed full concentration on the details of the descent. He wondered later whether this was a premonition.

Das continued down, kicking his heels into soft snow, until he reached a large boulder. He turned to face the rock and, belayed by Sah, reached the base three metres below. He looked up to see that Singh had joined Sah. Singh again had one hand in his pocket, and he seemed to get a crampon caught in the rope. He began to hop on his right leg and swing the left in order to free it. He lost his balance, plunged over the edge, first pulling Sah off, and after a momentary delay, dragging Das off the mountain as well. The three men fell four hundred metres. Das remembered only "waiting for the interminable end of the fall," and that he had attempted to protect his face with his hands. They were still all roped together when they finally came to a rest. Indeed, Singh and Sah were lashed together, end to end, by the tangle of rope. Das, who was badly bruised but otherwise uninjured, heard Singh groaning. Das asked "Any bones broken? Any pain?" Singh, in shock, responded: "*Aap Kaun Hai*?" ("Who are you?")[41] He had a face wound and complained that his left leg was broken. Das then turned his attention to Sah, who was lying with his face in the snow. There was no response, so he grabbed his hood and pulled him over. Sah's face was horribly injured, and blood from gaping wounds stained the snow. His neck was broken and the unusual shape of his rib cage indicated that he had suffered severe internal injuries. Sah was dead.

Das tried to free Singh, but he was unable to do so, and the climber remained bound tightly by the rope to Sah. Das straightened the injured man out by shifting Sah's body, and was able to relieve some of the pressure on Singh's legs. However, Das realized his surviving colleague was deteriorating rapidly, and there was little he could do about it. He was in a precarious situation, without an ice axe, crampons, or extra clothing. Das covered his bare hands with extra socks. Shivering and stamping his feet, he shouted out to try to attract the attention of a rescue party.

Das concentrated on keeping up his friend's spirits and on his own survival. He looked at the time: It was only 8:30 P.M. He was determined not to fall asleep. Shortly after midnight, he became aware that "someone, a friend,"[42] was sitting to his right. From that point on, Das felt the presence of another being:

> This presence was around me and at times I talked to him
> and it urged me to concentrate on my survival, which I was
> doing. It was not a ghost-like apparition but like a
> companion. A presence.[43]

Before sunrise, but with diffuse light leaking into the sky, Das, addressing both his "friend"—the presence—and Singh, said he would go for help. He descended by an avalanche chute (a path carved by successive avalanches) and continued until he was within thirty metres of where three other climbers were camped. He then sat in the snow to rest, and began to speak again to the presence, who had descended with him and "was sitting safe, out of avalanche danger, on [my] right."[44] Das, by then, had been spotted by the other climbers, and two of them were hurrying towards him. Just then, "the Presence disappeared from my sphere of consciousness." Singh was carried down a short time later by the rescuers, but died half an hour after reaching the tent. Two decades after his encounter with the presence on Bhagirathi II, Das told me the experience remained "intense, and very personal."[45] He said it had never had any sense of unreality about it, just the opposite. A month after I last heard from him, on September 24, 2005, he was killed with four other climbers during a severe snowstorm while attempting to climb Chameo Moho in Sikkim.

GREG CHILD WAS AWARE "SOMETHING ALIEN was going on within me." With Peter Thexton, Child was climbing the main summit of Broad Peak, the twelfth-tallest mountain in the world, which straddles the border of China and Pakistan. They were at 7,900 metres, and had just reached Broad Peak's fore-summit, when Child, a skilled Australian climber, began experiencing headaches that suggested the onset of cerebral edema, a form of altitude sickness that leads to an accumulation of excessive fluid in the brain. He felt a sense of dislocation, followed by momentary blackouts. He would emerge from these absences a short time later, but reality had altered. It was all, he felt, "like a dream." His symptoms worsened. He had a throbbing headache, and his capacity to speak had eroded to the point that he could hardly string together a series of sensible words. They were a mere six or seven vertical metres from the true summit, but Child knew he had to quit. Thexton urged him to continue, but Child was adamant: "Lost control…. Too high, too fast." In fewer than three days, they had ascended more than three thousand metres. Thexton, who was a physician, was forced to accept the need to descend. But soon, he too was experiencing worrying symptoms. "I can't breathe properly," Thexton whispered to Child. This was possibly an indication of pulmonary edema, where the fluid buildup is in the lungs. "Are my lips blue?" he asked. They were, indicating oxygen starvation. Thexton and Child needed to retreat quickly.

Their immediate goal was their tent, six hundred metres below. The light was fading. While Child's symptoms improved, Thexton's condition rapidly deteriorated. His breathing became laboured, and he was struggling to continue. When they reached a snowfield, Child said he would plough ahead, making a new track. He urged Thexton to follow as quickly as he could. Thexton nodded, but after one hundred metres, Child turned to see that Thexton had barely moved. Child was forced to return for his partner as the last light drained from the sky. At times, Thexton would crawl a couple of metres. At other times, Child had to drag or carry him. Through it all, Child had a "strong feeling as if someone is peering over my shoulder keeping an eye on me."[46] In fact, with Thexton failing, Child felt as if he had help: "Someone was leading the way." More than that, he felt someone "must have lent a hand in carrying Pete."[47]

At 10 P.M., Thexton lost his sight, and soon he could almost not move. The situation was critical. Child was forced to use a rope to lower him down the slope. Both men were exhausted. They had been without food and drink for a day, and were climbing in darkness. Conditions worsened as a windstorm engulfed them. They were, Child later wrote, "completely lost on the vast west face of the world's twelfth-highest mountain." Yet, throughout the descent, Child continued to sense that a presence accompanied them. He later wrote in his journal: "My watcher checked every move and decision. I kept turning around, expecting to see someone."[48] Child wrote that "the experience of travelling with a third presence was powerful and calming." He felt confident: "Pete and I were being led to our tent."

He was right. At 2 A.M. they reached the tent where they were aided by two other members of their expedition. Thexton and Child, who had been climbing for twenty-two hours, now had a chance to recover. After a warm drink, Thexton appeared to pick up, and something of his wry humour returned. He and Child then slumped into sleep. In the morning, Thexton awoke and asked for water, but when a cup was pressed to his lips a few minutes later, he was already dead. Child, however, survived, and despite the horrific experience, he continued to climb. This seems to be the practice of many climbers. Child still wonders about the origin of the invisible ally who had seen him through the worst night of his life. It was, he told me, "not a fearful sensation, not a sense one might expect to have if confronting something supernatural."[49]

This occurred in June 1983, and Child encountered it again three years later, during his successful Gasherbrum IV expedition: "It had come to me in the snow cave first, then last night as well, in the small hours of the morning, the same sensation of someone familiar, an old friend, lying close to me, wrapping his arms around me, lending his warmth." Child wrote in his book, *Thin Air*, that he had, to that point, "an explanation for every sensation up here, as some symptom of oxygen starvation, dehydration, fatigue, or chemical imbalance." But as to being accompanied by the Third Man, he had no ready explanation. It was, he felt, "so vivid," and far "more real" than merely an hallucinatory episode caused by decay of brain function.

FRANK SMYTHE'S EXPERIENCE ON EVEREST, the world's greatest peak, those of Hermann Buhl and Reinhold Messner on Nanga Parbat, the ninth highest, and that of Tony Streather on Haramosh, occurred in situations of undoubted extremity. These are four of the most celebrated climbs in history: They were undertaken at extreme altitude, under adverse conditions, and at enormous risk. Parash Moni Das on Bhagirathi II, and Greg Child on Broad Peak, also confronted altitude and other stresses. Yet there is one other factor that connects them all. In each of these climbs, the stress of loss played a role. The Third Man appeared after separation from, or following the serious injury or death of, a companion. In such situations, where an individual is already isolated, and confronting great hardship and acute danger, the loss of a partner has the effect of a serious trauma. This raises an intriguing possibility: that adults are responding to stress in the same way that children do. Macdonald Critchley first made the link to imaginary playmates. Here too, the Third Man appears to be responding to stress by filling the void left by another. Not only do studies show that children under stress are more likely to experience an unseen friend, but there also is a series of studies that provide important evidence that the stress of loss can evoke a presence among adults, even in much more mundane circumstances than those described in this book. One of these investigations involved widows in Arizona.

In 1988, researchers at the University of Arizona at Tucson questioned five hundred widows over the age of sixty-five, and found that about half of them had sensed the presence of their deceased partner. This result surprised the researchers, because "sensing the presence of deceased people is considered an aberrant behavior caused by disassociation with reality. Consequently, many people are reluctant to disclose these experiences."[50] But theirs was not the only study to produce such a result. In fact, according to a British study, it is "commonplace": "At its weakest it is a feeling that one is somehow being watched; at its strongest it is a full-blown sensory experience."[51]

A survey of 227 widows and sixty-six widowers in Wales produced a similar finding. Almost half said they had sensed their late spouse, and the incidence was similar in men and women. What is more, "the hallucinations often lasted many years." That study, by W. Dewi Rees in the *British Medical Journal*, found that most people who had the experience reported they had visits intermittently throughout the day, while 10 percent said they "felt the dead spouse was always with them." All said they sensed the presence of the deceased; a few also said they actually saw or heard him. Rees found the experiences were in no way frightening, and concluded, "these hallucinations are … normal and helpful accompaniments of widowhood."[52] Research into widows of men killed in automobile accidents in Japan found the incidence even higher, and there, too, the researchers concluded the presence "may be a positive sign in helping them adapt to the loss."[53]

In fact, one study concluded that: "The imaginary companion of the aged may not differ in purpose and content from that of childhood." One eighty-one-year-old Canadian widower routinely cooked for his deceased wife, and would become panicky when he was unable to find her in the house. On one occasion he organized a dinner party for family members in her honour. Though he firmly held to the idea that she had joined them for the meal, he had "a rather bemused attitude towards the fact that his wife was still visiting after her death and recognized that others found this belief unusual."[54] In another case a widow, while aware that her husband had died and was buried, claimed that he "had returned to live with her within a few days of his death. For fear of 'upsetting him,' she didn't question this turn of events and carried on 'without comment.'" A few months later, however, she discovered her late husband had "mysteriously disappeared" and she became distraught at his departure and "suspected that he might have found another woman."[55]

A much larger survey in the U.K., conducted in 1995 and involving 1,603 people of all ages, found that about 35 percent "had gained some such sense of the presence of the dead." This study did not just look at widows or widowers, but a cross-section of society, revealing that the continuation of an important relationship after death is not confined to those who have lost a spouse. This often also involved the presence of a parent, as well as other family members, such as a grandparent. Some people have also reported sensing the presence of a dead friend. In one case, a girl, after the death of her father, "lay down in his bed to keep her mother company. After some days, she declared she would no longer sleep there because she felt the presence of her father: she had the impression that he was walking around the bed."[56] Usually the presence of the deceased is a comfort, although in this instance even though, "the girl was convinced that this impression did not correspond to reality the fact caused her anxiety." The prevailing scientific explanation is that "these experiences are illusory—symptoms of broken hearts and minds in chaos." This may account for the fact that most people do not disclose the experience, and if they do, it is only to close friends or relatives, for fear they "might become or be considered insane."[57] However, there is an alternative view among researchers, one that "allows the phenomenon to be seen as 'real' and 'natural.'"[58]

The feeling of a presence is most common in the first months of bereavement; about half of the subjects in one study reporting it during the first three months.[59] The incidence declines after a year, but only slightly, with 42 percent still reporting feeling the presence. The incidence of those who report more fully realized experiences, including speaking to, hearing, seeing, or being touched by the presence of the deceased, was significantly lower, and also declined precipitously as the months passed. Notably, a study at a hospital in Sweden found that, "when analyzing the relationship to grief reactions, hallucinations or illusions were more frequently found in subjects suffering from severe loneliness, crying, and memory problems one month after bereavement."[60] In other words, there is a greater incidence among those experiencing greater stress.

In a life-and-death struggle, such as that which often faces climbers, the loss of a climbing partner—or even the threatened loss of a climbing partner—has a dramatic impact. This effect was vividly demonstrated during the conquest of Annapurna, in the Himalayas, in 1950 by a team of French climbers. In this case, it is possible actually to trace its onset to the physical collapse of one climber. When he was returning from a reconnaissance of Dhaulagiri, a nearby peak, expedition leader Maurice Herzog could feel the strength ebbing from him. He realized that he could not keep pace with his climbing partner, Marcel Ichac, who was pressing ahead. Every ten steps, Herzog found himself stopping, then lying down in the snow. Ichac, frustrated by this behaviour, would then curse him, which seemed to provide the impetus for Herzog to continue. When they finally reached their camp, Ichac explained a "queer thing" that had happened. He said that as he ploughed along through the snow, he became aware of the presence of another climber with them. Said Ichac:

> I thought I heard someone else behind me … a third man. He was following us. I wanted to call out to tell you. I couldn't. I glanced behind me rather furtively, to set my mind at rest. But like an obsession, the feeling of someone else there kept on coming back to me.[61]

Ichac's encounter with the presence happened at the same time that Herzog had begun to collapse. Then, with Herzog's recovery, the immediate crisis passed and the presence was gone.

In the case of Reinhold Messner, it was first the threatened loss, and then the actual death, of a brother that led to the feeling of a presence. For many others the climbing partner may not even be a close friend; sometimes it is only a casual acquaintance. Yet, when confronting extremity, the absence of companionship still has profound consequences. This occurs at great altitude, but it also happens in routine environments, after the death of a loved one. The Third Man is not restricted to harrowing adventures, but can take the form of children's imaginary friends, and the awareness of the deceased experienced by their loved ones.

For Messner, that companionship came from a Third Man who provided, he told me, "psychological help to stem the loneliness.... The body is inventing ways to provide company."[62] This is the widow effect. It's the ultimate and beautiful illustration of the extent to which we are social animals—that in our time of deepest solitude and need, there is a way to reassure us that we are not alone, and provide us with that feeling of shared humanity that makes the difference between life and death.

CHAPTER NINE

Sensed Presence (II)

IN 1976, THE AMERICAN PSYCHOLOGIST Julian Jaynes provided a context in which the Third Man could be viewed as the product of brain processes. Jaynes is a controversial figure because of his theory that consciousness, as we now understand it, is a late development in human evolutionary history. According to Jaynes, in earlier times people experienced the products of their right cortical hemisphere as external events, as if they were taking place in the real world. Until about three thousand years ago, the human brain was divided into a right-brain "god-side," which appeared like an omnipotent being or authority figure, dispensing admonitory advice and commands by way of visual and auditory hallucinations, and a left-brain "man-side," which appeared to be a supplicant, listening and obeying. "All early civilizations we know of seem to have been ruled by such hallucinations or gods,"[1] Jaynes argued.

He outraged classicists by pointing to Homer's *Iliad* as an example of the persistence of what he called the "bicameral mind," saying there is no evidence of true consciousness—of thinking, feeling, or being aware—in the original text: "People are not sitting down and making decisions. No one is. No one is introspecting. It is a very different kind of world." Instead, whenever a decision has to be made, "a voice comes in telling people what to do," such as when Apollo recommends that Hector avoid battling Achilles. "These voices are always and immediately obeyed. These voices are called gods. To me this is the origin of gods. I regard them as auditory hallucinations."[2]

The idea that a physical split between the brain hemispheres could account for voices heard in the head is not so radical, in light of some unusual brain effects recorded by neurologists. For example, scientific studies report cases of "Dr. Strangelove syndrome," where people who suffer organic brain injuries have a hand that seems to take on a life of its own, like that of Peter Sellers' character in the classic film, and will not follow brain commands. One woman had a hand that kept trying to strangle her, forcing her to fight to subdue it using her second hand. The woman explained it this way: "I suppose there must be an evil spirit in it." A study published in 2000 described another unusual case, this time involving a man who, after suffering a stroke, had one hand that engaged in involuntary masturbation. This would occur in public as well as private situations, and was observed in a clinical setting. Needless to say, "the patient's wife ... expressed deep concern."[3] Only the man's left hand was involved. In such cases, a part of the brain appears to function outside of a person's will, and so it seems as if the errant hand has become possessed of an external, or alien, force. In the context, Jaynes' theory of bicameralism hardly seems outlandish.

Jaynes, who taught at Princeton University, was criticized in part because rather than publishing in peer-reviewed journals, he largely opted to set out his radical theory of bicameralism in his 1976 book, *The Origin of Consciousness in the Breakdown of the Bicameral Mind*, written for a general audience. By combining neurology, anthropology, archaeology, theology, and the classics, he trod where few scholars dared and, consequently, sometimes found himself pursued by fierce critics at academic meetings. Yet, Jaynes' ideas have endured, leading one reviewer to ask: "How many students of cognitive science have read this deeply unfashionable book under, as it were, the bed-covers?"[4]

Jaynes argued that there was a hair trigger for hallucinations in pre-conscious humans, and even the "slight stress of making a decision in a novel circumstance" would have been enough to bring one on. The intervention of this personal god was required for "anything that could not be dealt with on the basis of habit."[5] While they looked and often behaved much as modern humans do, pre-conscious humans were in this important way very different. Jaynes attributed the subsequent breakdown of the bicameral mind and emergence of a more unified consciousness to several factors, including literacy, which, "in relaying the commands of the gods weakened the power of auditory hallucinations."[6] Only then did people perceive the processes of both hemispheres as their own, and not as coming from some external source.

There is a great deal of evidence in antiquity that would seem to support Jaynes' thesis, such as an ancient carving of the King of Assyria kneeling before an empty throne, from which his god is conspicuously absent, leaving him without divine guidance. A tablet from the period reads: "My god has forsaken me and disappeared. My goddess has failed me and keeps at a distance. The good angel who walked beside me has departed." The Old Testament also provides evidence that ancient peoples heard voices. The Hebrew prophet Amos was a shepherd, and was in a solitary setting, tending his flock in the fields, when he heard a voice: "I am not a prophet ... I am merely a herdsman and dresser of sycamore-figs. But Yahweh took me as I followed the flock, and Yahweh said to me, 'Go and prophesy to my people Israel.'"[7]

Jaynes saw a persistence of bicameralism even today, including in children's imaginary playmates, which he said should be called "hallucinated playmates," and also the voices heard by schizophrenics, many of whom experience "command hallucinations," where voices direct them to commit certain acts. Jaynes pointed to a study showing that, when a system was developed for communicating with institutionalized quadriplegics who had never been able to speak, they were asked about the possibility of hearing voices. Most of the patients, "gave startled expressions followed by excited 'yes' signals. The voices were usually of the same sex as the patient, sounding like a relative but identified as God. They spoke as from outside the patient."[8] He also said, "the 'voices' gave authoritarian commands that told the residents how to behave and to which the residents feel compelled to respond."[9]

For modern humans generally, however, the stress threshold for triggering a bicameral hallucination is much higher, according to Jaynes: "Most of us need to be over our heads in trouble before we would hear voices."[10] Yet, he said, "contrary to what many an ardent biological psychiatrist wishes to think, they occur in normal individuals also."[11] Recent studies have supported him, with some finding that a large minority of the general population, between 30 and 40 percent, report having experienced auditory hallucinations. These often involve hearing one's own name, but also phrases spoken from the rear of a car, and the voices of absent friends or dead relatives.[12] Jaynes added that it is "absolutely certain that such voices do exist and that experiencing them is just like hearing actual sound." Even today, though they are loath to admit it, completely normal people hear voices, he said, "often in times of stress."

Jaynes pointed to an example in which normally conscious individuals have experienced vestiges of bicameral mentality, notably, "shipwrecked sailors during the war who conversed with an audible God for hours in the water until they were saved."[13] In other words, it emerges in normal people confronting high stress and stimulus reduction in extreme environments. A U.S. study of combat veterans with post-traumatic stress disorder found a majority (65 percent) reported hearing voices, sometimes "command hallucinations to which individuals responded with a feeling of automatic obedience."[14] During his extraordinary voyage from Sydney to Los Angeles, the first recorded solo west–east crossing, the Latvian sailor Fred Rebell in 1932 heard "the Voice," an authoritative male voice speaking in English that gave him counsel he came to trust.[15] The British climber Joe Simpson, famous for his book and the film *Touching the Void*, reported experiencing a "coldly rational" voice in his head during his brush with death on Siula Grande, in Peru:

The voice was clean and sharp and commanding. It was always right, and I listened to it when it spoke and acted on its decisions. The other mind rambled out a disconnected series of images, and memories and hopes, which I attended to in a daydream state as I set about obeying the orders of the voice.[16]

The normally dominant left cortical hemisphere releases its grip on the mind, with a resulting decline in logical, linear thinking. Meanwhile, the right hemisphere, which is involved in imaginative thinking, seizes the opportunity to play a greater role, "and its products, which may include the perception of an imagined 'other,' enter consciousness."[17] Some studies of subjects exposed to profoundly restricted environmental stimulation also describe a shift in hemispheric dominance. While Jaynes focused on auditory hallucinations, he argued, "visual hallucinations may be fitted into the real environment, the figures walking about." It is perhaps not coincidental that among the explorers who have experienced Third Man Factor, four I have spoken to—Jim Sevigny, Ann Bancroft, Reinhold Messner, and Parash Moni Das—offered without prompting that the presence was on their right side.

ONE OF THE RESEARCHERS WHO TOOK JAYNES' THEORY and applied it to the real world is Peter Suedfeld, a psychologist at the University of British Columbia in Vancouver and one of the world's foremost investigators of psychological responses to extreme and unusual environments. His research is concerned with how human beings adapt to and cope with novelty, challenge, stress, and danger.

Suedfeld came by his specialty honestly. A Holocaust survivor, he was eight when his parents were taken away. His mother died at Auschwitz, and his father survived the concentration camp at Mauthausen. Peter went into hiding, and ended up in an orphanage, where an employee gave him a new name to conceal his identity. After the war, an aunt found him after a long search. It was, he said, "the happiest day of my life."[18] Now a professor emeritus, Suedfeld has spent much of his career studying the effects of isolation. He was director of the Canadian High Arctic Psychology Research Station, has worked in Antarctica, and has advised NASA on the psychology of capsule environments for long duration space missions. Suedfeld was intrigued by Jaynes' belief that "stress is the basis for the re-emergence of bicamerality." In the late 1970s, when writing a book on sensory deprivation, Suedfeld was looking for material on reduced sensory and social stimulation situations outside the laboratory. He turned to narratives of polar explorers, solo sailors, mountain climbers, and religious hermits, where he began to discover reports of "hallucinations of other people or superhuman entities, usually felt to be helpful, supportive, and capable of saving the hallucinator."[19] None of the reports involved schizophrenics or people with another psychosis. To the contrary, all came from "otherwise mentally normal, physically healthy individuals, many of them adventurous and of outstanding achievement."[20] As far as Suedfeld was concerned, their experiences provided "an example of bicamerality."[21]

There was something else that interested him. Suedfeld found "the impression of help or encouragement by the phantom presence lends the experience great psychological immediacy and makes the phenomenon important to a description of coping mechanisms."[22] He was struck both by "the immediacy to the individual, in that the presence is so real, alive, active, and knowledgeable and/or powerful," but also "the immediacy to survival, which the presence makes possible, or at least facilitates."[23] They sometimes do not offer only companionship, but also useful information or advice, and at other times seem to take a direct hand in improving the chances of survival.[24] It is, he argued, a dramatic phenomenon, and the variety of circumstances that can provoke its appearance underscores its significance: "This is so common, across so many types of travellers—Western sailors, Inuit hunters, native Indian adolescents—that it demands attention."[25]

It is impossible to estimate just how prevalent the occurrence is, but it is even more common than we think, because it is almost certainly underreported. Suedfeld said that some people would "deny such phenomena" out of embarrassment—an unwillingness to admit to an experience that they fear might imply that they were coming undone by physical and psychological challenges. But Suedfeld, in his important study (with Jane Mocellin) of the phenomenon, "The 'Sensed Presence' in Unusual Environments," rejected such thinking: "People who may encounter the evoking conditions, as well as scholars and mental health professionals, should be warned against assuming that the experience is a symptom of actual or imminent breakdown."[26] It is quite the opposite, he argued, "an adaptive response, a normal reaction to an abnormal situation." He continued:

There is no factual basis for categorizing it as a psychiatric symptom, aside from its superficial similarity to some

psychotic hallucinations ... The sensed presence should be
added to, and therefore extends, the recognized range of
normal coping behaviours in certain unusual situations.[27]

Under extreme stress and in monotonous environments, the
dominant left hemisphere of the brain becomes less dominant,
which he said reduces "the preponderance of logical, linear, reality-
oriented thinking. The right hemisphere, which (to put it simplis-
tically) governs creative, imaginative, non-linear cognition, assumes
a greater role than usual; and its products, which may include the
perception of an imagined 'other,' enter consciousness."[28] Suedfeld
resisted the tendency to look at brain anatomy for all the answers,
and urged that attention be paid instead to the mind. He called for
"a more psychologically oriented explanation for the experience
than one based exclusively on neurochemical changes."[29] As
Suedfeld put it, "the conscious experience cannot be disregarded."[30]

ANOTHER RESEARCHER TO HAVE BUILT on Julian Jaynes' theory
is Michael Persinger, a psychologist at Laurentian University in
Sudbury, Ontario. Persinger and his Behavioral Neuroscience
Laboratory have become well-known in the rarified discipline of
neurotheology (a term coined by Aldous Huxley in his novel
Island, meaning the study of the neural basis for spirituality), and
even in the popular media, for having developed a device that has
been dubbed the "god helmet," because it is said to induce
religious experience by stimulating the brain with low doses of
complex, low-intensity magnetic fields, less intense even than
those a hair dryer generates.

In 1988, Persinger suggested the existence of a link between hallucinations and electromagnetic disturbances, whether produced internally by the brain, or externally by other natural sources such as solar flares and seismic activity, or by man-made sources such as microwave transmissions and electrical devices. There is, he and his colleagues wrote in the *International Journal of Neuroscience*, growing evidence to suggest that "the right hemisphere of the normal brain may be more sensitive to changes in geomagnetic activity."[31] He theorized that these fluctuations cause micro-seizures that in turn produce altered states, notably the sense of a presence nearby. A number of other studies have connected geomagnetic activity to certain brain responses. One revealed a statistically significant correlation between the solar wind, with its embedded magnetic fields, and historical reports of hallucinations, both of which peak in the months of March and October.[32] And in her study of the sensed presence reports at the Esperanza base in Antarctica, psychologist Jane Mocellin suggested that two environmental factors seemed to trigger the sensed presence among the Argentine crew: The incidents always occurred at the generator of the station, which creates powerful electrical fields, and Esperanza base is located near a very strong local magnetic anomaly that caused ships and aircraft compasses to fail.

Following on Jaynes, Persinger argued that the sense of self is normally mediated by the brain's left hemisphere, but when the "normal state of reciprocal inhibition between the two hemispheres" is altered by factors like drugs, psychological trauma, or magnetic patterns, there can be transient intrusions by the right hemisphere. These are detected by the left-brain self, which then attempts to make sense of a non-existent entity. Wrote Persinger:

> During periods when consciousness was significantly altered ... the bicameral characteristics partially emerged again. In secular men and women, the right hemispheric (ego-intrusive) phenomenology might be reported as a presence, entity, or force while in religious men and women the same process might be reported as a spirit, angel, or culture-specific god.[33]

The god helmet was Persinger's way to test his hypothesis. "If all experiences are generated by brain activity, then experiences of God and spirits should also be produced by the appropriate cerebral stimulation," he said. For more than fifteen years, his experiments have demonstrated that "the sensed presence of a 'Sentient Being' can be reliably evoked by very specific temporal patterns of weak transcerebral magnetic fields."[34] Subjects were asked to sit in a comfortable chair in an acoustic chamber. They would have a blindfold placed over their eyes, and wear a modified motorcycle helmet, with four sets of solenoids (electrified magnets) embedded on each side of the helmet, exposing the subjects' temporal lobes to a weak magnetic field. The resulting inter-hemispheric changes "have produced reported experiences of sensed presences in about 80% of participants."[35]

Most of the subjects reported a vague sensation of being watched. Persinger wrote that some presence experiences were confined to simple statements like, "I feel there is someone in the room behind me," but sometimes involved more complex observations like, "I began to feel the presence of people, but I could not see them; they were along my sides. They were colourless, grey-looking. I know I was in the chamber but it was very real." Few of the accounts seem to match the giddy popular-media reports of Persinger's work that invariably flowed from his novel research. An article in *Wired* magazine, for example, reported full-blown religious experiences: "Elijah, Jesus, the Virgin Mary, Mohammed, the Sky Spirit."[36] However, in one journal article, Persinger did describe a subject who encountered "a religious entity" during an experiment, and Persinger himself wrote that the sense of a presence "can be considered the phenomenological basis for most reports of visitations by spirits, gods, and extraterrestrial entities."[37]

Some of the accounts Persinger has published are strikingly similar to the descriptions of the Third Man given by explorers and others in extreme and unusual environments:

> I felt a presence behind me and then along the left side. When I tried to focus on its position, the presence moved. Every time I tried to sense where it was, it moved around. When it moved to the right side, I experienced a deep sense of security like I had not experienced before. I started to cry when I felt it slowly fade away.[38]

Among the writers and journalists who have visited Persinger at his laboratory in Sudbury and donned the god helmet, or more properly, the "transcranial magnetic stimulator," is the British arch-atheist and Oxford zoologist, Richard Dawkins, who went there in 2003 for the British Broadcasting Corporation's science program, *Horizon*. Dawkins, best known for his book, *The God Delusion*, agreed to try the technique to see if he could have a religious or mystical experience. But the magnetic fields only induced some strange tinglings and twitchings. "It was a great disappointment," said Dawkins:

> Though I joked about the possibility, I of course never
> expected to end up believing in anything supernatural. But I
> did hope to share some of the feelings experienced by
> religious mystics when contemplating the mysteries of life
> and the cosmos.[39]

Persinger acknowledges that there are differences in individuals' susceptibility to the phenomenon, and suggests that the temporal lobes of some people are more responsive to naturally occurring electromagnetic fields than those of others. Persinger explained Dawkins' failure to experience any entity by observing that, before the experiment, he was given a psychological test to measure proneness to temporal lobe sensitivity and had scored poorly.

There may be another explanation. In 2005, a group of researchers in Sweden published a paper arguing that suggestibility, not exposure to the weak complex magnetic fields generated by Persinger's helmet, was responsible for the sensed presence and mystical experiences gathered in his laboratory. They had been unable to replicate his results,[40] but Persinger disputed the Swedish group's findings, saying they omitted reference to two major studies he had conducted, involving 148 subjects, where double-blind conditions were adhered to. In a statement posted on his website, Persinger further suggested the Swedes had not followed his laboratory's procedures exactly, and had "applied the software through a Pentium computer that would have distorted the magnetic configurations through the solenoids. This would produce noise rather than a bioeffective pattern."[41]

Persinger remained unbowed by the criticism. I met him briefly on March 10, 2006, at the interval during a standing-room-only discussion at the University of Toronto, titled "Belief and the Human Brain: Is God All in Your Head?" organized, appropriately enough, by the Toronto Secular Alliance. A gaunt man, he seemed overdressed for the occasion (and judging from other accounts for most occasions), in a three-piece suit. One of his colleagues has admitted that he had "never seen Persinger dressed other than in a three-piece suit, even when he was mowing his lawn."[42] At his talk, Persinger said again that the sensed presence is the prototype for supernatural beings, from gods to space aliens. "Nature's been doing it forever. We're not doing anything fancy. All we have done like all science is simply take the scientific method, measure what nature does, duplicate it in the laboratory and then replicate it under controlled conditions."

His talk was well received, and Persinger did not reveal any frustration with his skeptics. But in a posting on his website, Persinger plaintively addressed the Swedish study: "Sadly, this is another example in the history of science of how the scientific explanation for a very important phenomenon, in this instance the brain basis to the sensed presence, the prototype for god experiences, may be disrupted by social and personality factors." The *Economist* magazine weighed in to suggest that it will likely take a third party to undertake yet another set of experiments to settle the dispute: "The origins of religious experience are one of the most mysterious phenomena in brain science. It would be nice to get a straight answer."[43]

What is clear is that the studies of both Suedfeld and Persinger fit neatly into Jaynes' theory, according to which such encounters are normal mental experiences rather than evidence of brain function deterioration.[44]

CHAPTER TEN

The Muse Factor

IN THE LATE SEVENTH CENTURY BC, HESIOD, in the first lines of "Theogony," a poem about the gods of ancient Greece, described how he had pastured his sheep on the slopes of Helicon, a large mountain in central Greece, when he encountered the Muses. They "breathed into me a divine voice," wrote Hesiod. "They have made Helicon, the great god-haunted mountain, their domain." To Julian Jaynes, the evidence was clear: "The poet was not out of his mind…. Rather, his creativity was perhaps much closer to what we have come to call bicameral…. And loneliness can lead to hallucination." Hesiod's account was, Oxford University classicist E.R. Dodds argued in his 1951 study, *The Greeks and the Irrational*, not "allegory or poetic ornament, but an attempt to express a real experience in literary terms." The Muses actually did speak to Hesiod. Dodds identified other manifestations of an unseen presence in ancient Greek religion, such as Pindar's vision of the mother of the Gods during a thunderstorm in the mountains, and Philippides' vision of Pan, which he experienced on "one of the wildest and most desolate tracks in Greece," while crossing the pass of Mount Parthenion. Each occurred in mountainous areas and involved "fatigue coupled with loneliness in the face of Nature." As Dodds wrote:

> These three experiences have an interesting point in common: they all occurred in lonely mountain places.... That is possibly not accidental. Explorers, mountaineers, and airmen sometimes have odd experiences even today: a well-known example is the presence that haunted Shackleton and his companions in the Antarctic.[1]

The "mountain metaphor in religion" is widely recognized, but in the journal *Medical Hypotheses*, Shahar Arzy and three co-authors, all neurologists from Swiss or Israeli universities, suggested that mountains are more than simply a metaphor. They categorized "feeling of a presence, hearing of a presence" among "reports of revelation-like experiences in high altitude mountaineers" as experiences that might help explain the link between mountains and religion. It is to the mountaintop that wise men go to seek enlightenment, and the peaks—Olympus in Greece, Kailas in Tibet, Fuji in Japan, T'ai Shan in China—represent both the powerful forces of nature and the sacred. In particular, Arzy and his colleagues wrote: "the revelations to the founders of the three western monotheistic religions—Moses, Jesus, and Mohammad—occurred on mountains":

> On Mount Sinai Moses experienced his first revelation in the burning bush, and encountered the Hebrew God three more

times. Jesus was transfigured "up a high mountain apart"—
identified as Mount Tabor or Mount Hermon—and
appeared to Peter, John and James in a cloud of glory. In
Islamic tradition, Prophet Mohammad had received the
Qur'an while in solitude on Mount Hira by a revelation of
the archangel Gabriel.[2]

The neurologists suggested "prolonged stay at high altitudes,
especially in social deprivation … might affect functional and
neural mechanisms, thus facilitating the experience of a revelation." When Joe Simpson heard a voice during difficult conditions
on Huascarán, he immediately attributed it to routine explanations: "I thought I might have left my Walkman on with the
volume turned down. On checking, I found it switched off and
carefully wrapped in a scarf in the top pocket of my sack. I pulled
back the balaclava exposing my ears to the icy wind, thinking that
it might be the rubbing sounds of the fabric. The voices were still
there …"[3] For people living in ancient times, the routine explanations for such experiences would not have been a Walkman, they
would have been religious.

The paper in *Medical Hypotheses* makes a second important
point: that revelatory experiences have also occurred on mountains
of low or moderate altitude. Helicon is 1,749 metres; Sinai is
2,600 metres; Hermon is 2,841 metres; Hira is 2,600 metres; and
Tabor is a mere 588 metres. Compared to the high-altitude climbs
undertaken today, these mountains are very small indeed. There is
neither extreme cold, nor lack of oxygen. The critical factors that
Griffith Pugh identified are absent. So how is it that some people
still experience the Third Man at much lower altitudes, or even at

sea level? The neurologists have an intriguing explanation: that for "subjects who are prone to mystical experiences … moderate altitudes are sufficient."[4]

Altitude can trigger the Third Man, but it is not required for people to have the experience. The mountaineering cases that follow stand in contrast to those of Smythe, Buhl, Streather, Messner, and the others, and persuasively contradict Pugh's contention that "decay of the brain functions" underlies the experience. In some, the stresses are serious, and in others they are comparatively moderate, but none of them involve hypoxia. Is the explanation of the differences, then, that some people are prone to mystical experiences, while others are not? That point is arguable, but this much appears certain: External conditions are not the only factor. Something else is at play, and evidence suggests it involves an internal psychological variable—a muse factor.

EXTREME ALTITUDE WAS NOT A FACTOR for American climber Rob Taylor in the struggle that followed his failed attempt to ascend the Breach Wall of Kilimanjaro in January 1978. The mountain itself, which rises 5,895 metres from the plains of Africa, is not a difficult ascent despite its height. Tourists without climbing experience can pay guides to take them up its slopes. The Breach Wall is different: a technically demanding climb which, in the first weeks of 1978, was more challenging than usual, thanks to one hundred metres of rotten ice near the top. To the depth of one metre, the ice had the consistency of sugar. Taylor had to scrape the ice crystals away before securing his ice screws. He realized that in such conditions a fall was a real possibility, and compensated by securing closely placed ice screws. The fall came anyway, when the ice Taylor was holding onto collapsed. He fell into space, but was saved by climbing ropes. He was immediately aware of a sharp pain in his left foot. He had broken his ankle when he lurched back into the ice wall following his sudden drop. The arch of his left foot was twisted grotesquely so that it touched his inner calf, and his boot began filling with blood. He struggled for control as the haze of shock threatened to envelop him. First he had to try to get the bones of his shin and foot back in place. Climbing partner Harley Warner grabbed hold of Taylor's left boot and held firmly. Taylor pulled, and after several minutes of agony, his fibula popped into place. He then used the shaft of an ice axe as a splint. In other circumstances, his would have been a serious, but manageable injury, but at 5,500 metres elevation, 120 kilometres from the nearest medical help, the twenty-three-year-old suddenly found himself in a race against infection, and the possible onset of gangrene.

With Warner, Taylor was forced first to bivouac, and then begin the hazardous and laborious descent early on January 15. Initially, Warner lowered the injured climber down the mountain, but as the steepness of the descent gave way to sloping ground, Taylor lost whatever mobility he had. Warner could not carry him far, so Taylor had to drag himself, "grovelling only a few metres at a time on my chest." Yet the rappel down the Wall, and the subsequent creep down from the glacier's edge, for all its agonizing hardship, was not the worst of Taylor's ordeal. On January 17, Taylor was deposited on the lee side of some large boulders at the base of Kilimanjaro. He crawled into his sleeping bag and "bivvy" (bivouac) sack and waited while Warner went for help. Warner assured him the rescue party would be there the following morning at the latest, and Taylor had no reason to doubt him. With the immediate danger of the descent past, he felt relaxed, at times even elated. But no one came the next day, and Taylor's deteriorating situation was made worse when his small butane stove ran out of fuel, and he could no longer melt snow for water.

Then Taylor noticed a male figure crouching fewer than fifty metres from him. He at first thought it might be a member of the rescue party, and began yelling for assistance. But there was no response. "Who are you? What do you want? Answer me!" he shouted. He felt confusion, then anger, and frustration at the failure of the figure to respond. He was desperate for help, he was waiting for help, he was expecting help—but no help was forthcoming. Taylor threw rocks in the direction of the figure in order to elicit a response. Some seemed to pass right through it: "Clearly I make out his form, yet never can I distinguish exact features through the snowy haze. So taut are the general lines of his body, he appears devoid of clothing, like a dancer in a leotard." Taylor found it impossible to categorize the experience—"my mind does not know what to do with him"—but he began to accept that the figure, which sat serenely on a boulder, was simply there to keep him company. "Hour upon hour this companion watcher, as I call him, peers out at me through the curtain of snow." With darkness, he directed his headlamp in the direction of his companion, and found him still acting as a silent sentinel.

That night, Taylor awoke suddenly, as if an alarm had been sounded. He realized that he not only felt no pain in his injured foot, but nothing at all. Pulling off his sleeping bag, he was hit by an overwhelming smell of decay. He tried to wrench the boot off his injured foot, but it would not come free. He then began hacking at it with his ice axe, before prying the boot off. His foot was severely infected, and once freed, jets of yellow pus shot from the wound. The foot had swollen in the boot, cutting off circulation, which allowed the infection to take hold. With the restoration of blood flow, he had feeling again in his ankle, foot, and toes. Taylor set about cleaning the wound. He believed that if he had not discovered the infection until morning, it would have been too late to save his foot. He asked: "What woke me? Was it my companion watcher? Was he sent to me as a messenger?... Someone, some being, guides me on my journey."[5] Before lying back down, Taylor cast the beam of his headlamp to look for this friend. He stared out into the darkness, searching for the presence, and saw him again, this time much closer.

Two more days passed, and two more nights. Something had happened to Warner. He was not coming back. There would be no rescue team. Fever set in; thought, reality, and the apparition all seemed to merge. His companion moved closer, yet still Taylor could make out no details. He could see a brow, the shape of the chin, but nothing more. He thought it odd that, despite the snowfall, there was no snow on the figure, yet "it took up absolutely solid space like a stone or anything else." Finally, the figure was, "right at the foot of the sleeping bag." At the end, Taylor felt the being "was very benevolent and very positive ... it was peaceful and definitely reassuring."[6] Then, after waiting with him for days, the presence departed, and Taylor was alone.

Minutes later, he heard his name being called. It was the rescue team. Taylor's life—and foot—were saved. Warner had taken a different route on his hike to get help, and had managed to get lost, accounting for the long delay. Taylor later wrote of his encounter:

> I don't often talk about my companion watcher these days. He is a creature out of place here, misunderstood. After the Breach when I first spoke of him to people, they reacted quite predictably: "What an imagination!" "Your fever had you hallucinating." At first I persisted in my stand: "He was real. There in the flesh or at least in some concrete form I could see." Later I left him out altogether. It was easier than trying to define or defend him to people who could not understand. Now I know this and say this to you: He was there and as real as you or I. I do not know to this day his purpose, but I sense that it was good.[7]

IN MAY 1981, JIM WICKWIRE, a forty-year-old Seattle attorney and a skilled climber who had already been to the summit of K2, set out to climb Mount McKinley's imposing Wickersham Wall. It is one of the largest mountain faces in the world, rising 4,200 metres from the Peter's Glacier to the 6,194-metre North Peak. Because of avalanche hazard, it had not been climbed since 1963, but Wickwire and a younger climber, Chris Kerrebrock, felt it was not an insurmountable challenge. They were deposited by aircraft at the mountain's main landing site, and then made their way around to the remote north side. They negotiated some tricky ice cliffs and a bergschrund—a large crevasse at the foot of the glacier—and then made their way down the Peter's Glacier towards the base of the Wickersham Wall.

They were travelling slowly across the glacier in the middle of the afternoon on May 8, hauling a sledge of supplies. They were roped together. Kerrebrock was leading, when a crust of ice concealing a crevasse collapsed, sending him headlong into the opening. Wickwire, who did not see the fall, was grabbed and thrown into the air by the force of Kerrebrock's weight on the rope. He remembered thinking, "I'm about to die," before he and the sledge both hurtled into the crevasse and slammed on top of Kerrebrock, who was alive, but lodged face-down between the walls of the crevasse, buried underneath his large pack, which had been compressed to half its normal width by the force of impact. Wickwire, stunned by what had happened, gathered himself up, and shoved the sledge off Kerrebrock. All Wickwire could see of Kerrebrock were his legs. He was still wearing his snowshoes. Kerrebrock said: "I can't move, Wick, you've got to get me out!" Wickwire had broken his shoulder, but was able to edge himself up, using an ice hammer with his good arm to make small indentations into the ice, onto which he placed the front points of his crampons. Gradually, he was able to climb out of the crevasse. It took an hour to ascend a 7.5-metre shaft. He finally emerged and lay on the snow, gasping for breath.

Wickwire immediately began to work to free Kerrebrock, first taking up the slack of the rope and, despite his injuries, pulling with all his might—but his partner did not budge. He tried again, but could not pull Kerrebrock free. He realized that he would have to re-enter the crevasse. He tied a rope to a picket that he drove deep into the hard snow, and then lowered himself in. He first tried to pull on Kerrebrock's pack, then tried tying the rope to the pack's accessible cross-straps, and pulled on them. When that failed, he took his ice hammer to the pack, trying to cut the material, thinking that by removing some items in it he would relieve the compression that held it fast.

Nothing he could do had any effect. After six hours of failed attempts, interrupted by radioed pleas for help that went unanswered, both men realized that Wickwire had exhausted all options. Kerrebrock said: "There's nothing more you can do, Wick. You should go up." Wickwire could not believe that Kerrebrock was going to die, and that he was utterly helpless to prevent it. When he emerged from the crevasse again, Wickwire was physically spent, but also burdened with sadness and guilt. Lying at the edge of the opening, he pulled himself into a nylon bivouac sack. Kerrebrock died that night from the cold and trauma. He spent his last hours in delirium from his injuries and the bitter cold. At one point, Wickwire heard Kerrebrock singing what sounded like a school song. At 2 A.M., Wickwire heard Kerrebrock for the last time.

Wickwire's own ordeal was not over. A scheduled rendezvous with a bush plane would not occur for two weeks. Most of the supplies, including tent, stove, and the bulk of the food, remained in the crevasse. Wickwire waited for rescue with twelve sticks of beef jerky to eat and only his bivouac sack for shelter. He later re-entered the crevasse, and was able to collect more food from the sledge, but it was not enough. Sitting beneath soaring ice cliffs, on a vast glacier, he began to suffer from dehydration. He had a water bottle and was able to melt some snow by holding it against his body, and on some days the warmth of the sun helped. The pilot who had flown them in had promised a flyby to check on their status, and Wickwire waited for sound of the aircraft. Several times he thought he heard light planes, but they were far away. After seven days, the threat of an avalanche forced him to move. In doing so, he twice nearly fell into crevasses.

Wickwire wrote in his journal: "At times the past week I've almost turned to talk to someone—a sense that a second person is here."[8] He wondered whether the being was "part of my personality disengaging from itself? Or Chris's spirit? Or was it just my fear and loneliness?"[9] Wickwire was not threatened by this other existence; in fact, "it was comforting, it was reassuring me.... It was a companion, a sense of support. It was also a signal to me that I was in an extreme situation, it was kind of a confirmation of that."[10] He decided that if he were to survive, he had to continue moving towards the climbers who congregated on the other side of the mountain.

He crawled, probing the crust of the glacier with his ice axe, this way avoiding each crevasse in his path. He made steady progress, and with the crevasses behind him, thought he was about a day away from reaching help. Then a blizzard struck, and he was forced to stop. The temperature dropped, he was buffeted by winds of up to 120 kilometres per hour, and snow piled up on him. Wickwire was now down to one stick of beef jerky. He craved food, but it was not only hunger that gnawed at him. He suffered episodes of unbearable loneliness. Yet during the four-day storm, the presence returned, and remained close by. Wickwire felt "comforted by the sense that I was not alone, that someone was there with me." He ascended to the upper glacier, and the danger posed by the crevasses lessened. He finally made radio contact with the pilot. The plane was approaching when he reached down to pick up his pack and one foot punched through yet another crevasse. He lunged forward to safety, but it was too much. It was almost as if the glacier was determined not to allow him to escape. In the end, Wickwire sat on the ground and wept. The pilot landed nearby, and Wickwire did escape. He was eleven kilograms (twenty-five pounds) lighter than when he and Kerrebrock had been dropped off only three weeks earlier.

MOUNT FUJI, A DORMANT VOLCANO that, at 3,776 metres, is Japan's highest peak, is not normally associated with any sort of extremity. During climbing season, July and August, it is a mountain that non-climbers can easily summit, and crowds of people do. A national symbol, visible on clear days from Tokyo, only one hundred kilometres away, the mountain has acquired special meaning for the Japanese for its resident deities and spiritual powers. However, off-season climbs are recommended only for skilled climbers, and from October to May, the Japanese government warns that climbing to the summit is highly perilous due to extreme wind, the danger of severe weather, and the risk of avalanches. Walter Welsch, a forty-three-year-old geodesy professor from Munich, Germany, who was in Japan to attend an academic conference, tackled the mountain on May 6, 1982. Welsch was an experienced climber, and judged Fuji a relatively easy climb even at that time of year. It was his first full day in the country, and he embarked on the climb alone. Early in the ascent, he became concerned because of rising winds. He found the mountain huts, built to provide a respite for climbers, all locked. He persisted, despite the winds that gradually rose to strong gusts. The altitude was not bothering him and the temperature was mild. He was calm, and felt neither anxiety nor loneliness. His attention was focused on climbing, which became increasingly difficult as he encountered snow. At one point, he stopped to drink a tin of tomato juice, and was "surprised, that no one was there with whom to share the drink." He realized then that there had been a palpable sense of another, an "invisible companion," with him, registering it as "strange."[11]

At 3,400 metres, the storm worsened. His footing was uncertain, and he had to be careful not to be blown off the mountainside. At 3,600 metres, he got down on his hands and knees, but continued to ascend on the "bone-hard" snow. He reached a series of *toriis*, or shrine gateways. With the last of these just thirty paces ahead, he was forced to pause because of the weather, before he resumed his struggle. By this time, he was creeping forward on his stomach. Welsch reached the crater plateau, at 3,720 metres, but then drew back. The conditions made the last fifty-six metres of elevation impossible. He felt he had done his best and the storm conditions were now acute. The descent was tricky. The gale blew constantly. He kept his face to the mountain and moved cautiously down in thick twilight. Several hundred metres down, he reached a hut and huddled behind it for protection from the wind, shivering, and waiting for the conditions to improve. He dozed for a while, and then at 9 P.M. decided to resume. Again he found himself turning around and offering juice to his invisible companion. He also described having "to check that no one was really there." Odd, he observed, since there really was no one there, that he did not in any way feel lonely: "I felt always as if I was in company with my usual climbing friends."[12] It was only when the conditions began to improve, and the snow moistened, that he "missed the unseen companion." It soon began to rain and the winds died down. He had reached safety.

PAUL FIRTH, A SOUTH AFRICAN, HAD A SIMILAR experience on Aconcagua, a 6,962-metre-high peak in the Argentine Andes. The highest mountain in the Western Hemisphere, Aconcagua is located in the western part of the country, close to the border with Chile. In late February 1996, Firth, a twenty-eight-year-old physician, made several attempts to reach the summit with climbing partners. Each failed. On day ten of the expedition, Firth prepared to try again, this time alone. He first removed his thick gloves briefly to take apart his tent, concerned that it was being battered by strong winds as a storm blew in. He then ascended rapidly, and finally reached the summit in late afternoon.

He was very weary on the descent, drained by his series of summit bids, and growing concerned about the lateness of the day. While resting at 6,700 metres, exhausted and alone, he stopped to photograph the sunset, and discovered five fingers were blackened by frostbite. Soon the mountain was shrouded by darkness. He realized that if he failed to make it back to camp, he risked dying of exposure: "I was in extreme danger."[13] Shortly after this realization, he "abruptly developed a powerful sensation"[14] of the presence of another person:

> I was sitting there, and then I suddenly felt like there was somebody behind me. The hair went up on the back of my neck, and I jumped up and I turned around to look for this person. And there was nobody there. I thought, gee, that's kind of odd, and I sat down, and then thought, "there's somebody with me" and I got up again and turned around and looked up the slope.[15]

In all, he got up and looked around three times, "but there was nobody to be seen on the windswept slopes."[16] Firth then continued down Aconcagua, but lost his path and was unsure where he was going. All the while, "my invisible companion following behind me, encouraging me to keep on going." The presence was that of a man, but no one Firth knew, and he was friendly, urging Firth on, and dispensing practical advice.[17] Said Firth: "The guy's saying 'just focus on where you're going, just put one foot in front of the other, don't panic, just keep going.' I was walking along and I'm having this mental conversation with this person."[18]

His condition was deteriorating, and he began to develop a sense that his body had changed shape. He looked at his feet and they seemed much farther away, as if he was above himself looking down at them. The presence remained with him, always behind him, over his shoulder: "Like two guys were walking down the path, and one guy was following the other. It felt like he was maybe six feet behind me." Conditions gradually improved as he descended. He found his path and felt warmer and as if he had more energy: "Lower down on the mountain I felt stronger, and my follower disappeared as mysteriously as he had arrived."

EXTERNAL TRIGGERS ARE NOT THE ONLY FACTOR involved in appearances by the Third Man. There is an internal psychological variable at play: Psychologists call this openness to experience, but I call it the muse factor. Openness is an aspect of personality, and one of the five factors of the so-called Big Five theory of personality that appear in psychological literature. The others are: neuroticism (the tendency to experience negative emotions, to be moody, angry, or easily disturbed); extroversion (an inclination to be enthusiastic, talkative, assertive, and the centre of attention); agreeableness (possessing an optimistic view of human nature, being friendly and generous); and conscientiousness (having task-oriented characteristics, such as being dependable and orderly, and seeking success through purposeful planning). Openness to experience distinguishes imaginative, independent individuals from unimaginative conformists, and is based on a person's "willingness to explore, consider, and tolerate new and unfamiliar experiences, ideas, and feelings."[19] Some contempt for bodily comfort and a need for stimuli derived from exploration are parts of everybody's makeup, but these characteristics are most strongly associated with individuals who rate highly on measures of openness.

People with this characteristic typically are full of ideas, quick to understand things, have unconventional values, aesthetic sensitivity, and a need for variety. "Openness is seen in the breadth, depth, and permeability of consciousness, and in the recurrent need to enlarge and examine experience."[20] It is associated with functions of the prefrontal cortex, a part of the brain linked to what is often called "executive system" functions—abstract thinking, the organization of actions and inhibition of inappropriate actions—and personality.

There is another concept that might help to explain why some people have presence encounters and others do not: a state of heightened awareness called "absorption." Two psychologists, Gilbert Atkinson and Auke Tellegen, defined the trait and developed what has come to be known as the Tellegen Absorption Scale, a means of measuring an individual's capacity for absorption, that is, their ability to become involved or immersed in events. Tellegen defined it as "a state of receptivity." Among the components of absorption is a heightened sense of reality, so, for example, an object, "either perceived or imagined, grasped in one's intentional focus is experienced as being present and real."[21] Absorption has been found to be a reliable indicator of hypnotic ability. It may yet prove to have a link to the Third Man. Intriguingly, researchers found that people exposed to the isolation of the brief summer field season in Antarctica developed "significantly increased absorption scores."[22] The study explained this as an adaptation to an isolated environment. Some people are able to develop this capacity more than others.

So people who experience all the necessary situational challenges, but are low in openness, may not interpret the effects as involving the Third Man. On the other hand, people high in openness may have a lower threshold of "sufficient" precipitating environmental conditions for experiencing the Third Man. Similarly, people may become absorbed with an idea that there is an unseen being in close proximity to them during times of great isolation and stress. Those high in openness or absorption possess the muse factor.[23] As Shahar Arzy and his three co-authors argued in *Medical Hypotheses*, for "subjects who are prone to mystical experiences … moderate altitudes are sufficient."[24] Of course, the stress and the suffering experienced by Taylor and Wickwire were no less severe than those encountered by climbers at extreme altitude, just different. Welsch and Firth also felt very real stress, but less extreme than Streather or Messner would have felt. Why can some people access this peculiar instrument of escape, while others must undergo much greater duress to achieve the same result? The muse factor represents the difference between those in EUEs who are left alone to fight for their survival, and those who are able to conjure up help and encouragement.

CHAPTER ELEVEN

The Power of the Saviour

DURING THE SECOND WORLD WAR, A SEAMAN gunner spent twelve hours floating in the North Sea. The explosion that had destroyed his ship had blown off all of his clothing, except his socks, belt, life jacket, and the sleeve of his coat. It was April, and he was "pretty cold." Four other surviving crewmen were in the water nearby. As night descended, he began to fear they would die before any rescue reached them. He suddenly began to experience bioscopic playback. He saw his fiancée, a pet dog from his childhood, scenes from his schooldays. These were all episodes he had experienced, but had long forgotten. He began to scream, terrified that he was dying. The episode ended when one of the other crewmen slapped his face. Not everyone in need of a benevolent companion will experience one. Some survivors in life rafts have disorienting hallucinations that not only fail to aid them, but also endanger their lives, or actually contribute directly to their deaths.

In one instance, a survivor announced that he was a rabid dog, and tried to bite others. In another, "a boy of sixteen protected himself for three days with an axe against the delirious aggression of the only other occupant of a tiny raft."[1] Such cases are very different from reports of the Third Man, a difference sometimes attributable to drinking salt water.

Shipwreck survivors see attractive tropical islands, or ships steaming to their aid. In one instance, after only three days adrift in the North Atlantic, a group of survivors "suffered from the most cruel delusions. Some thought that they were back … in their homes; some stretched out their hands towards green fields and shady plantations; some saw sumptuous repasts spread before them; some had hailed imaginary ships, or cried out that they were close to a magnificent harbour and that the shore was beckoning."[2] In such situations, where people are in a state of delirium, they often drown: "One said he had just made some tea and was going below to get a cup: he dived over the side and was lost. Another thought he saw a row of houses a couple hundred yards away: he, too, went over the side and was not seen again."[3] They swim towards what they believe to be the source of their salvation, unaware that it is a cruel hoax. For survivors at sea, such delirious behaviour is extremely dangerous, the danger compounded by the plausibility of the visions: "Lilliputian hallucinations, elaborate visions of faces and animals, distorted scenes, a sense of alarm, strangeness, or incomprehension, do not occur."[4] Instead, what is before desperate survivors appears to be the source of their rescue and ultimate survival: tables of food, beckoning ships or land—often presented with "great sensory vivid-ness"—making these hallucinations an invitation to extinction.

Clearly not everyone experiences the phenomenon of a benevolent companion; what is striking is that so many do. The experience at sea is not confined to shipwreck survivors—individuals who are lost at sea and for whom the involuntary ordeal is invariably terrifying—but has also been reported by solo sailors or sailors who are involved in long-distance yacht races. In the one case, the persons visited are shocked by the situation they find themselves in; in the other, they are well prepared for a journey they have embarked upon willingly. In these respects they are very different experiences, and yet they are bound by common stresses: monotony, loneliness, sleep deprivation, and exposure. There are also the psychological effects of cumulative mental and physical distress. And here, as with climbers and polar explorers, the human response can be extraordinary. Wrote E.C.B. Lee and Kenneth Lee, the authors of *Survival and Safety at Sea*: "There are many instances where survivors have felt an Unseen Presence, helping and comforting them, even telling them what to do."[5] Unlike the delusions, "the third man does not come to mock or make mischief."[6] There are, consequently, two classes of vision encountered in extremity: the saviour and the destroyer. What follows are examples of the power of the saviour.

IT IS HARD TO IMAGINE A MORE HORRIFYING SAGA than that suffered by Kenneth Cooke, a merchant seaman aboard a freighter, SS *Lulworth Hill*, after it was torpedoed by a German U-boat on March 19, 1943, off the west coast of Africa, to the east of Ascension Island. The ship, bound for Britain from Cape Town with a load of explosives, aircraft engines, rum, and sugar, had been pursued for hours by the enemy, but its end was sudden. Severed by powerful blasts, the *Lulworth Hill* sank in a minute and a half, allowing only fourteen of her crew of fifty-seven to reach life rafts. They were adrift in shark-infested waters, more than twelve hundred kilometres from land. What followed was a saga of unremitting cruelty. From the beginning they were, Cooke wrote, "a sorry-looking lot," their faces blackened by fuel oil and their clothing torn to shreds by the explosions. From their location, they calculated that it would take thirty days before they would be rescued. One by one the survivors, burnt by the unrelenting equatorial sun, starved from only the barest of provisions and, for some, driven by thirst to drink seawater, cast off any hope of survival. They lay side-by-side, their bodies covered with salt-water boils, their tongues swollen, living only for the horizon. Sharks stalked them relentlessly.

On the fifth day, a building chorus of despair reached fever pitch: "We've had it." "We'll never be picked up, nor reach land neither." But it soon trailed off, and by the eighth day, Cooke observed that no one had said anything for forty-eight hours. Later in the second week, the noise level rose again, the situation having deteriorated so badly that there was a constant din on the raft: muttered curses, gibberish, sobbing, and moans of agony. On April 6, after nineteen days on the raft, came the first death. The mate, Basil Scown, had spent a terrible night, raving throughout. He twice tried to get over the side, but was so weak that a single hand could restrain him. At 4 P.M. he seemed to pick up. He opened his eyes and asked for water. Cooke gave him two ounces, holding the cup to his parched lips. The mate looked peaceful and became lucid, telling the others they were "a good lot of men." He then smiled faintly. A few minutes later he seemed to mumble something, and Stewart, the cabin boy, bent his head to the officer's lips to try to make out what he was saying. "Suddenly the kid screamed, and began beating the Mate about the head with his fists." Tears streamed down his face as he sobbed: "He's dead, I tell you." Cooke began to wonder who would be next. "We were all looking at each other quite openly now, measuring our own strength and endurance against the others'." He felt like a participant in a macabre game, but there were no winners unless an "extra day of torment" could be considered a prize. A second death followed on the ninth of April, and a third man died on the eleventh. They had been adrift for twenty-four days.

For Cooke, the death of John Arnold, an apprentice who had passed his eighteenth birthday on the raft, was the hardest to accept. The boy, he wrote, "actually radiated goodness and sweetness." Arnold had a profound faith, and led the survivors in prayer. For some time before Arnold's death, Cooke was haunted by the young man's gaunt face: "I knew that face, I had kept telling myself. I had seen it before." Later on, he realized that John's face had, in his own mind, become one and the same as that of Christ crucified, as painted on the wall of a chapel Cooke had attended as a child. On April 12, the twenty-fifth day, Arnold called faintly to Cooke, a sea-hardened ship's carpenter ten years his senior. "May I pray?" he asked. He then prayed for some time, before opening his eyes and looking at Cooke peacefully:

"I am going to die," he said. "I have been talking to God.
Some of you are going to be saved, and I think you will be
among them. I want you to give a message to my mother and
dad. Will you?"

"Of course, John. Anything. Anything!"

"Tell them I died a good Christian."[7]

Cooke held him and watched, helplessly, as Arnold's life ebbed
away.

More deaths quickly followed so that, Cooke decided, "death
was no longer an event. He was our constant companion on the
raft." They died, he felt, "like flies." Some passed in horrible
convulsions, retching from collapsed bellies, choking to death on
swollen black tongues, screaming obscenities. Others died silently;
their lives slipping away like rainwater running into a culvert. On
April 17, a man named Bott sprang up, crazed and exhibiting
maniacal strength; he grabbed the men on either side of him and
jumped overboard, taking the two men with him. Cooke and
others on the raft tried to get their hands on the two victims. They
succeeded in pulling one man back on board, but before they
could reach the second, "a shark flashed in at him and ripped off
his right leg above the knee." Bott, who was flailing about insanely,
managed to keep the sharks temporarily at bay. No attempt was
made to pull him in. They had no choice: Even if they could have
reached him, they could never have overpowered him. They left
Bott to the sharks. After a few moments of thrashing and
screaming, the water around the raft became calm.

On April 22, a man named Platten died. He was a meticulous
man, chief steward on the *Lulworth Hill*, and, Cooke thought, he

had steeled himself for thirty days adrift. When the thirtieth day passed, he simply gave up. Cooke wrote in his log, which was scratched onto a piece of canvas, "eight more men passed on." The last two survivors, Cooke and an able seaman named Colin Armitage, struggled to push Platten's body into the ocean. When it did finally go overboard, it immediately slid underneath the raft. The corpse remained there for three days, "thumping and banging horribly." Finally it slipped away.

The last two men were sustained on the barest rations, which had been stretched further by each death. But for Cooke there was something else that helped to sustain him. On April 23, day thirty-six, he saw John Arnold, and again heard his words, that he would be saved. On the fortieth day on the raft he wrote, "I saw John Arnold's face again and again today. His presence as much as the water and chocolate and pemmican kept me alive." Death was calling, however. Periods of coma had overtaken their times of awareness. On the forty-second day, Cooke was watching some gulls circling around them and muttered, "If only we had wings." Then Armitage gave a whoop. Cooke thought he was mad, but Armitage said: "Don't you realize these are the first birds we've seen since we've been on the raft?" They thought they must be near land.

On the forty-third day the two survivors struck a suicide bond. They determined to tie themselves together and roll into the sea where sharks would finally end the slow torture. Then Cooke heard a voice: "Some of you are going to be saved." The words were so clear and distinct, he thought at first it was Armitage speaking. But Armitage was looking idly out to sea, and shortly drifted back into unconsciousness. Then Cooke realized who had spoken:

Maybe it can be scientifically explained, and that voice was simply my subconscious mind telling me not to be a fool. I don't know. Perhaps so, perhaps not. All I do know is that at the time I was convinced that it was eighteen-year-old John Turney Arnold who was speaking. What is more, I could feel his invisible presence sitting there comfortingly beside me in that lonely little raft lost so hopelessly in the vast Atlantic. [8]

"He's right," Cooke said to himself. "He's right. They always say the darkest hour's before the dawn."

The intervention forestalled any suicide bid, and that same day the survivors heard two aircraft fly overhead at great altitude. Finally, on May 7, 1943, they were spotted and rescued by the crew of a British warship, HMS *Rapid*. Tragically, Armitage died soon after, leaving Kenneth Cooke the sole survivor of the SS *Lulworth Hill*. After that he lived away from the sea, working as a gamekeeper in Yorkshire. He would sometimes have nightmares that he was back on the raft, and would wake up screaming. He published his account of the horrors he had been through seventeen years after the ordeal ended. He felt he had come to know those men on the raft in a way that few could understand. He had admired their courage and endurance, and he had seen the worst in them and in himself, "the craven fear, the hysterical grasping at life." But Arnold had been the best of them. Wrote Cooke: "I know that John's example and his presence saved and altered my life."[9]

ADRIAN HAYTER, A RUGGED INDIVIDUALIST raised on an extremely isolated island off New Zealand, went to sea in part to escape the padded crib of the welfare state. But he admitted also that his decision to sail his thirty-two-foot yawl *Sheila II* solo from England, by way of the Mediterranean and the Red Sea, east across the Indian Ocean, to his native New Zealand, was more than a "physical adventure." It represented a "search for something greater." It may not have been what Hayter anticipated, but he did encounter something out of ordinary experience as he left the Arabian Sea and entered the Indian Ocean.

Four days out of Al Mukalla, in Yemen, Adrian Hayter entered a monsoon. The continual gale-force conditions meant that for the next three weeks *Sheila*'s decks were always wet from sheets of spray, and the constant soakings caused saltwater boils to develop over much of Hayter's body. Then a splice holding a main lower shroud to the crosstrees on the mast let go. Hayter had to climb the mast, which was swinging wildly, to save it. As he gripped the mast tightly with his legs, the motion tore the skin off his inner thighs, causing the boils to burst. Afterwards "[I] went below to the cabin . . . and I sobbed with the agony of my diseased, bleeding legs. Leaving *Sheila* hove-to, I made no more attempt to sail more that day."

He fell into a deep depression that, Hayter felt, was a sign "that the end of endurance was near." It was early August 1951, but he was not even midway in his voyage. To break the dark mood, he pulled on his oilskins and forced himself back to the helm. By 4 A.M. he was again soaked, aching from his efforts to steer in the gale, and could no longer tolerate the pain of sitting. So he "gave up, beaten." *Sheila* was again hove-to and Hayter went to his bunk and slept. Only two hours later, he was awoken with a start by a stern voice: "Get up. It's your turn at the helm." He recognized the voice. It was the same one he had heard much earlier on the voyage, a voice that had warned him that he was on a collision course with a large steamer. He got up this time, refreshed despite the short sleep,

> and wondering how on earth the man had got on board, I went to relieve him at the helm. There I checked the compass, altered sail, and put her on course. Somehow my friend had passed me on the narrow companion-way and was then in the galley, bending over the primus as if about to get breakfast.[10]

"Where do you keep the eggs?" the man asked. Hayter laughed and replied aloud, "You know bloody well we haven't got any eggs." At the same time, he thought to himself, "This is very strange. No one else *can* be here, but he *is* here. I am awake and feel wonderful. Who is he?" Hayter studied the face of his mysterious guest intently, and was struck by his blue eyes. Deciding there had to be an explanation for the mystery, he went below to confront the man:

> The cabin was empty; feeling foolish but knowing I had seen him I looked in the fo'castle, the only other place on the ship he could have been. It was empty . . . I felt a little sad, but his cheerful vitality remained, I felt strong and confident, glorying in the sea and *Sheila*, as she surged ahead of the wind as joyfully confident as myself.[11]

Hayter failed to record "this strange event" in his log, "perhaps because I felt that to 'publicise' it would be a kind of sacrilege, like breaking a confidence; perhaps because at that time I was afraid of inviting ridicule—not of myself, but of it." But his mood had changed irrevocably, and he rededicated himself to his distant goal.

Hayter was a deeply spiritual man, who believed that when you'd really given your all, and when you were nearly beaten, "something else comes in."[12] He overcame further hazards on his voyage—a cyclone, sailing through a minefield, exposure and starvation—to reach Westport, on the South Island of New Zealand in May 1956.

ON FEBRUARY 23, 1953, TWO DESERTERS from the French Foreign Legion jumped ship while en route to Saigon, where they were to fight the Communist Vietminh. They had tossed a raft and a few basic supplies overboard, including food and wine to last them a couple of days. They were in a busy shipping lane, and expected to be picked up almost immediately. Instead, they found themselves on the raft for weeks, beginning in the Straits of Malacca, but drifting westward, carried ever deeper into the Indian Ocean. At times, violent storms laced them with ice water and vicious gales pummelled the raft. During one tempest, they had to struggle just to remain aboard as the raft was tossed from one wave crest to another. At other times they baked under a relentless equatorial sun.

In time, they were driven to the point of despair by thirst and hunger. The psychological pressure of their desperate circumstances exacted a terrible toll. One of the men, a twenty-three-year-old Swede named Fred Ericsson, began to exhibit strange behaviour: "He had an imaginary box of matches and kept going through the act of striking and holding the non-existent light up to a real cigarette between his lips." At another point, there was a heavy splash and Ericsson disappeared. The other man, a twenty-four-year-old Finn named Ensio Tiira, cried out: "Ericsson,

Ericsson, where are you?" At that moment Ericsson surfaced along-
side the raft. He clambered back aboard and demanded: "Why did
you push me overboard?" Said Tiira: "Push you? Don't be a fool.
I've been sitting on my side of the raft looking for ships. I didn't
touch you." Ericsson was adamant: "Someone pushed me."

The ordeal dragged on from days to weeks. One day Ericsson
cried out suddenly as a shark burst through the canvas floor of the
raft. The men clung to the floats and beat it with their paddles
until it finally sank back into the ocean, leaving a hole wide
enough for a man to fall through. A second shark then tore another
large hole in the hull. A dozen times, one side or the other of the
raft was pushed up at a forty-five-degree angle as sharks struck.
Sometimes the attacks were coordinated and up to three would
strike at once. For hours the onslaught continued, and for hours
the two men fought back. Finally the sharks broke it off, and
resumed their pattern of circling the raft, Tiira and Ericsson
collapsed with exhaustion. Said Tiira: "My eyes ached and my
mouth had no drop of moisture. My temples and heart throbbed.
I couldn't move. I was done."

They endured sixty-hour stretches without water. Then rain
would fall and they would collect enough to gulp ten mouthfuls
each. And then the drought would return. They were dying in
increments. The horror of their situation was compounded by the
passing of several ships that failed to spot their desperate signals.
On one occasion, they awoke at night to see the lights of three
ships, all steaming to the west and none more than five kilometres
from their location. Ericsson grabbed his flashlight and began
flashing in Morse code: SOS, SOS, SOS. One ship, within half a

mile, seemed to signal back. They felt a surge of hope and joy. Ericsson flashed again, SOS, over and over. But there was no further signal from the ship; it did not deviate from its course. They sat in stunned silence, and then slept.

In the first days adrift they had shared stories, and with time their conversation grew morbid. After several more days had passed, they stopped talking altogether; there was nothing left to say, nothing worth the effort. Said Tiira: "We were dying of exposure, heat, thirst, and starvation." They could feel their lives winding down. Even their beards stopped growing. By the sixteenth day their bodies were covered by deep ulcers, caused by the salt water and the unrelenting sun. Ericsson was very weak. At noon on the seventeenth day rain fell, but it was not enough, and two hours later Ericsson began calling out for more. At one point, he asked Tiira to get him to a hospital. Soon the pleas for water ended and he was only groaning softly. It rained briefly the next day, and Tiira collected some using a plastic bag. He called on Ericsson to wake up, but Ericsson had lapsed into unconsciousness, and from there slipped seamlessly into death. Tiira found the resulting loneliness almost unbearable. He kept Ericsson's body on the raft, as he had promised to do, in order to return it to land for burial. The body, lolling against the ropes, also served as company of a sort. But it began to desiccate in the equatorial sun, and then sharks came for it. To save himself, Tiira was forced to roll the corpse into the ocean. A feeding frenzy began within a metre of the raft.

Tiira had been reduced to a living skeleton, his skin covered with sores. He lay dying a slow agonizing death, barely able to move, enduring what he termed "the horror of the raft." And yet, in his account of the ordeal, *Raft of Despair*, he wrote that he was not alone:

> I didn't pray, and I'm not a religious man usually, but for the whole voyage I'd had the strange feeling that someone else was with me, watching over me, and keeping me safe from harm. I sensed it in the storm, when we nearly overturned, and many other times. It was as if there were sometimes three people on the raft, not two. With Ericsson dead I felt it more strongly than ever.[13]

He wondered if the source of this feeling was his mother's prayers, if it was possible that "this strong bond between us came to my mental rescue." Two weeks passed by and Tiira lapsed in and out of unconsciousness, but each time he was about to let go, something would bring him back, a cool night breeze, or a splash of water. Of the thirtieth day, he wrote: "No ships. No rain. No clouds. No hope." On the thirty-first day at sea, he confronted the certainty that he was about to die:

> I'd lost all sense of a second person being in the raft. The guardian angel who kept me company after Ericsson's death left the raft with my own loss of hope.[14]

But help had arrived. A British freighter, the *Alendi Hill*, was steaming 480 kilometres off the island of Ceylon (now Sri Lanka). Tiira's flashlight was dead. There was no way to signal them but to beat his paddle on the side of his raft. It was just after midnight when two officers heard the sound. In the moonlight, they saw a human figure on a small raft. They went to the captain who ordered the ship to search for him. Ensio Tiira had drifted one thousand kilometres across the Indian Ocean from the Straits of Malacca. He had been on the raft for thirty-two days. He weighed twenty-five kilograms (fifty-six pounds). Tiira felt he could not have lived another day.

IN 1954, WILLIAM WILLIS, A VETERAN AMERICAN seaman, set out in a raft from Peru to test his theory that castaways, with minimum equipment, could survive long periods adrift. He embarked from Callao, Peru, and after a voyage across the Pacific Ocean, made land at Pago Pago, in American Samoa. The journey was not without hardship, despite his plans. Willis suffered a mysterious pain that afflicted the solar plexus, the hollow below the breastbone where the ribs meet. The pain became so severe that he hoped he would become unconscious, and then thought seriously about taking a knife and cutting the pain out of his body: "I felt death in the wind that buffeted the cabin." It lasted for thirty hours before the pain gradually began to release its grip.

He was also battered by severe storms, and at one point had to confront the possibility that his raft, which was made of balsa logs, was gradually sinking as the wood became saturated. Then, on August 6, forty-five days out from Callao, Willis discovered that his freshwater supply had been gradually leaking into the sea, because the seals on the containers were faulty. Of the supply he was able to salvage, he calculated he had enough only for one cup of water a day for three months. He was sailing close to the equator in unremitting heat. In addition to these immediate crises, he suffered from sleep deprivation, near exhaustion, and solitude. He felt he had grown to accept being alone, but there remained "moments of suffering, too; a vague uneasiness which comes when one realizes that he lives on the edge of the abyss. Man must talk to someone and hear the sound of human voices." When the loneliness became almost unbearable, he began to sing, and wondered at the strange power of sound.

Willis eventually slipped into a kind of stupor. He all but stopped thinking and he began to function at a very basic level. At times, he felt as if his spirit was "off somewhere, looking down at my body and watching it at its labour." On the forty-sixth day, he lay crumpled beside the wheel. The raft was sailing on its own, or was it? Wrote Willis:

> Into my subconscious came the impression that somebody was busy on deck, handling the raft. I often had this impression. At times it seemed to be Teddy [Willis' wife], or someone from the distant past—my mother or sister. As I began to regain my senses, this impression became more definite and I felt relieved of all responsibility.[15]

He then realized that dark clouds had gathered in the sky, and the seas were rising. He felt as if his "shadowy partners" had left, and that he was "alone in space, severed from the earth." The phenomenon was repeated on the seventy-first day. Willis had dozed off. He awoke with a start, believing that the raft was among rocks, and that he was in mortal peril. Then he regained a sense of calm: "Someone was at the wheel, taking care of the raft." Hours later, the sea had come over and nearly washed him off the raft, and just as it hit, "there had been the shadowy figure of my mother near the wheel again."

On October 15, Willis completed a 115-day solo voyage across the Pacific Ocean.[16]

DOUGAL AND LYN ROBERTSON SOLD THEIR SMALL dairy farm in England, parlayed the proceeds into a fifty-year-old, thirteen-metre schooner named *Lucette*, and, with their young family embarked on what was intended to be an around-the-world voyage. Dougal had spent twelve years at sea before he started farming, and held a foreign-going master mariner's certificate. His wife, Lyn, with whom he had sailed before, was a registered nurse. They wanted to expand their children's horizons, and with their eldest children, Douglas and Anne, approaching the age when they would leave school, and the twins, Neil and Sandy, at eleven, old enough to benefit from such a journey, the time seemed right. Their course took them from Falmouth to Portugal, the Canary Islands, then across to the West Indies. By February 1972, they had completed the Atlantic crossing. In Nassau, Anne opted to leave, but the others, together with twenty-two-year-old Welshman Robin Williams, who joined them in Panama, passed through the Panama Canal and pushed into the Pacific Ocean.

From the Galapagos Islands, they sailed on June 13 for the Marquesas Islands, five thousand kilometres to the west. Two days later, their plans were altered irrevocably by "sledge-hammer blows of incredible force" striking the hull. Someone shouted, "Whales!" The noise of impact was followed by inrushing water. The hull had been breached in two places from the broadsides of killer whales, and Dougal issued the order to abandon ship. In the few moments before the *Lucette* sank, they threw everything they could lay their hands on into a self-inflatable raft. They also launched a fibreglass dinghy, *Ednamair*, but it became totally submerged as they tried to board it, so they swam to the raft, and tied a line to the dinghy. They didn't have much: a bag of onions, a tin of biscuits, some oranges and lemons, and a survival kit containing vitamin-fortified bread, glucose tablets, eight and a half litres of water, eight flares, fish hooks, a knife, a signal mirror, and three paddles. They had neither compass nor nautical charts.

After the shock of what had happened set in, Lyn, who was devout, raised in the Church of England, led them in the Lord's Prayer. She then said quietly to Dougal: "We must get these boys to land." Dougal replied: "Of course, we'll make it." The answer came from his heart, but he later confessed: "My head was telling me a different story." He felt despair, because they had lost most of their possessions in the *Lucette*, and also guilt, because his unorthodox approach to parenthood had led to their current predicament. Dougal estimated there were supplies enough to last the six of them for ten days, although he hoped they would be able to supplement their diet by fishing and capturing sea turtles. Nevertheless, they were 320 kilometres downwind of the Galapagos Islands, and the coast of Central America was more than sixteen hundred kilometres to the northeast, on the other side of the doldrums—a region known both for lack of wind and sudden storms. Dougal calculated that their only chance would be to sail north, into what he hoped would prove to be a shipping lane.

That first night they remained in shock. The raft was raised and then dropped by five-metre swells. Neil and Robin were seasick. They were given pills to try to prevent any further fluid loss. In the morning some of the scarce provisions were carefully divided. Each had a biscuit, piece of onion, and sip of water. They had difficulty keeping the raft inflated, so they worked to re-float the *Ednamair*, and then crowded onto the three-metre dinghy. They used their knives to cut apart the raft, and used the remnants to protect themselves from sun and rain. They had not been in the dinghy many days when hopes soared. Douglas yelled: "Quiet!" Then he said: "Engines." They heard a muted beat of what sounded like a propeller. Dougal sent off a round of flares, but there was no response, and the noise slowly abated. Their hopes diminished and they returned to their immediate concern, which was bare survival. They were able to capture flying fish and had pulled several large sea turtles aboard. They were thirsty enough to drink turtle blood by the glass.

The worst of it came on the twenty-third day. In the early afternoon, they noticed dark clouds banking on the northern horizon, and they knew from experience that they were in for a blow. Soon they could see whitecaps under the clouds, but what they did not know, and could not have anticipated, was the brute force of the storm. They were in an extremely fragile situation, with only about fifteen centimetres of freeboard. They were packed, six of them, into a boat that was designed for three, drifting in the middle of the Pacific Ocean, without secondary means of flotation. If they were swamped, they would die.

Dougal operated a mechanism he had devised that steered the boat using the sail. He needed to be vigilant, because he had to point the bow into the waves and, as darkness fell, he had little notice that a wave was approaching. Lightning did help him to see, but even then, occasionally, they were hit by a rogue wave, broadside on, at ninety degrees to the other waves, and water would slop on board. Three of them, Lyn, Douglas, and Robin, bailed frantically to keep up, a situation made worse by heavy rainfall. They were nearly overwhelmed. In the middle of the night, a squall hit them like a hammer blow. The storm intensified and left them floundering under a constant torrent, more water for a time than the bailers could keep up with. Dougal had to fight to control *Ednamair*. At one point, Douglas shouted: "Sing!" And they did, everything from "Those Were the Days" to "God Save the Queen."

Dougal, who had been at the steering position for eight hours, was suffering from severe cramps, and started moaning, a long, low moan, followed by another moan, followed by another. Lyn, who also was cold and exhausted, endeavoured to help. It was while trying to assess his condition that she saw a Third Man above his left shoulder, as if another being had joined them to help in their struggle for survival. She counted the number of people on the *Ednamair*, and there were seven, so she immediately counted again—because she knew there were only six. Again she counted seven. She drew enormous comfort from this guiding presence. Her faith was certain: She believed it was Jesus Christ, and she understood. His presence meant that, even though they were in great peril, they would prevail. The message was clear: "You will be alright."[17]

After they had battled the squall for twelve hours, it eased to a normal downpour, and the seas calmed. At dawn they were still bailing wearily, but they were past the worst of the storm. Later, they all drifted into fitful sleep. When they awoke they ate some dried turtle meat and biscuit. As they huddled together under a sheet, Lyn told the others she "had counted seven people in *Ednamair* in the night," adding she "had had a vision of a presence rather than a person," who had helped to fight the storm. Dougal greeted her account with skepticism, saying it was "silly," and adding they could not risk their survival on "spooks, ghosts and things," but were responsible for their own survival. Recalled Douglas: "My father denied it. He denied that such a vision could appear, but the rest of us, well, we believed our mother. My mother was absolutely emphatic."[18] The presence had saved Lyn, who by extension was able to help save everyone. Later, Dougal acknowledged: "If this had helped her in the midst of that terrible storm, then it certainly had made a great contribution to our survival. We had been close to death many times in the night and the failure of any one of us to play our part could have meant destruction for us all."[19]

After that low point, the situation began to improve. They were catching enough fresh food, and collecting enough water, that they no longer thought constantly about a rescue. They had adapted to a humble sort of sea life. Dougal noted the change: "Not only were we surviving, we were improving our physical condition." It was not until thirty-eight days after the loss of the *Lucette*, that the ragged group was sighted by a crewman aboard a Japanese fishing vessel, and they were spared.

EVEN BEFORE HIS AROUND-THE-WORLD SOLO VOYAGE in his boat, the 12.8-metre schooner *Galway Blazer II*, which had been custom-built for the arduous forty-five-thousand-kilometre circumnavigation, William "Bill" King was already considered by some to be Britain's greatest living sailor. A sinewy man with patrician looks for whom home is the fifteenth-century Oranmore Castle, near Galway, Ireland, King has the distinction of having been the only British submarine captain to survive all six years of combat in the Second World War. He later added a case-full of sailing trophies to his war decorations. But nothing could prepare King for the terrifying experiences he endured when he embarked on his journey from Plymouth. At one point, his boat was dismasted during a tremendous hurricane. After making the necessary repairs, King again faced a battle for survival, this time an attack by a killer whale that inflicted hull-shattering blows on the *Galway Blazer II*, while she was eight hundred kilometres from land. King prevailed, only to then confront the unremitting terrors of the Drake Passage, a 480-kilometre-wide channel that lies between Cape Horn, at the southern tip of the Americas, and Antarctica.

King had wanted to sail around Cape Horn since he was a boy. Bringing a boat through the passage, he said, "represented a challenge for which I thought myself particularly well fitted." He understood the dangers, that the channel would act "like the spillway of a dam," and approached it from the west with a mixture of exhilaration and dread. He was buoyed by the conditions he had encountered crossing the Pacific, in the two months immediately preceding his February 1973 attempt to navigate the Drake Passage. Winds blew hard for more than eight thousand kilometres, and he was able to reel them off, all the while meditating on the mysteries that surrounded him. As King later put it: "You cannot cover the whole Pacific alone and remain as you were before." But as he drew nearer to South America, he felt the lightheartedness seep out of him. He became acutely aware of the continent's fractured coastline, as yet unseen, and sensed ice in the air. As he approached Cape Horn, King found himself in black seas and thick fog. He felt he could not wait for conditions to improve because the variability of the weather in Antarctic waters was extreme: "As I approached the tip of South America I reckoned the sooner I rounded it the better." Suddenly, a gale roared out of the northwest: "With visibility nil, I became seriously worried about getting sights. One could have no peace of mind with this freezing mist and the sea became extremely rough." He had anticipated huge seas and constant wind change, but the mist was an unexpected test. It was February 4, and the Drake Passage still lay before him.

To help him stay alert, King filled two Thermoses with coffee. He was growing ever more anxious about the "basalt fang of the Horn" which lurked nearby. The black cliffs of the cape reach 424 metres, and mark a graveyard of an untold number of ships, a place where the alabaster corpses of drowned sailors once washed up in heaps on the rocks. Said King: "The hours went by, black and icy and wild. I stared furiously into the grey dawn and literally craved the moment when I could dare turn left." The storm clouds descended on him, until they merged with the spume thrown up by the tempestuous sea. For two days and two nights, King fought on through ceaseless squalls, battling in a curtain of darkness, unsure of where he was. He later said: "I began to be afraid." He started to think in prayers, but his lips were numb with cold, and he could not even mouth the words. Such was the storm that battered him, that he thought of the two oceans as sharing a mutual hatred, and that his small boat was "being buffeted by their fists." During the second night, on February 5, after twenty-four hours without sleep, King began "to stiffen, both mentally and physically. In fact, I began to wonder if I was going to die of cold and exhaustion."

Off the top of a fifteen-metre wave, King managed to take a non-latitude sight of the sun that would enable him to pass safely between two groups of small islands at Cape Horn. He went down below to work out the position, but hesitated, and thought to himself: "I should go up top and have a look-out for land."[20] Then he remembered: "*He* is up there."[21] King later wrote: "Someone was up front keeping a lookout. In this most lonely hour of my life there was no sensation of being alone."[22] King was able to calculate his position, a necessary step, because he was certain that someone else, a companion, was riding out the storm with him:

> … a strange sensation as if someone were in the boat with me. How can I explain it—not a mystical experience, just a calm feeling of assurance that *someone* was there helping and sharing tasks. Looking back, I do not feel that my mind became deranged—I was just quite certain that I was not alone.[23]

So tangible and pervasive was this sense that King began to demonstrate consideration for the needs of his unseen companion, the sort of consideration one would normally reserve for a flesh-and-blood friend. When he thought he could chance it, he crept below deck, half-frozen, but moved quietly, aware that "he"—this other being—might be off watch and asleep:

Who? I saw nothing; I only felt that radiation which comes from a good companion.

This curious mental warmth sustained me, my fatigue lessened and so did that nagging fear that in this total blackness with mast-high waves and roaring wind we might hit an island.

As *Galway Blazer II* emerged from the Drake Passage and steered into the Atlantic, it remained enshrouded by a thick ice fog. The wind only intensified, as if, King felt, each blast screamed angry rebukes at him. Throughout it all, "the sense of an unseen companion stayed with me." King began to refer to "we" rather than "I." He felt the presence shared in the terrors he faced, but also the dawning sense of elation as *Galway Blazer II* entered the Atlantic: "I was very tired by now, but obviously we were around the Horn. Had we not been, we would have hit it." Finally, when the winds eased, King dropped below and slept for twelve hours: "My companion left me and never returned." Later, King described his unusual encounter to Mike Richey, director of the Royal Institute of Navigation. "Oh," Richey replied, "we all know about *that*."[24]

WHEN HE SET OUT ON A SOLO VOYAGE from Nova Scotia to Scotland, Angus MacKinnon was steeled for every eventuality. Yet even an expert mariner can be humbled by the sea, he believed, and as a Presbyterian minister, he recognized there were other, greater forces at play: "There is still the x factor of Providence." MacKinnon sailed in fair weather from the Northern Yacht Club in North Sydney, on June 23, 1995, in a small ocean racer called *Research II*. His first test came quickly. A severe storm left him "nearly broken," he wrote in his narrative of the journey, *Atlantic Challenge*. A second gale followed, however, and he was hit by waves so large they made the boat stagger and drenched him with ice-cold water. He also lost radio contact.

On the night of July 12, twenty days into his journey, the weather moderated to a semi-gale, though the seas remained rough. He was below, in the cramped cabin, when he became aware that he was not alone. He had a sense that his wife, Mary, was with him: "Several times I had to get up and re-orientate myself to realize that she just could not be." Yet the impossible persisted. Three days later, he was again in the cabin lying down, when he became aware that she was there. "It seemed quite natural. We were talking to each other." Then he heard her say distinctly to "go out on deck." He looked for her, but saw no sign of her and lay back down, then she spoke again: "You've got to go at once." Just then the boat jerked violently and *Research II* jibbed right around so that the yacht was sailing in the opposite direction.

The gale continued for days, the boat bobbing like a cork on the ocean. At one point, it was hit by a mighty wave that sent him flying into a heap on the cupboards, as the boat rolled over on her side. None of these terrors was enough to shake his faith that God and *Research II* would see him through. And yet lack of sleep and a pervasive homesickness added to the burden of an already difficult passage. On July 24, his wife again visited him. He was sleeping. He woke up to hear a voice in the cabin, a warning: "I found it very hard to believe that she was not there. There was a powerful sense of her being there in spirit." It happened again the next day. He had the sense of speaking to her in the night, but in the morning he heard himself say, "Mary, you are there aren't you?" Wrote MacKinnon: "There was a silence. But even the absence of her voice did not dispel the sense of her presence."

MacKinnon wrote that he loved the visits, and it made him ponder the question, "What is our presence?" What constitutes a presence when it's possible to chat by telephone across thousands of kilometres, or even to see one another across similar distances? And here the minister found a lesson in faith: "Why should skepticism narrow down our cognition to exclude fields of knowledge that we are simply too uneducated to understand? The fallacy that 'seeing is believing' as a foolproof principle of inductive inquiry is glaringly obvious to an open mind."[25]

GIZMO, A NINE-METRE J BOAT (a brand of recreational sailboat), was built for speed, but not for racing across an ocean. Yet when the sport boat departed from Newport, Rhode Island, on the inaugural Legend Cup race on May 9, 1996, the goal of her crew was not to round some buoys in the harbour and then retire a few hours later to the lounge of the Newport Yacht Club. They embarked on a gruelling, twenty-one-day Atlantic crossing, with the goal of being first to reach the English port of Plymouth. Derek Hatfield, captain of Gizmo, and crewmen Andrew Prossin and Bill Russell sailed out into the Gulf Stream, and rode it north towards Newfoundland. The first two days were uneventful. The temperature was moderated by the warm waters of the Gulf Stream, and they were sailing fast with the current. But in the Cabot Strait, between Newfoundland and Cape Breton Island, *Gizmo* was becalmed for three days, in cold and wet conditions. It was there that the crew began to experience the first real hardship of the journey.

The sailboat was small, and because it was designed for racing, it was hard to find a way to stand up. Indeed, because of the boat's design and the ocean swell, all three men were either in a crouched position, or, more often, crawling on their hands and knees, for most of the twenty-one-days at sea. In Cabot Strait, they also were exposed to constant near-freezing temperatures and dampness. Prossin, a twenty-seven-year-old Cape Bretoner and experienced sailor, found himself shivering almost without respite for the three days, unable to warm up. He became hypothermic, and was unable to keep watch for longer than half an hour at times. It was in these conditions, Prossin said, that "I started having these feelings … I started to count four people instead of three."[23] He noticed it first when it was his turn to cook. He prepared four portions of freeze-dried food instead of three. He also set out an extra mug and spoon. "At first I thought it was a mistake, and then I noticed I was doing it all the time," said Prossin. It was not a mistake. He actually would count out the people on *Gizmo*, and the number totalled four. At other times, when he was at the helm, he would expect to be relieved not by Hatfield or Russell, but by the fourth man.

As the race continued, the conditions only deteriorated. They sailed to the north of the Gulf Stream, intending to ride a series of lows that they hoped would propel them across the Atlantic. It was an unusually harsh spring, and the conditions were often extremely rough. At times the waves reached fifteen metres, dwarfing *Gizmo*'s 11.5-metre mast. The sailboat was repeatedly knocked over, and its transom was open so, when waves washed over, it would fill with water. Yet when Prossin was at the helm by himself, with the other two sealed below because it was so rough, he was never afraid, and never felt alone, even at night in the pitch darkness:

> On the really rough times we'd sometimes have a second person sitting in the cockpit facing aft to warn where the waves were breaking. In this little quick boat your best bet was trying to race away from the breaking waves, because you didn't want them crashing on the boat because it was built pretty lightly. And when there wasn't someone there I still felt like there was someone out there watching the waves. I didn't see anything, but I definitely felt like someone was helping me ... telling me to turn certain ways. And so many times, it was reinforced, because I'd do that, and I'd hear an explosion, and look back in the direction and there'd be 15 feet of foam there, where the breaker was. I felt like there was a pilot there telling me to move.[24]

A day out of Plymouth, with yet another storm bearing down on them and in the lee of the Irish coast, Prossin wanted to lay off, and allow the storm to pass. Hatfield, however, ordered that they sail hard for Plymouth. Prossin became extremely concerned, feeling that they were pushing too hard. "Something caused me to be afraid," he said. After failing to convince Hatfield, Prossin actually spoke aloud to the unseen member of the crew. In the end, *Gizmo* was the only one of the seven boats competing for the

Legend Cup to finish. One had been dismasted in a squall and had to be towed back to Newport. Another suffered major structural damage after purportedly hitting a sleeping whale. And a third, a trimaran, was dismasted in the mid-Atlantic. For Prossin, the fourth crewmen was a near constant on the crossing, an existence equal to his own, so tangible that he felt this Third Man, too, needed to be fed. And yet, he did feel the presence represented something greater than what just another crewman could offer. Said Prossin: "I did see it as a sign of some sort of guiding force, or guardian angel."

WHY IS IT THAT SOME PEOPLE ENCOUNTER a benevolent friend and helper, while others experience destructive fantasies? Why do some meet their saviour, and others the destroyer? There are different theories. Drinking salt water can cause disorienting hallucinations. Another holds that certain people experience a sort of "blinkers effect," and are able to set the worst of their ordeal aside, and focus on their survival. Undoubtedly a critical factor is an individual's ego strength, the saviour "being more common for individuals who believe in their ultimate rescue throughout their ordeal,"[25] while the destroyer placidly dispatches the rest. "There are no grounds for doubting the importance claimed for this sheer determination to endure."[26] This attitude, a faith in one's ultimate survival, seen in so many of the cases in this book, is the power of the saviour.

CHAPTER TWELVE

The Shadow Person

THE JAYNESIAN NOTION, THAT THE THIRD MAN is the product of right-brain intrusions into the left hemisphere, was disputed by Swiss neuroscientist Peter Brugger. In a 1996 study, Brugger and two colleagues analyzed reports of "unilaterally felt presences" among thirty-one brain-injured or disordered subjects (involving conditions like migraine, tumour, schizophrenia, and acute hypoxia), and found no clear association between the phenomenon and right-hemisphere dysfunction. In fact, a large number of the cases he looked at were traced to the left brain. Brugger proposed another explanation for the "illusion of being accompanied by an invisible being," suggesting the experience is a full-body equivalent of the sensation described by amputees.[1]

After the loss of a limb, the brain creates the sensation that the missing appendage is still there. Amputees actually feel it in certain positions. They know where it is in relation to the rest of the body. Sometimes, even pain or other sensations are felt. More than

90 percent of amputees have these experiences. Donald O. Hebb argued the phantom limb is evidence that own-body perception is an hallucination that just happens to usually agree with reality. Brugger argued, in a similar way, that the Third Man was actually a phantom double, or doppelgänger, "an extension of one's own corporal awareness into extracorporeal space."[2] The brain external-izes own-body awareness, and then detects a false sense of another being nearby.

Brugger thought it telling that "exhausted mountaineers frequently overcome hopeless situations by caring for 'the other' who climbs with them"; he mentioned the example of Frank Smythe sharing his Kendal mint cake on Everest. There are many other similar cases. The Polish climber Jerzy Kukuczka had a comparable experience when he was climbing alone on Makalu, the fifth-highest mountain in the world, located twenty-two kilometres east of Everest. Kukuczka dug out a platform in the snow at 8,000 metres, and pitched a tent in the face of a strong wind. Inside, the climber started brewing some tea when he suddenly realized he had company: "Just then I experienced a quite inexplicable feeling that I was not on my own, that I was cooking for two people. I had such a strong feeling that someone else was present that I felt an overpowering need to talk to him."[3] Reinhold Messner, during his historic 1980 ascent of Mount Everest's North face, had a similar experience. He could barely bring himself to eat or drink, and instead sought to preserve his energy, "just to fight against fear and inertia." But then he heard a voice: "'Fai la cucina,' says someone near me, 'get on with the cooking.' I think again of cooking." He had the feeling of being with an invisible companion. "I divide the piece of dried meat which I take out of the rucksack into two equal portions. Only when I turn do I realize that I am alone."[4]

Brugger's theory is that, in such cases, people are actually caring not for the Third Man, but for themselves.[5] In a similar way, when the Third Man seems to be actively assisting someone in need, it is, in fact, a case of someone looking after their own immediate needs, as when American Steve Swenson, during a 1994 climb of Mount Everest, was forced to spend a second night at 8,200 metres. Swenson had decided, because of the increasing dangers posed by altitude, not to sleep: "Sleep would slow down my respiratory rate. I was afraid that I'd wake up in some kind of respiratory distress. I thought I had better just sit there and stay awake and monitor myself." Despite his efforts, he began to doze off. As soon as he did, he was awoken by a person saying: "No, you need to stay awake." He looked over his left shoulder into the face of a kindly Asian woman. She was very gentle, and nurturing, and urged him to have a cup of tea. Swenson saw only her head, but was not startled by her unexpected appearance. He knew why she was there: "Her job was to keep me awake, and I was dozing off and on. When I'd doze off she'd wake me up. She'd be behind me, saying 'have a cup of tea, it's important to stay awake.'"[6] The presence of the Asian woman stayed with him throughout the night. Said Swenson: "Everything, every piece of advice I was getting, was exactly what I needed to do." Another example was reported by the Australian climber Michael Groom, who found himself in great distress while spending the night at high altitude on Kangchenjunga in 1987. "I felt the presence of someone in the

tent next to me. He knelt close by my right side, placed a firm
hand in the middle of my back and lifted me into an upright
position. My breathing now became easier as I rested my dizzy
head between my knees but I still felt the presence of someone
watching over me."[7]

Brugger also noted some people report a synchrony of
movement, that the Third Man can operate in tandem with the
observer, seeming to imitate his every action. On Nanga Parbat,
Reinhold Messner described his "third climber" as keeping a
"regular distance a little to my right and a few steps away from
me." Brugger also noted that while unidentified, the unseen being
is sometimes still familiar, and Messner, in fact, wondered whether
the Third Man was not actually himself, viewed from "a different
plane of existence." Brugger pointed to a case cited by Critchley,
involving an elderly woman with bilateral cortical atrophy, who
experienced an intense feeling that someone was in the room with
her even though she was alone. She felt strongly that she knew the
person, but was at a loss to identify her, although at other times,
"it would dawn on her that this person was none other than
herself." Sandy Wollaston had a similar experience while being
fitted by a bespoke tailor in London: "There in the mirror was the
mystery man Sandy had followed in the jungle, the doppelgänger
who had saved his life."[8]

Brugger related these encounters to full-blown "autoscopic"
hallucinations where people come face-to-face with themselves. An
example involves the French writer Victor Ségalen, who encountered a phantom companion while on a topographical and archae-
ological expedition to the borders of China and Tibet. After

trekking for two months into the western depths of China in 1909, Ségalen, who was travelling with a companion and guides, reached what he termed "the extreme point" of his travels. He was in the Qinling Mountains, a ragged spine that runs east-to-west in the eastern province of Shaanxi. Turning south, the expedition had crossed a pass at an elevation of three thousand mètres through heavy snow, and then followed a narrow path along the edge of the gorge of the Heishui River. On November 17, Ségalen found himself at the foot of the last buttresses of a plateau, at high altitude. It was, he wrote, "harsher than the most ragged peaks of Europe … a landscape quivering with streams and howling winds." He was in a state of exhaustion, having trekked, apparently, "a little farther than I was allowed to," when, quite suddenly, a "desire to weep from distress gave place to an unexpected lucidity." Wrote Ségalen: "Myself and the other met here, at the most remote point of the journey." It was an almost fantastic encounter. Ségalen found himself face-to-face with a colourless, nearly transparent figure, through whom he could see the landscape, "the wreckage of rocks and torrents," beyond.

"The other," Ségalen wrote, was "silently barring the path stretched out in front of me." Despite its transparency, he recognized the figure as a youth, dressed in out-of-fashion European clothing. Ségalen had overcome great hardship to reach this place, but the other seemed untouched by the effects of temperature or altitude. He found himself saying these words: "You don't belong to this landscape. Your waistcoat is out of place, and your shoes and your pale face with no tan. Aren't you cold? You don't look as if you're used to high altitudes …" The figure failed to acknowledge him: "He presented himself obliquely, without looking at me, and perhaps not seeing me. I questioned him without expecting an answer, an answer that would have astonished me more than his silence. And in fact, he did not reply." The figure then seemed to be absorbed into the landscape, but in the moment before its dissolution, Ségalen believed he recognized it. Ségalen, who was thirty, thought the strange figure was himself, a phantom double, but younger, "a naïve memory of youth." He was astonished by what he had seen, and wondered at its occurrence, "in this place, for me the most removed in the world." With it came a message: He decided he had travelled far enough, that his unexpected meeting signalled it was time to withdraw from the brink: "Having come to the end of my path, I would return ... I reoriented myself to the homeward trip."

Ségalen provided an account of his encounter in *Équipée*, a literary work, part documentary and part novel. However, a notation in Ségalen's papers makes clear that this was an experience that was lived.[9] He added that to have repeated the experience would be unbearable, making the "rare phantom, a need, a lifelong companion."[10] Brugger suggested that such overt experiences of a duplication of one's own body are rare, but added that "a number of observations support the notion that the 'stranger beneath' is no one else than one's invisible doppelgänger."[11] He emphasized that in accounts of a sensed presence, "a feeling of familiarity or of close psychological affinity with the 'presence' is frequently mentioned." No matter that the presence is distinct from the self, indeed that people often go out of their way to make clear that the unseen being was a specific distance from their own body, or sometimes assign an identity to it. For Brugger and his colleagues, it is still a case of a neurological mechanism projecting oneself into extracorporeal space; that when a person encounters the Third Man, he is encountering him or herself.

THERE IS ANOTHER CONTEXT IN WHICH THE PRESENCE of an unseen being is often felt: during sleep-paralysis episodes. Scientists distinguish among several stages or levels of sleep. Rapid-eye-movement (REM) sleep, during which dreams occur, is recognized as essential to health. A feature of REM sleep is the immobilization—a kind of natural paralysis—of the sleeper. A different kind of sleep paralysis occurs when the immobilization persists even though the individual is awake, with the result that a person can be fully aware, yet unable to move. Sleep paralysis is a brief event, and researchers have differed on how many people have experienced the phenomenon at least once over the course of their lifetime. Estimates range from 30 to 50 percent of normal individuals. The episodes often are accompanied by the sense of an unseen presence. In some cases, the presence is described as a neutral impression of another person in the room, but without any corroborating evidence provided by the senses. People say, "I've never seen it but there's definitely something there."[12] In other cases, people describe "shadowy presences." And in about half of cases, people report someone, or something, was watching or monitoring them. Some feel the presence is evil, and is threatening them, evoking fear.

In his study of sleep paralysis, researcher J. Allan Cheyne, who works in the psychology department at the University of Waterloo, argues that this fear is experienced as "an unspeakable dread of an unknown power." Cheyne theorizes that during sleep-paralysis episodes people experience an extreme "hyper-vigilant" defensive state: "the sensed presence is the experiential component of a threat detection mechanism that gives rise to interpretive efforts to find, identify, and elaborate sources of threat."[13] The fear is understandable, given that during sleep paralysis, the person is "paralyzed, helpless, and typically supine and in the dark."

In a later study, Cheyne, and co-author Todd A. Girard elaborated on the idea that a "Threat Activated Vigilance System" is set off by such episodes. "Predator detection and risk assessment mechanisms are among the most fundamental evolved strategies of organisms," they wrote. "The function of such mechanisms is, in the presence of uncertain, hidden, or partially obscured threat, to acquire information about potential predators."[14] Cheyne and Girard wrote that humans are "extraordinarily sensitive" to cues for the existence of some external agency, such as a predator or possible human assailant, even at the risk of false positives. As an example, they pointed to the rustling of leaves as something that can be perceived as the presence of a threat: "Any sudden unexpected movement with no obvious external cause will trigger a sense of the presence of an agent."[15]

Psychologist Justin L. Barrett referred to this function of our minds as HADD—the hypersensitive agent detection device. He said that all that is required for HADD to identify something as an agent "is for the object to move itself (or in some other way act) in a way that suggests a goal for its action."[16] It is, Barrett argued, one reason people believe in "gods, ghosts, and goblins." Cheyne does not only link cases of a sensed presence during sleep paralysis to HADD, but also suggested it could apply to those involving "other altered states of consciousness." He noted that "agency detection devices come especially to the fore in emergency situations, in which thresholds are lowered and agency detection bias is increased."

But Tore Nielsen, of the Dream and Nightmare Laboratory at Montreal's Sacré-Coeur Hospital, offered an alternative explanation, namely that "the paralysis attack enables activation of hallucinatory social imagery" in the form of a presence. Nielsen pointed out that the conditions under which presences occur are not particular to sleep paralysis, but vary widely: "They are evoked by recent births and deaths, sensory deprivation conditions, and brain disorders such as epilepsy and tumours. They arise in a variety of extreme environments, such as polar trekking and mountain climbing over 6,000 metres." Furthermore, he argued: "Any experience of the presence of a spiritual entity such as God, an angel or a spiritual guide reflects this capacity."[17] In his list of presence experiences, Nielsen also mentioned imaginary companions, and a fascinating dream-associated behaviour affecting postpartum women called "baby-in-bed," in which the presence of a baby in the bed is strongly felt and, although the infant may be sleeping peacefully in a crib nearby, often results in the mother frantically searching for it in the bedding.

Nielsen's point is that the "felt presence is a variant of normal social imagery," that occurs in many circumstances other than during sleep-paralysis episodes. Social imagery itself is a common, "basic, albeit under-appreciated, dimension of human cognition."

He further noted that in some of these situations, the presence is sometimes "encouraging, comforting, offering hope." In his view, it is the "uncanny nature" of sleep paralysis that evokes fear and trepidation, and "distress if the individual is prone to anxiety disorders." Nielsen suggests that the "occurrence of both fearful and non-fearful felt presences in a multiplicity of situations, other than sleep-paralysis attacks, supports the notion that they are hallucinatory variants of social imagery and that they are not necessarily bound to threat-activated vigilance."[18] As for the presence itself, Nielsen suggests it may "constitute the spatial skeleton of all imagined entities—a type of orientational scaffold."[19]

RESEARCHERS IN LAUSANNE, SWITZERLAND, were treating a patient with epilepsy, probing her brain with electrodes to determine whether her symptoms could be reduced by surgery. When they stimulated the left "temporo-parietal" junction, about 2.5 centimetres above and behind the ear, with a mild electric current, the twenty-two-year-old woman, a student, turned her head to the side. When they did it again, she turned her head again. "Why are you doing this?" she was asked.[20] The woman replied she had experienced "the strange sensation that somebody is nearby when no one is actually present." When the researchers turned off the current, she said the presence had gone away. The electrical stimulation was repeated, and again "produced a feeling of presence in the patient's extra-personal space." With further stimulation, the woman began "describing the 'person' as young and of indeterminate sex, a 'shadow' who did not speak or move, and whose position behind her back was identical to her own."[21] However, she came to conclude it was a man, and said "he is behind me, almost at my body, but I do not feel it."

During the next stimulation, the woman sat and hugged her knees with her arms. "She noted that the 'man' was now also sitting and that he was clasping her in his arms, which she described as an unpleasant feeling."[22] To confirm the relationship between the woman's body position and that of the illusory person's body, the researchers applied the stimulation again when she was lying down, either on her right or left side. In each case she felt the "person" was also lying down, "taking the same position as my position, the same place as my place." When she was lying on her left side, however, she also noticed something else: "somebody touches my right thigh." When asked whom she thought it was, she replied: "probably the same person."[23] The researchers applied further stimulation while the woman was seated and performing a language test, using a card held in her right hand. She again described a presence sitting behind her to her right. She felt the presence was trying to interfere with her task, and said: "He wants to take the card…. He doesn't want me to read."

The researchers, including Shahar Arzy and Olaf Blanke, are part of a group centred at the Presurgical Epilepsy Unit of the Department of Neurology at University Hospital, Geneva, and the Brain-Mind Institute, Lausanne, engaged in groundbreaking investigations into cognitive neuroscience. In a September 2006 paper in the journal *Nature*, they explained how they had been able to artificially induce an "illusory shadow person" during this clinical examination. One of the authors, Blanke, had come across the phenomenon before. Several years earlier, he had studied a sixty-five-year-old nun who was admitted to hospital with complaints about vision and speech problems. The patient soon began describing auditory hallucinations, that she was "hearing a presence." In 2003, Blanke and his colleagues published an account of the unusual case in the journal *Neurocase*. While attending a service in the hospital chapel, the nun suddenly had the feeling that two people were whispering behind her. "She became progressively more annoyed by their continuous whispering. Since their conversation did not end, she finally turned around to tell them to be quiet. However, to her surprise there was no one sitting behind her." When she looked away the whispering resumed, and it continued until she left the chapel.

Similar episodes followed in her hospital room, where she not only heard but felt a presence. "She often had the sudden feeling as if someone were standing behind the chair talking to her." This person was always on the right side. She also described the presence of what she called a "shadow": "Sometimes she experienced a complete human shadow. She described the figure as three-dimensional, not as an image, and grayish-black." She felt that the shadow person was a woman, and had the feeling that it was following her, and that it moved when she moved. Blanke attributed the nun's symptoms to "damage to the parieto-temporal junction." In other words, it involved the same area of the brain as that which produced a presence in the twenty-two-year-old when provoked by electrical stimulation.

This area, where the temporal and parietal lobes of the brain are joined, is involved in our awareness of our physical self, and helps us to distinguish between ourselves and someone else. The parietal lobe integrates and organizes sensory information, such as sight, sound, and body image. Researchers have found a change in parietal activity at the height of meditative experiences, at a point when subjects reported a "greater interconnectedness of things," which supports the view of some that the temporo-parietal junction is also a prime node for religious experience.[24] It has been previously reported that lesions in this area can produce a sense of an unseen presence, and the hyperactivity of the temporo-parietal cortex of schizophrenics can result in their believing their own body is someone else's, hence their common attribution of their own actions to others.

Independent research involving epileptics has resulted in very similar reports. One case involved a young Swedish man, who described it as "a feeling that someone stands behind me, someone with a distinct wish to support and comfort me. This person will follow me anywhere I would like to go."[25] He found the sensation "pleasant." The patient's cerebral blood flow was being monitored and "a distinct local increase in activity of uncertain origin in the left frontoparietal area" was detected.

Further insight came from Paul Firth, the climber who encountered the Third Man in 1996 on Aconcagua. Firth's qualifications placed him in a special position to analyze what had happened to him. He was an instructor in anaesthesia at Massachusetts General Hospital, Boston, and subsequently produced a study of his experience in the journal *High Altitude Medicine and Biology*. Soon after the encounter, Firth realized that "my guardian angel … was no more than a neurological short circuit." His theory was consistent with Blanke's later report:

> An area of the brain that integrates sensory input into a
> cohesive picture is the parietal cortex.... The integration of
> multiple sensations—sight, sound, bodily position sense—
> allows us to maintain a continuous perception of where we
> are in space.... [D]ysfunction in a highly specific region of
> the brain can produce disturbances to our perception of
> bodily position. Disruptions of the oxygen supply to this part
> of the brain, such as during a near-death experience or when
> climbing vigorously at extreme altitude, may cause loss of
> this integration of position sense. Hallucinations of floating,
> or of a phantom presence may arise from this.[26]

In Firth's opinion, "The hallucination of a 'sense of presence'
is an example of a broad range of perceptional dysfunctions of
personal space and self-position."[27]

Blanke and his colleagues gathered six other examples
involving patients with epilepsy or migraine. The odd episodes
included, not only the sense of a presence, but also out-of-body
experiences. Blanke wrote that out-of-body experiences, too, are
related to a failure in the ability of the brain to successfully
integrate sensory information, including a person's location in
space, sense of touch, and visual inputs. As he wrote in the *British
Medical Journal*: "This may lead to the experience of seeing one's
body in a position (that is, on the bed) that does not coincide with
the felt position of one's body (that is, under the ceiling)."[28] Once
again, Blanke found, "these experiences are related to an interfer-
ence with the temporo-parietal junction of the brain."

Blanke and his colleagues were familiar with the phenomenon
of a sensed presence in psychiatric and neurological patients. They
were also aware that healthy people have experienced it. The

twenty-two-year-old woman had an otherwise normal psychiatric history, and was as surprised as the researchers that they could induce a "shadow person," through "a very simple switch in the brain."[29] They decided that the woman's brain projected her own movements onto a phantom figure it had conjured up. "It is quite astonishing—she definitely realized the 'person' was taking the same posture as she did, but she didn't make the connection," said Blanke. At no time did she recognize that the presence was an illusion of herself. "To her it remained a different person, an alien— exactly what you find in schizophrenics."[30] The paper in *Nature* proposed that the electrical stimulation of the temporo-parietal junction interfered with the integration of sensory information leading to "an own-body illusion of another person." What is more, Blanke speculates that a similar or related process may account for experiences described "in mountaineers, outcasts."[31]

It's one thing, however, to use neuro-stimulation on a part of the brain to induce the Third Man in a clinical setting. But how does this happen to people in extreme environments? There are no electrodes in the brains of people on mountainsides, hauling sledges over ice, or adrift on the ocean. In a British study published in 2002 in *The Lancet*, Dennis Chan and Martin N. Rossor speculated on the origin of the Third Man in such cases: "The hallucinations might indicate the brain's attempt to create the perception of a person from partial sensory stimuli during states of increased arousal (fear, paranoia). The combination of a heightened state of environmental awareness and physical privation might go some way to explaining the prevalence of extracampine hallucinations in … shipwreck survivors and mountaineers."[32] The brain may be attempting to form a complete human form from "incomplete sensory data." It is, then, attempting to create a companion.

What would provoke the brain to do this? That is where other factors come in, such as the pathology of boredom and the principle of multiple triggers. And why would the experience be of constructive emotional significance? Here the widow effect, the muse factor, and the power of the saviour offer some clues. This mechanism is not a fluke of human brain structure, and it seems an unlikely by-product of decaying brain function. Rather, it can be interpreted differently: It is there to do precisely what it does for people in need. It is possibly even an evolutionary adaptation. Imagine the advantage for primitive man, perhaps separated during a hunt, alone far from his tribal group, to have the guiding hand of a companion pointing the way home.

CHAPTER THIRTEEN

The Angel Switch

EACH OF THE EXPLORERS AND SURVIVORS in this book had, as Sir Ernest Shackleton put it, "pierced the veneer of outside things." They were engaged in an endeavour that pushed them to the bare limits, and they reached the point of sufficient extremity to have experienced an additional unaccountable companion on their journeys.

The Third Man has been called many things: a sensory illusion or hallucination caused by extreme physical exertion or monotony; a medical condition attributable to low blood glucose, high-altitude cerebral edema, or cold stress; a ghostly apparition or mediumistic experience; a manifestation of a guardian angel, or a psychological "compensatory figure" that embodies "inner resources that the beleaguered person is not able to call on in the ordinary way."[1] One explorer even confided to me privately that he had wondered at times whether there is "just one Third Man, a single entity," who has through time intervened to help those most in need. "Have you ever found," he asked, "that this being has been in two places at one time?" I had to answer that I have not, and he nodded knowingly.

As the climber Greg Child said, solving the mystery of the Third Man is like a "detective stalking the invisible man; there is no fingerprint, no solid evidence at all. The clues lie deep within us."[2] Increasingly, that is where the evidence leads: within us, to a mechanism of the brain, activated in those who cross the line of physical or psychological tolerance. The most recent scientific research is compelling. By electrical stimulation of the left temporo-parietal junction, a part of the brain involved in organizing sensory information, Olaf Blanke and his colleagues at École Polytechnique Fédérale de Lausanne were able to evoke in the laboratory a presence in a twenty-two-year-old woman who suffered from epilepsy. Each time they stimulated this area of the brain, the woman vividly felt the presence return. When they stopped, the shadow person abruptly departed. In the context of Blanke's research, this mechanism has been called a "switch."

For most people going about the business of everyday life, the capacity to access this power lies hidden and dormant. The switch remains off. But for some of those who reach the limits of endurance, either through some traumatic event or while doing the seemingly impossible, the switch is turned on, and it is suddenly and tantalizingly before them: a startling awareness of being in the presence of some ineffable good.

Stephen Venables, a celebrated British climber, had the experience in 1988 when he was a member of a four-man team that discovered a new route up Everest's biggest wall, the Kangshung face. In the final stage, Venables was breaking trail. As he struggled towards the summit, he was essentially alone, with the others lagging some way behind. It was then that he became acutely aware of a presence with him. Venables felt that it was an older person: "I never identified him, but this alter ego was to accompany me on and off for the rest of that day, sometimes comforting me and advising me, sometimes seeking my support."[3] On the descent, Venables, gasping with exhaustion and struggling in severely limited visibility, fought his way towards the South Col. He was rejoined by "my invisible companion, the old man ... together we moved forward, determined not to die." It was nearly dark, and after confusion about the correct route, "the old man suggested that we should stop here for the night and wait for daylight to reorient ourselves." He later explained the experience this way: "He seems to have been acting as a kind of guardian angel—a wiser self prompting caution and, perhaps, stimulating instinctive self-preservation."[4]

In the summer of 1986, disaster struck a group of skilled Himalayan veterans on K2, among them the Austrian climber Kurt Diemberger. A blizzard closed in on the climbers early in the descent, while they were still at great altitude. They believed the storm would blow over, but it remained at hurricane force for five days, without let-up. They grew weaker and weaker. It became a protracted battle for survival as food and water supplies ran out. The ferocity of the weather meant that Diemberger, and the other climbers, became helpless observers of a cruel drama that ultimately claimed the lives of five of the seven. Diemberger was one of the two who eventually reached base camp. He later revealed that the whole time he had "the sensation that there is an invisible presence watching over me, a force around and within me, a guardian being…. It has been with me for the last few days, up there in the tent …"[5]

The Third Man may behave like a guardian angel; it may be described by climbers as a "kind of guardian angel"; but when asked whether it is in fact an angel, most who have experienced it say not. Reinhold Messner was emphatic on the point: "No, no, no. I think it is quite natural, and I think all human beings would have the same feelings or similar feelings, if they would expose themselves to such precarious situations. The body is inventing ways to let the person survive."[6] Peter Hillary had a similar reaction. He felt the experience was produced by the brain as a coping mechanism: "It didn't surprise me or frighten me. I didn't think 'where did you come from?' because I believe it's a projection of what was happening inside my mind. I think it was probably all in my mind."[7] As Greg Child said, "It was not a fearful sensation, not a sense one might expect to have if confronting something supernatural. I felt its origins are within the self, not without."[8]

There is, then, "a benevolent being assigned to each of us on a permanent basis, who sometimes works in the background like a discreet family servant, but who sometimes emerges in response to specific needs, whether momentary—as in a physical emergency—or continuous, as in the case of childhood companions."[9] Except that this benevolent being exists not outside of us, but within. It is a real power for survival, a secret and astonishing capacity of mind, part of our social hardware. I call it the angel switch.

ONE STRIKING ASPECT OF SUCH STATES is that they are sometimes shared. States of mind, it seems, are contagious. Whether via subtle personal cues or some other mechanism, it has been shown that strong shared beliefs can provoke actual changes in the body, such as rashes or allergic reactions. This is especially true with respect to states of the mind, such as the "psychic epidemic" of the Middle Ages known as the St. John's dance.

The dance involved wild leaping, mad gesticulations, and screaming, giving its practitioners all the appearance of insanity. The spectacle attracted large gatherings, and, strangely, many people who began by watching soon joined in the dancing mania. In one case, a single St. Vitus' dancer, dancing day and night over the course of a month, infected four hundred people with his confused and bizarre behaviour. Medical causes may explain the actions of some of the dancers, but the epidemic appears to have been fuelled by mass hysteria. As with the shared encounters with the Third Man, the St. Vitus' dancers appeared in Europe at a time of "particular stress and travail," in this case, "when men were awed and terrified by the ravages of the Black Death, and disturbed by the instability of society."[10]

There is a possibility that a beneficent state of mind is also contagious. Sir Ernest Shackleton, Frank Worsley, and Tom Crean, all experienced the presence on South Georgia. Harry Stoker and his two companions did the same in Turkey. In his book *Beyond Risk: Conversations with Climbers*, Nicholas O'Connell reported a similar case involving Polish climber Voytek Kurtyka, and his climbing partner, Robert Schauer, during their brush with death on Gasherbrum IV in 1985. They spent two nights unable to move because of severe weather conditions. As Kurtyka told O'Connell:

> What was possibly the most amazing thing about this is that both I and Robert Schauer had [it] at the same time. It was so striking, so tangible, this sense of a third person, that at one moment I tried to talk about it with Robert, and the moment I started, I could not express myself, I just said something like "Robert, I would like to tell you something, but it's very strange."
>
> "I know what you mean," he said. "You sense him, the third person."
>
> "Yes. Do you?"
>
> "Yes."[11]

Finally, a well-known American mountaineer with wide experience, Lou Whittaker, and his wife, Ingrid, shared what he called a "metaphysical experience" on Kangchenjunga in 1989. Ingrid was trekking in the area, but spent three days in her husband's tent at base camp during his climb, suffering from a severe altitude headache. During her illness, "a two-dimensional Nepalese woman appeared in the tent. The woman manifested as a dark shadow." She was a helpful, nurturing presence. "She placed her hand on Ingrid's forehead in a soothing way, and she stayed with her in the tent for the entire three days." Although she thought she was hallucinating, "Ingrid felt very comforted by her." Several months later, when they were both home in the United States, she told Lou what had happened. He had had the same experience in the tent: "I'd climb into the tent at night and have the sensation that somebody was there…. It hadn't been an intimidating feeling at all. It had been comforting."[12]

So are beneficent states of mind also contagious? That is one possibility, certainly, but there is another: Did they, as Shackleton's party felt they had, simply share some sort of "metaphysical experience"? Is it possible they reached, independently, a state of extremity that caused a simultaneous psychological or neurological response in the form of the Third Man?

THERE WAS A MOMENT IN EACH OF THESE JOURNEYS when all appeared lost. In such circumstances, how many people would have given up hope? Heroic expiration in the face of such extreme obstacles is no indignity. Yet, for most normal people confronted with abnormal conditions, the will to live is a powerful source of strength, as is that "indefinable, but all-important factor— morale."[13] If we have learned anything from the survival stories in this book—from James Sevigny's shamble down the Valley of the Four Peaks after being swept six hundred metres down a mountain face by an avalanche that killed his friend and left him with terrible injuries; or from Tony Streather's climb out of the snow basin on Haramosh; or from Ensio Tiira's thirty-two days adrift in the Indian Ocean, while wasting away to just twenty-five kilograms— it is that human beings, in general, are tougher and more resilient than we tend to think.

Consider the widely reported ordeal endured by a slender and fit twenty-seven-year-old, Aron Ralston, in April 2003. Ralston's arm was pinned by a 360-kilogram boulder when he was rock climbing solo in Utah's Bluejohn Canyon. Very suddenly he faced the ultimate test of survival. He tried throwing the weight of his body against the boulder but it did not move. He improvised a hoist using rope and pulleys from his climbing gear. He also tried chipping away at the rock using a pocket knife. Nothing worked. It was April 26. Three days later, his food and water nearly exhausted, Ralston concluded his only hope of survival would be to cut off his arm. He prepared a "surgical table." He set out a knife and first-aid kit, and tied a tourniquet around his bicep. The knife was so dull, he could not break the skin, and he realized that it would be impossible to cut through the bone. He nevertheless worked at the grim procedure determinedly over the next few days, puncturing the skin and muscle of his forearm, and finally using his body weight to first break the radius, and then the ulna, the larger of the bones of the forearm. Ralston wrapped his stump in a plastic bag, and rappelled down an eighteen-metre rock face using one arm. He drank from a puddle, and then walked for ten kilometres before he encountered two hikers, who helped him. Ralston later told reporters he had become aware of "presences" with him in the canyon: "I believe that there was a greater presence there than just me in that canyon. I felt the presence of several of my friends and family. I didn't sleep the whole time, so it was almost like waking visions."[14]

It can happen just as readily after a natural disaster, or in a time of war. Take the case of Airey Neave, a British prisoner of war who encountered an unseen presence after his daring 1942 escape from the Third Reich's most secure military prison, the notorious Colditz Castle. After days on the run, Neave, together with a Dutch escapee, crossed snow-covered fields near the border with neutral Switzerland. Suddenly, he "felt a figure beside" him. Neave "turned to see my old Colonel marching in the snow in his uniform and field boots. I spoke to him and addressed him respectfully."[15] His Dutch companion was startled, and said: "What the hell?" prompting Neave to end the conversation. A short time later they made a dash across no man's land to freedom.

Then there's the experience of Israeli soldier Avi Ohry. On October 6, 1973, the Egyptian army launched a massive attack on a line of fortifications Israel had constructed along the Suez Canal after occupying the Sinai. The attack marked the start of the Yom Kippur War. At the Israeli outpost at El Firdan, only a handful of soldiers survived the initial onslaught, and subsequent summary executions conducted by Egyptian soldiers. One of the survivors was Ohry, a twenty-five-year-old medical officer.

What followed was a virtual death. He was subjected to long periods of sleeplessness. He endured beatings, and mock executions. He was forced to stand, or to sit bound, for lengthy periods of time. Two weeks into his "battle to survive," Ohry sat blindfolded, his arms tied behind his back, in a small cell, when he became aware of a vivid presence. It was his wife, who was in Geneva at the time. He spoke with her. A short time later he had a similar visit, and the presence this time was a close friend from medical school. In each case, "I urged them to save and evacuate me from that miserable situation."[16] The presences were comforting, but suddenly disappeared when the interrogators' steps were heard: "I could not understand how they managed to enter safely the jail and how they succeeded in leaving." The visits "encouraged me. I had the impression that I would be released soon."[17] Ohry was eventually repatriated to Israel.

Nicholas Tu was among the hundreds of thousands of refugees, known as the boat people, who fled Vietnam in an exodus driven by economic desperation and a desire to escape communist repression. In March 1987, Tu left in a small boat with ten others. A terrible ordeal followed. Thai pirates ransacked the boat and raped the women. The boat was later hit by a fierce storm. In his book *The Purple Storm (One of the Bastards)*, Tu described being helped by the presence of a dead brother, "right there in the deep dark purple water around me.... It seemed to me that he was next to me, listening to my crying, comforting me at the toughest moment of my life."

More recently, in Somalia, a survey of former combatants, war widows and children for the United Nations Development Programme, found the "sensed presence" was among the coping strategies used to survive the horrors of that war.[18]

EVEN IN THE MIDST OF DISASTERS, an overwhelming majority of people adapt and cope, help themselves and each other. In situations where panic might be expected, it is often not found. Peter Suedfeld has characterized *Homo sapiens* as "the Indomitable Species." Wrote Suedfeld: "the fact is that most survivors have demonstrated surprising ability to endure, recover from, overcome, and even be strengthened by, events that to outside observers seem overwhelmingly destructive."[19] He concluded that while an inordinate amount of attention is paid to those whose problems overwhelm them, there is a tendency to "downplay or ignore the strengths of survivors." Great emphasis is usually placed on post-traumatic stress, loss, and grief—much less so on the capacity for coping. The typical reaction to disaster is not defeatist, but a determined struggle to survive, even in the face of the most overwhelming adversity. In some ways, people return stronger, Suedfeld said. "In general, it is true—people who come back from space or from polar research stations have a better sense of values, a better sense of purpose, a better sense of what's important, a better balance in their lives. Most survivors of even extreme trauma, such as the Holocaust and other genocides, construct new, contented, and well-adjusted lives, even if they continue to experience occasional symptoms of stress." No more eloquent testament to this resilience can be found than the Third Man. When the usual methods—resourcefulness, courage, and endurance—are exhausted, a mysterious power can still be called upon.

But does the angel switch, when thrown, guarantee a person's survival? No, it does not, as Maurice Wilson, an Englishman who attempted Everest in 1934, demonstrated. Wilson had no climbing experience, and his struggle was one of undeniable courage, but it had the pall of tragic inevitability about it. Wilson was rebuffed on his first attempt at Everest by severe weather. On May 12, 1934, accompanied by two Sherpa porters, he set out to try again. This time he reached the 1933 British expedition's Camp Four, and hunkered down for days through hellish winds, snow, and cold. When the weather improved, he announced his intention to continue, but his porters refused to accompany him. The situation was already perilous. They had concluded that to proceed would be to invite certain death. Their will to live had kicked in. On May 27, as he fumbled into his sleeping bag, partially snow-blind, and suffering from exhaustion, Wilson was overwhelmed by the sensation that he was not alone in his tent, that someone was at his side. "Strange," he wrote in his diary, "but I feel that there is somebody with me in tent all the time."[20]

He should have quit then. It was a desperate situation, but Wilson was determined to make it worse. The following day he embarked on one last try. He told his two Sherpa porters: "Wait for ten days. Then if I don't come back, return by yourselves." Wilson began his ascent slowly and deliberately. His last diary entry was May 31: "Off again. Gorgeous day." From that point his diary fell silent. Wilson did not make it very far, and the extremity of his suffering in his final hours can only be deduced. His body, and diary, were found in 1935, a year after his death, at 6,700 metres, by Eric Shipton and Charles Warren, members of another British Everest expedition. They sat and read the "pathetic document," then wrapped Wilson's body in a tent and placed it in a crevasse. It is unknown if his invisible companion stayed with him during his final hours. Wilson's sad story emphasizes something important: There is no saving the life of one who will not be saved. The Third Man requires a willing partner.

The key to overcoming seemingly insurmountable obstacles in order to survive begins, then, with a simple belief—call it a faith— that an individual will somehow triumph over his or her immediate appalling situation; that he or she is going to live. That is the premise with which most people begin their ordeal. It is when that faith is severely tested, and failure—even death—seems inevitable, that the Third Man appears. What changes? What turns the growing certainty of defeat into the miracle of survival? It begins with belief, a belief that a companion stands with them. Think of how amazing this is! Our brains have a kind of a placebo social sense, a humanity trigger. This is a new function of the brain, no doubt selected by evolution because it is so useful (our ancestors were no doubt much-stressed, and faced many more life-or-death situations than we do). It's the ultimate and quite beautiful example of how we are social animals—that in our time of deepest solitude and need, our brain or mind finds a way to reassure us that we are not alone, and that fellow-humanity feeling is what ultimately makes the difference between life and death.

PETER SUEDFELD PREDICTS THAT INTERACTIONS with the Third Man will only intensify in the years ahead with the "increasing exploration and exploitation of hitherto inaccessible sites," under the sea, at the poles, as well as a result of the growing popularity of extreme sports. But it is in space that the Third Man has the greatest potential to be of assistance. More than anything the Earth has to offer, space travel beyond the Moon represents the potential for great stress, real danger, absolute isolation, and also crushing monotony.

A human expedition to Mars would not compare to any other endeavour human beings have attempted. At the closest point, the distance between Earth and Mars is 55 million kilometres. A mission to Mars would result in unprecedented periods of confinement. The astronauts would be away for up to three years. They would be isolated, not only away from family and friends, but even communication with mission control would take up to forty-four minutes. And they would live with the knowledge that if anything went wrong, there would be no chance of rescue. While there would be episodes of intense activity on board the spacecraft, most of the flight would involve monotonous routines. Any free time likely would be frittered away on make-work projects designed to fill the void. Here human beings would experience the full pathology of boredom. There are also the unknowns. While the experience of seeing Earth from space is thought to have resulted in the increase in references to spirituality by many astronauts,[21] the psychological or religious impact of "the Earth-out-of-view phenomenon, which has never been experienced before," is unknown.[22] All of these factors could have profound effects on astronauts. It is not hard to imagine that joining the crew on the Mars mission will be other, unseen, beings.

The Third Man is multiplying, and as exploration shifts to the solar system, and people push the limits of endurance ever farther, there is every reason to believe that more and more humans will experience the phenomenon. As the apparition of a missing astronaut, a non-corporeal David Bowman, says in Arthur C. Clarke's film *2010: Odyssey Two*, something is happening: "Something wonderful."

IN THE FIRST CHAPTER, I WROTE OF MY OWN strange childhood experience when confronted by a rattlesnake. I noted that Wilfrid Noyce, in his book *They Survived: A Study of the Will to Live*, became intrigued with the phenomenon when, struggling over the Geneva Spur of Everest without oxygen, he had first-hand experience with what he judged to be a rudimentary manifestation of the Third Man, a simpler "sense of duality," encountered at very high elevation. The British mountaineer Doug Scott had a similar experience on Mount Everest: "a curious out-of-body sensation where part of my mind separated from my tired self and gave me protective advice."[23] These examples seem to fit the theory that the presence is the product of own body duplication.

But intriguingly, very few people see the Third Man as another them. Instead for most it is someone else, a friend and helper. This is Noyce on the subject:

> When we are alone or in difficulty it can appear as a person-ification, though dim, of what we need in order to escape our isolation or helplessness. Because of human association and past experience stored in subconscious memory, it takes the form of another person. I believe that it may indeed be another person, summoned from the deep in which, unknown to conscious mind, we are joined with those others who provided that association and that experience.[24]

To Noyce, this suggested the possibility that "the teeming cells of which we are composed sent an SOS into the farthest interior and beyond." He felt it pointed to the existence of a little-under-stood capacity to reach out beyond oneself to a collective uncon-scious: "The survival situation struck a spark which in many lay unsuspected or dormant. This spark seems to me to have some essential connection with other people."

What if that capacity exists in every one of us? What if there is a brain mechanism that allows us, when we are most alone, to suddenly be in the company of another? It may not literally be another person summoned from the collective unconscious, but it is no less startling and revelatory: We have the capacity to conjure up a companion when one is most needed. It is a stirring thought. We evolved yoked into a network of people. Even our dreams are full of them. We are hardwired for people!

This raises another fascinating question. Can the Third Man, the guiding companion called upon by polar explorers, mountaineers and other adventurers, and those in the throes of a disaster, be summoned to help people facing crises of a more mundane nature? Imagine the impact on our lives if we could learn to access this feeling at will. There could be no loneliness with so constant a companion. There could be no stress in life that we would ever again have to confront alone. How far-fetched is this idea? Lonely children or kids under stress summon company in the form of an imaginary friend. So do some people who lose their spouses. Cultures considered more primitive than contemporary Western culture have been doing the same thing for thousands of years. So have religious mystics. Consider the implications of this: When lonely or somehow compromised, we could—as neuro-feedback suggests—learn to provoke the area of the brain that produces the Third Man, and thus give ourselves that extra survival boost.

But is it only the brain that is involved? The Third Man impresses those who experience the phenomenon with the vivid belief that they have come into contact with an unseen being of compassion and beauty, and, for some, a greater power. Paul Firth, the physician and climber who was joined by a Third Man on Aconcagua, argues that even if we accept prevailing neurological explanations for the Third Man, a mystery endures:

> A biological explanation does not preclude a benign metaphysical origin—an explanation of "how" does not answer the question of "why." Whatever the physiological details of these experiences ... who can say why these helpful ghosts wander in the penumbral world of the edges of our perception?[25]

Yes, an angel switch exists in the brain—but the fact that it is a brain response to extreme and unusual environments doesn't take away from the experience itself, which is still a potent force for survival. Richard Dawkins and other atheists seem to be arguing that religious or mystical impulses are somehow worthy of contempt—yet here is something with every appearance of being a religious or mystical experience that can save your life.

The Third Man represents something extraordinary. His appearance has always signalled a moment of transcendence over an explorer's, adventurer's, or survivor's immediate, dire situation. The Third Man is an instrument of hope, a hope achieved by a recognition that is fundamental to human nature: the belief—the understanding—that we are not alone.

The Church Army Gazette

WITH WHICH IS INCORPORATED *THE CHURCH EVANGELIST.*

No. 1,846. (NEW SERIES.)   WEEK ENDING FEBRUARY 7, 1920.   [ONE HALFPENNY.

THREE MEN—

OR FOUR?

SIR ERNEST SHACKLETON
the great Antarctic Explorer says,

"I KNOW

that during that long and racking march over the unnamed mountains and glaciers of S. Georgia

IT SEEMED TO ME OFTEN THAT WE WERE

FOUR—NOT THREE.

I said nothing to my Companions, but afterwards Worsley said to me:

'BOSS, I HAD A CURIOUS FEELING ON THE MARCH THAT THERE WAS ANOTHER PERSON WITH US.'"

"Three were they—who hath made them four?   And sure a form divine He wore,
Even like the Son of God."

This has been the experience in all ages of the men who trusted God, for

"IN ALL THEIR AFFLICTION HE WAS AFFLICTED, and THE ANGEL of HIS PRESENCE SAVED THEM;

IN HIS LOVE and IN HIS PITY HE REDEEMED THEM."   Is this your experience too?

ACKNOWLEDGMENTS

I would like to thank the following explorers and survivors who shared their remarkable stories with me and allowed me to quote from their published and unpublished accounts: Ron DiFrancesco, Jerry Linenger, Peter Hillary, Doug Scott, Rob Taylor, Jim Wickwire, Commander William King, Tony Streather, Reinhold Messner, Jim Sevigny, Ann Bancroft, Stephanie Schwabe, Sir Ranulph Fiennes, Robert Swan, Greg Child, Avi Ohry, Douglas Robertson, Dr. Paul G. Firth, Capt. Brian Shoemaker, Andrew Prossin, Steve Swenson, Walter Welsch, Alan Parker, and the late Dr. Parash Moni Das. I am also grateful to the late Nicholas Wollaston, son of Sandy, Rebecca Hayter, daughter of Adrian, and to Ralph Barker.

Peter Suedfeld is a leading authority on the subject of the sensed presence in extreme environments and was an enormous help and inspiration. I feel honoured to have collaborated with Peter on an essay on the subject. Thanks also to Jane S.P. Mocellin, Peter Brugger, Allan Cheyne, Tore Nielsen, Olaf Blanke, and Michael Persinger.

Thanks to Heather Wilson, Toronto Reference Library; Gerstein Science Library, University of Toronto; Massey College; Robarts Humanities Library, University of Toronto; State Library of New South Wales; Alexander Turnbull Library, National Library of New Zealand; British Library; Paul D. Fleck Library and Archives, The Banff Centre; National Library of Canada; T. Butcher, National Post Library; Library, National Hospital, Queen Square, London; Anne Morton, Hudson's Bay Company Archives, Provincial Archives of Manitoba.

This book would not have been possible without the encouragement and insight of many people, including my agent Patrick Walsh of Conville and Walsh, and Andrea Magyar at Penguin Books Canada. Thanks also to Dianna Symonds, Karen Cossar, Susan Folkins, Sam Hiyate, Jonathan Webb, and Carl Honoré. Jeff Warren read the manuscript and provided sound advice, as did Kate Fillion and Sean Fine. Gerald Owen gave a lesson in angelology. Leila Hadley Luce gave a lesson in courage.

I would like to thank those other friends and individuals who have accompanied me on this journey, provided assistance or advice: John R. Smythies, Vincent Lam, Margaret Atwood, Gavin Fitch, Andrew Duffy, Dr. Rhodri Hayward, Master John Fraser of Massey College, Anna Luengo, Prof. Abraham Rotstein, Dr. Denis St-Onge, Veikko Kammonen, Robert Burton, Colin Haskin, Fr. David Harris, Nicolas Jiménez, and Tony Hendrie. Also Peregrine Adventures, now Quark Expeditions.

I am grateful to Edward Greenspon, editor-in-chief of *The Globe and Mail*, for seeing "idiosyncratic pools of knowledge" as a good thing.

Finally, I want to thank Shirley and Eddie Keen, Dr. K.W. and Jean Geiger, Becky Geiger, and especially my sons, Alvaro and Sebastian, and Marina Jiménez, who travelled this long journey with me and shared in the miracles, wonder, and loss.

COPYRIGHT ACKNOWLEDGMENTS

My Father, Sandy by Nicholas Wollaston. Used by permission of Short Books.

Karluk by William Laird McKinlay. Reprinted by permission of Weidenfeld & Nicolson, an imprint of The Orion Publishing Group.

What Cares the Sea? by Kenneth Cooke, published by Hutchinson. Reprinted by permission of The Random House Group Ltd.

Atlantic Challenge by Angus MacKinnon, published by Catalone Press. Reprinted courtesy of Mary MacKinnon.

Illustration © British Library Trustees. All rights reserved. *The Church Army Gazette*, February 7, 1920.

Sheila In The Wind by Adrian Hayter (London: The Companion Book Club, 1959).

ENDNOTES

Chapter One

1. Brian Clark, "Above the Impact: A Survivor's Story," *Nova Online*, http://www.pbs.org/wgbh/nova/wtc/above.html.
2. Andrew Duffy, "Last One Out Alive: A 9/11 Survivor's Tale," *National Post*, June 4, 2005.
3. Ibid.
4. Dennis Cauchon and Martha T. Moore, "Machinery Saved People in WTC," *USA Today*, May 17, 2002.
5. Andrew Duffy, "Last One Out Alive."
6. Brian Clark, "Above the Impact."
7. Ibid.
8. Andrew Duffy, "Someone Told Me to Get Up," *National Post*, June 6, 2005.
9. Ron DiFrancesco, interview with John Geiger, August 23, 2005.
10. Ibid.
11. http://www.freerepublic.com/focus/news/689589/posts.
12. Ron DiFrancesco, interview with John Geiger, August, 23, 2005.
13. Ibid.
14. Andrew Duffy, "Someone Told Me to Get Up."

15. See also Dennis Cauchon, "Four Survived by Ignoring Words of Advice," *USA Today*, December 18, 2001.

16. James Sevigny, interview with John Geiger, November 14, 2003.

17. James Sevigny, letter to John Geiger, December 22, 2004.

18. James Sevigny, interview with John Geiger.

19. Allan Derbyshire, letter to John Geiger, February 14, 2006.

20. *Calgary Herald*, April 1983.

21. Milbry Polk and Mary Tiegreen, *Women of Discovery* (New York: Clarkson Potter, 2001).

22. Stephanie Schwabe, letter to John Geiger, March 6, 2007.

23. The text describing this incident first appeared in John Geiger, "I Was Two People in Two Places," in Jason Schoonover, *Adventurous Lives, Adventurous Dreams* (Vancouver: Rocky Mountain Books, 2007).

24. Wilfrid Noyce, *They Survived: A Study of the Will to Live* (London: Heinemann, 1962).

25. Claude A. Piantadosi, *The Biology of Human Survival: Life and Death in Extreme Environments* (New York: Oxford University Press, 2003).

26. Rob Schultheis, *Bone Games* (New York: Breakaway Books, 1996).

27. Reinhold Messner, interview with John Geiger, January 13, 2004.

Chapter Two

1. Oliver Shepard, "Virginia Fiennes," *The Guardian*, February 24, 2004.

2. Ranulph Fiennes, *To the Ends of the Earth* (London: Hodder and Stoughton, 1983).

3. Ranulph Fiennes, interview with John Geiger, February 10, 2006.

4. Ranulph Fiennes, *To the Ends of the Earth*.

5. Weston La Barre, *The Ghost Dance: Origins of Religion* (New York: Delta, 1972).

6. G. Daniel Steel, "Polar Moods: Third-Quarter Phenomena in the Antarctic," *Environment and Behavior*, vol. 33, no.1, January 2001.

7. Lawrence A. Palinkas and Deirdre Browner, "Effects of Prolonged Isolation in Extreme Environments on Stress, Coping, and Depression," *Journal of Applied Social Psychology*, 25, 1995.

8. Peter Suedfeld and G. Daniel Steel, "The Environmental Psychology of Capsule Habitats," *Annual Review of Psychology*, 2000.

9. Jane S.P. Mocellin, "A Behavioural Study of Human Responses to the Arctic and Antarctic Environments," Ph.D. Thesis, University of British Columbia, Vancouver, 1988.

10. Jane S.P. Mocellin, "Transcriptions of Cases Related to the Third Person Phenomena," unpublished report.

11. Peter Suedfeld and Jane S.P. Mocellin, "The 'Sensed Presence' in Unusual Environments," *Environment and Behavior*, January 1987.

12. Graham Reed, *The Psychology of Anomalous Experience* (London: Hutchinson University Library, 1972).

13. Constanta Parhon-Stefanescu and Thea Procopiu-Constantinescu, "Considérations sur l'impression de présence," *Annales médico-psychologiques*, 125, 1967.

14. Weston La Barre, *The Ghost Dance: Origins of Religion*.

15. Woodburn Heron, "Cognitive and Physiological Effects of Perceptual Isolation," in *Sensory Deprivation: A Symposium Held at Harvard Medical School* (Cambridge, Mass.: Harvard University Press, 1961).

16. W. De la Mare, *Desert Islands* (London: Faber, 1947).

17. Constanta Parhon-Stefanescu and Thea Procopiu-Constantinescu, "Considérations sur l'impression de présence."

18. Leonard Zusne and Warren H. Jones, *Anomalistic Psychology* (Hillsdale, N.J.: Lawrence Erlbaum Assoc., 1989).

19. Peter Suedfeld, "The Sensed Presence Phenomenon," Keynote Address, Annual Meeting of the Society for Clinical and Experimental Hypnosis, San Antonio, Texas, October 2001.

20. Peter Suedfeld and Jane S.P. Mocellin, "The 'Sensed Presence' in Unusual Environments."

21. Leonard Tripp, memorandum for Dr. H.R. Mill, 1 March 1922; Alexander Turnbull Library, National Library of New Zealand.

22. Duncan Carse, *The Times* (London), March 16, 1956.

23. Harold Begbie, *Shackleton, A Memory* (London: Mills & Boon Ltd., 1922).

24. Robert Service, "The Call of the Wild" in: *The Spell of the Yukon and Other Verses* (New York: Barse & Co., 1916).

25. Harold Begbie, *Shackleton, A Memory.*

26. Leonard Tripp, memorandum for Dr. H.R. Mill.

27. John Keats, *Endymion: Book II*, lines 817-818:
    Let us entwine hoveringly—O dearth
    Of human words! Roughness of mortal speech!

28. Sir Ernest Shackleton, *South* (New York: Konecky & Konecky, 2001).

29. Ibid.

30. Sara Wheeler, *Terra Incognita* (New York: Random House, 1996).

31. Margery Fisher and James Fisher, *Shackleton* (London: Barrie, 1957).

32. A.J.P. Taylor, *The First World War: An Illustrated History* (London: Hamish Hamilton, 1969).

33. W.H. Salter, "An Enquiry Concerning 'The Angels at Mons,'" *Journal of the Society for Psychical Research*, December 1915.

34. Margery Fisher and James Fisher, *Shackleton.*

35. Harold Begbie, *Shackleton, A Memory.*

36. Margery Fisher and James Fisher, *Shackleton.*

37. Frank W. Boreham, *A Casket of Cameos* (London: Epworth Press, 1926).

38. Boreham was not the only one to relate Shackleton's Fourth Presence to the "form of the fourth" in Daniel. The *Church Army News* cited a poem by John Keble, an Anglican priest, professor of poetry at Oxford, and Church reformer, whose "thoughts in verse" were popular hymns at the time. Keble's version read: "Three they were— who hath made them four? And sure a form divine He wore, Even like the Son of God." See: John Keble, *The Christian Year* (1927).

39. Hugh Robert Mill, *The Life of Sir Ernest Shackleton* (London: William Heinemann Ltd., 1923).

40. Peter King, *South: The Story of Shackleton's Last Expedition 1914–17* (London: Pimlico, 1991).

41. Roland Huntford, *Shackleton* (New York: Carroll & Graf Publishers, 1998).

42. *Daily Telegraph* (London), February 1, 1922.

43. Among climbers, the phenomenon is called the "Third Man," the "third man factor," or the "third man syndrome." See Gavin Daly, "Peak Practice," *Sunday Business Post*, March 5, 2006.

44. T.S. Eliot altered the number of members in Shackleton's party from three to two, and in his "Notes on The Waste Land," the poet evoked Scripture, writing that the journey to Emmaus in the Gospel According to Luke serves as a theme in Part V of the poem, which he titled "What the Thunder said." In Luke 24:15–17, two men on the road to Emmaus encounter a presence and do not recognize it as the risen Christ:

> And, behold, two of them went that same day to a village called Emmaus, which was from Jerusalem about three score furlongs.
> And they talked together of all these things which had happened.
> And it came to pass, that, while they communed together and reasoned, Jesus himself drew near, and went with them.
> But their eyes were holden that they should not know him.

When Jesus blessed and broke bread at dinner, the disciples finally did know him, but Jesus then vanished. Eliot linked the events on the road to Emmaus with those on South Georgia. The tone of the account given in Eliot's poem is notably different, though, from Shackleton's published reference to a presence "very near to our hearts," and instead emphasizes the idea that they were "comrades with Death." Rather than inspiring a sense of the divine, one critic argues "the visitation in the poem inspires a feeling of dread."

45. Nicholas Roe, "Be Inspired by the View from the Top If You Can See Through Your Tears," *The Times*, May 14, 2003.

Chapter Three

1. Frank Smythe, *Camp Six: An Account of the 1933 Everest Expedition* (London: Hodder and Stoughton, 1937).

2. Ibid.

3. Frank Smythe, *The Adventures of a Mountaineer* (London: J.M. Dent & Sons Ltd., 1949).

4. Hugh Ruttledge, *Everest 1933* (London: Hodder and Stoughton, 1934).

5. Ibid.

6. Peter Gillman and Leni Gillman, *Everest: Eighty Years of Triumph and Tragedy* (Seattle: The Mountaineers Books, 2001).

7. Eric Shipton, *Upon That Mountain* (London: Hodder & Stoughton Ltd., 1943).

8. Wilfrid Noyce, *They Survived* (London: Heinemann, 1962).

9. Joshua Slocum, *Sailing Alone Around the World* (1900).

10. Joshua Slocum, "Spook on Spray," *Boston Globe*, October 14, 1895.

11. William Laird McKinlay, *The Last Voyage of the* Karluk (New York: St. Martin's Griffin, 1999).

12. A.F.R. Wollaston, "An Expedition to Dutch New Guinea," *Geographical Journal,* March 1914, vol. 43.

13. Nicholas Wollaston, letter to John Geiger, June 11, 2003.

14. Nicholas Wollaston, *My Father, Sandy* (London: Short Books, 2003).

15. Ibid.

16. H.G. Stoker, *Straws in the Wind* (London: Herbert Jenkins Ltd., 1925).

17. Peter King, "Who Was the Fourth Man?," *Fate*, March 1967.

18. Fred and Elizabeth Brenchley, *Stoker's Submarine* (Sydney: Harper-Collins, 2001).

19. H.G. Stoker, *Straws in the Wind*.

Chapter Four

1. Macdonald Critchley, "Idea of a Presence," *Acta Psychiatrica Neurologica*, vol. 30, 1955. Reproduced in: Critchley, *The Divine Banquet of the Brain and Other Essays* (New York: Raven Press, 1979).

2. E. Allison Peers, *The Life of Teresa of Jesus* (New York: Image Books/Doubleday, 1991).

3. Peter Suedfeld and Jane S.P. Mocellin, "The 'Sensed Presence' in Unusual Environments."

4. Aldous Huxley, "Visionary Experience," in *Moksha* (Rochester, Vermont: Park Street Press, 1999).

5. http://www.kagyu-asia.com/l_mila_life10a.html.

6. Ruth Fulton Benedict, *The Concept of the Guardian Spirit in North America* (New York: Kraus Reprint Corp., 1964).

7. Weston La Barre, *The Ghost Dance: Origins of Religion* (New York: Delta, 1972).

8. Ruth Fulton Benedict, *The Concept of the Guardian Spirit in North America*.

9. Wilfrid Noyce, *They Survived*.

10. Nathan L. Comer, Leo Madow, and James J. Dixon, "Observations of Sensory Deprivation in a Life-Threatening Situation," *American Journal of Psychiatry*, 124:2, August 1967.

11. Moon Ihlwan, "Dream Keeps Seoul Girl Alive for 16 Days," Reuters, July 15, 1995.

12. Dennis Cauchon and Martha T. Moore, "Miracles Emerge from Debris," *USA Today*, September 6, 2002. See www.usatoday.com.

13. Ruben V. Napales, "'I Actually Saw Jesus Coming Toward Me' – 9/11 Survivor," *Inquirer*, July 22, 2006.

14. Lynn Vincent, "Purpose-Driven Life," *World*, August 12, 2006. http://www.worldmag.com/articles/12122.

15. Pope John XXIII, "Meditation for the Feast of the Guardian Angels," October 2, 1959. www.catholic-forum.com.

16. The Book of Tobit, Revised Standard Version of the Bible, Old Testament Apocrypha.

17. First Part of *Summa Theologiae*, Question 111, Article 2.

18. Nancy Gibbs, Sam Allis, Nancy Harbert, and Lisa H. Towle, "Angels Among Us," *Time*, December 27, 1993.

19. Michael Murphy, *The Future of the Body* (Los Angeles: Jeremy P. Tarcher, Inc., 1992).

20. James Redfield, Michael Murphy, and Sylvia Timbers, *God and the Evolving Universe* (New York: Putnam, 2002).

21. Harold Bloom, *Omens of Millennium* (New York: Riverhead Books, 1996).

22. William James, *The Varieties of Religious Experience* (New York: Longmans, Green and Co., 1916).
23. Ibid.

Chapter Five

1. Peter Suedfeld, "Extreme and Unusual Environments," in D. Stokols, I. Altman (eds.), *Handbook of Environmental Psychology* (New York: Wiley, 1987).
2. Charles A. Lindbergh, *The Spirit of St. Louis* (New York: Charles Scribner's Sons, 1953).
3. Charles A. Lindbergh, "33 Hours to Paris," *Saturday Evening Post*, June 6, 1953.
4. Brian Horrigan, "'My Own Mind and Pen': Charles Lindbergh, Autobiography, and Memory," *Minnesota History*, Spring 2002.
5. Woodburn Heron, "The Pathology of Boredom," *Scientific American*, January 1957.
6. Peter Suedfeld and G. Daniel Steel, "The Environmental Psychology of Capsule Habitats," *Annual Review of Psychology*, vol. 51, February 2000.
7. W. Grey Walter, "The Human Brain in Space Time," in N.W. Pirie, *The Biology of Space Travel* (London: Institute of Biology, 1961).
8. Bianca C. Wittmann, Nathaniel D. Daw, Ben Seymour, and Raymond J. Dolan, "Striatal Activity Underlies Novelty-Based Choice in Humans," *Neuron*, 58, June 26, 2008, pp. 967–73.
9. John A. Sours, "The 'Break-Off' Phenomenon," *Archives of General Psychiatry*, November 13, 1965.
10. D.O. Hebb, "The American Revolution," *American Psychologist*, 15, 1960.
11. Stuart C. Miller, "Eco-Autonomy in Sensory Deprivation, Isolation, and Stress," *The International Journal of Psycho-analysis*, 43, 1962.
12. Leonard Zusne and Warren H. Jones, *Anomalistic Psychology* (Hillsdale, N.J.: Lawrence Erlbaum Associates, 1989).
13. Woodburn Heron, "The Pathology of Boredom."

14. D.O. Hebb, *Essay on Mind* (Hillsdale, N.J.: Lawrence Erlbaum Associates, 1980).

15. Mayme Evans, "I Never Flew Alone...," *Fate*, May, 1969.

16. Brian Shoemaker, interview with John Geiger, May 9, 2006.

17. Ibid.

18. Brian Shoemaker, correspondence with John Geiger, May 15, 2006.

19. Jerry M. Linenger, *Off the Planet* (New York: McGraw-Hill, 2000).

20. Woodburn Heron, "The Pathology of Boredom."

21. Jerry Linenger, *Off the Planet*.

22. Jerry Linenger, interview with John Geiger, July 19, 2005.

23. Ibid.

Chapter Six

1. Peter Hillary and John E. Elder, *In the Ghost Country* (New York: Free Press, 2003).

2. Roger Mear and Robert Swan, *In the Footsteps of Scott* (London: Jonathan Cape, 1987).

3. Robert Swan, interview with John Geiger, March 29, 2004.

4. Ibid.

5. Ibid.

6. Peter Hillary and John E. Elder, *In the Ghost Country*.

7. Ibid.

8. Peter Hillary, interview with John Geiger, October 31, 2005.

9. Liv Arnesen and Ann Bancroft with Cheryl Dahle, *No Horizon Is So Far* (Cambridge, MA.: Da Capo Press, 2003).

10. Ann Bancroft, interview with John Geiger, October 29, 2004.

11. Ann Bancroft, expedition journal entry, November 25, 2000, cited in Ann Bancroft, letter to John Geiger, November 11, 2004.

12. Ann Bancroft, interview with John Geiger, October 29, 2004.

13. Mera M. Atlis, Gloria R. Leon, Gro M. Sandal, and Michael G. Infante, "Decision Processes and Interactions During a Two-Women Traverse of Antarctica," *Environment and Behavior*, vol. 36, no. 3, May 2004.

14. E.Ll. Lloyd, "Hallucinations and Misinterpretations in Hypothermia and Cold Stress," in B. Harvald and H. Hansen (eds.) *Circumpolar 81: Proceedings of the Fifth International Symposium on Circumpolar Health*, (Oulu, Finland: Nordic Council for Arctic Medical Research, 1982).

15. Richard G. Hoffman, "Human Psychological Performance in Cold Environments," in K.B. Pandolf, R.E. Burr, C.B. Wenger, R.S. Pozos (eds.), *Medical Aspects of Harsh Environments, Vol. 1*. In: R. Zajtchuk and R.F. Bellamy (eds.), *Textbook of Military Medicine* (Washington, DC: Department of the Army, Office of the Surgeon General, and Borden Institute, 2001).

16. E. Llewelyn Lloyd, "Hallucinations in Hypothermia and Cold Stress and Their Neurochemical basis."

17. Ibid.

18. Fiona Godlee, "Walking Across Antarctica," *British Medical Journal*, vol. 307, no. 6919. December 18, 1993.

19. Mike Stroud, *Survival of the Fittest: Understanding Health and Peak Physical Performance* (London: Jonathan Cape, 1998).

20. Claude A. Piantadosi, *The Biology of Human Survival: Life and Death in Extreme Environments* (New York: Oxford University Press, 2003).

21. Fiona Godlee, "Walking across Antarctica."

22. Peter Suedfeld, "Extreme and Unusual Environments."

23. Peter Suedfeld and Jane S.P. Mocellin, "The 'Sensed Presence' in Unusual Environments."

24. Alan Parker of the Australian Antarctic Division was building field huts on the plateau of Macquarrie Island when he was caught in a whiteout during a severe storm in March 1968. It was not the cold alone, but also disorientation and helplessness, that produced a Third Man for Parker—urging him along, saying, "Don't worry, keep going."

Chapter Seven

1. David Miller, "Macdonald Critchley (1900–97)," *Journal of Medical Biography*, vol. 14, no. 3.

2. *British Medical Journal*, 316, February 7, 1998.

3. Macdonald Critchley, "Idea of a Presence," *Acta Psychiatrica Neurologica*, vol. 30, 1955. Reproduced in Critchley, *The Divine Banquet of the Brain and Other Essays* (New York: Raven Press, 1979).

4. Ibid.

5. Francis T. McAndrew, *Environmental Psychology* (Pacific Grove, Calif.: Brooks/Cole Publishing, 1993).

6. Macdonald Critchley, "Idea of a Presence."

7. Ibid.

8. Karl Jaspers, *General Psychopathology* (Chicago: University of Chicago Press, 1968).

9. Karl Koehler and Heinrich Sauer, "Jaspers' Sense of Presence in the Light of Huber's Basic Symptoms and DSM-III," *Comprehensive Psychiatry*, vol. 25, no. 2, March/April 1984.

10. Constanta Parhon-Stefanescu and Thea Procopiu-Constantinescu, "Considérations sur l'impression de presence."

11. Macdonald Critchley, "Idea of a Presence."

Chapter Eight

1. Hermann Buhl, *Nanga Parbat Pilgrimage: The Lonely Challenge* (London: Baton Wicks, 1998).

2. Ibid.

3. Karl M. Herrligkoffer, *Nanga Parbat* (London: Elek Books, 1954).

4. Hermann Buhl, *Nanga Parbat Pilgrimage: The Lonely Challenge* (London: Baton Wicks, 1998).

5. Karl M. Herrligkoffer, *Nanga Parbat*.

6. Herbert Tichy, *Cho Oyu: By Favour of the Gods* (London: Methuen, 1957).

7. Michael Hellier, "Mountain Ghosts," *San Francisco Chronicle*, January 18, 1971. See also: Curtis Fuller, "I See by the Papers," *Fate*, vol. 24, no. 8, August 1971.

8. Michael Hellier, "Mountain Ghosts."

9. Donald Heath and David Reid Williams, *Man at High Altitude* (Edinburgh: Churchill Livingstone, 1981).

10. Charles S. Houston, *Going High: The Story of Man and Altitude* (New York: The American Alpine Club, 1980).

11. Ibid.

12. Donald Heath and David Reid Williams, *Man at High Altitude*.

13. Ruth Seifert and Charles Clarke, "The Third Man" *World Medicine*, No. 15, December 1, 1979.

14. Peter Suedfeld and Jane S.P. Mocellin, "The "Sensed Presence" in Unusual Environments."

15. Greg Child, "The Other Presence," in Greg Child, *Mixed Emotions* (Seattle: The Mountaineers, 1993).

16. Macdonald Critchley, "Idea of a Presence."

17. M. Svendsen, "Children's Imaginary Companions," *Archives of Neurology and Psychiatry*, 32, 1934.

18. Julian Jaynes, "Verbal Hallucinations and Pre-Conscious Mentality," in Manfred Spitzer and Brendan A. Maher (eds.), *Philosophy and Psychopathology* (New York: Springer-Verlag, 1990).

19. D. Pearson, H. Rouse, S. Doswell, C. Ainsworth, O. Dawson, K. Simms, L. Edwards, and J. Faulconbridge, "Prevalence of Imaginary Companions in a Normal Child Population," *Child: Care, Health and Development*, 27, 2001.

20. Julian Jaynes, "Consciousness and the Voice of the Mind," *Canadian Psychology*, April 1986.

21. Inge Seiffge-Krenke, "Imaginary Companions in Adolescence: Sign of a Deficient or Positive Development," *Journal of Adolescence*, 20, 1997.

22. Hilary Evans, *Visions, Apparitions, Alien Visitors* (Wellingborough, Northamptonshire: Aquarian Press, 1984).

23. Eduardo Garrido, Casimiro Javierre, Josep L. Ventura, Ramón Segura, "Hallucinatory Experiences at High Altitude," *Neuropsychiatry, Neuropsychology, and Behavioral Neurology*, vol. 13, no. 2, 2000.

24. Ralph Barker, *The Last Blue Mountain* (London: Chatto & Windus, 1959). Available at **www.rippingyarns.com**

25. Ibid.

26. Ibid.

27. Wilfrid Noyce, *They Survived*.

28. Tony Streather, interview with John Geiger, January 31, 2004.

29. Ibid.

30. Ibid.

31. Wilfrid Noyce, *They Survived*.

32. Tony Streather, interview with John Geiger, January 31, 2004.

33. Tony Streather, correspondence with John Geiger, January 21, 2005.

34. Reinhold Messner, *The Naked Mountain* (Seattle: The Mountaineers Books, 2003).

35. Reinhold Messner, interview with John Geiger, January 13, 2004.

36. Reinhold Messner, *The Naked Mountain*.

37. Ibid.

38. Ibid

39. Reinhold Messner, interview with John Geiger, January 13, 2004.

40. Ibid.

41. Parash Moni Das, *Storms and Sunsets in the Himalaya: A Compilation of Vignettes from the Experiences of a Mountaineer* (Jalandhar City: Lotus Publishers, 2000).

42. Ibid.

43. P.M. Das, "Mountains and Mysticism," *Indian Mountaineer*, 1999–2000, http://www.123himachal.com/eco/26.htm.

44. P.M. Das, *Storms and Sunsets in the Himalaya*.

45. P.M. Das, correspondence with John Geiger, August 22, 2005.

46. Greg Child, *Thin Air* (Salt Lake City: Peregrine Smith Books, 1988).

47. Greg Child, "On Broad Peak," in Greg Child, *Mixed Emotions* (Seattle: The Mountaineers, 1993).

48. Greg Child, "The Other Presence," in Greg Child, *Mixed Emotions*.

49. Greg Child, correspondence with John Geiger, September 28, 2005.

50. Sherry Simon-Buller, Victor A. Christopherson, and Randall A. Jones, "Correlates of Sense the Presence of a Deceased Spouse," *Omega*, vol. 19, no. 1, 1988–89.

51. Gillian Bennett and Kate Mary Bennett, "The Presence of the Dead: An Empirical Study," *Mortality*, vol. 5, no. 2, 2000.

52. W. Dewi Rees, "The Hallucinations of Widowhood," *British Medical Journal*, October 2, 1971.

53. Joe Yamamoto, Keigo Okonogi, Tetsuya Iwasaki, and Saburo Yoshimura, "Mourning in Japan," *American Journal of Psychiatry*, 125, June 12, 1969.

54. M. O'Mahony, K. Shulman, and D. Silver, "Roses in December: Imaginary Companions in the Elderly," *Canadian Journal of Psychiatry*, 29, March 1984.

55. Ibid.

56. Constanta Parhon-Stefanescu and Thea Procopiu-Constantinescu, "Considérations sur l'impression de présence."

57. A. Grimby, "Bereavement among Elderly People: Grief Reactions, Post-Bereavement Hallucinations and Quality of Life', *Acta Ppsychiatr Scand*, 87, 1993.

58. Gillian Bennett and Kate Mary Bennett, "The Presence of the Dead: An Empirical Study."

59. Marshall McLuhan, the communications guru, is among the better-known dead to make their presence felt. McLuhan's widow, Corinne, said after her husband's death she continued to encounter him "big as life" in their rambling Toronto home. "She seemed to view Marshall as a guardian spirit." (Philip Marchand, correspondence with Gerald Owen, July 3, 2008.)

60. A. Grimby, "Bereavement among Elderly People."

61. Maurice Herzog, *Annapurna: Conquest of the First 8000-Metre Peak* (London: Jonathan Cape, 1952).

62. Reinhold Messner, interview with John Geiger, January 13, 2004.

Chapter Nine

1. Julian Jaynes, "Hearing Voices and the Bicameral Mind," *Behavioral and Brain Sciences*, vol. 9, no. 3, 1986.

2. Julian Jaynes, "Consciousness and the Voice of the Mind."

3. Benson Hai, G. Ong, and Ib Odderson, "Involuntary Masturbation as a Manifestation of Stroke-Related Alien Hand Syndrome," *American Journal of Physical Medicine and Rehabilitation*, vol. 79, no. 4, 2000.

4. Mike Holderness, "In Two Minds about Consciousness," *New Scientist*, July 17, 1993.

5. Julian Jaynes, *The Origin of Consciousness in the Breakdown of the Bicameral Mind* (Boston: Houghton Mifflin, 1982).

6. Julian Jaynes, "Verbal Hallucinations and Pre-Conscious Mentality."

7. Amos 7:14–15

8. Julian Jaynes, "Hearing Voices and the Bicameral Mind."

9. J. Hamilton, "Auditory Hallucinations in Nonverbal Quadriplegics," *Psychiatry*, 48, November 1985.

10. Julian Jaynes, *The Origin of Consciousness in the Breakdown of the Bicameral Mind*.

11. Julian Jaynes, "Hearing Voices and the Bicameral Mind."

12. Terry R. Barrett and Jane B. Etheridge, "Verbal Hallucinations in Normals, I: People Who Hear 'Voices,'" *Applied Cognitive Psychology*, vol. 6, no. 5, 1992.

13. Julian Jaynes, "Verbal Hallucinations and Pre-Conscious Mentality."

14. Douglas S. Holmes and Louis W. Tinnin, "The Problem of Auditory Hallucinations in Combat PTSD," *Traumatology*, vol. 1, no. 1, 1995.

15. Fred Rebell, *Escape the Sea* (London: The Travel Book Club, 1952).

16. Joe Simpson, *Touching the Void* (London: Jonathan Cape, 1988).

17. Peter Suedfeld and John Geiger, "The Sensed Presence as a Coping Resource in Extreme Environments," in J. Harold Ellens (ed.) *Miracles: God, Science, and Psychology in the Paranormal*, Vol. III (Westport, Conn.: Praeger, 2008).

18. *Psychobabble*, no. 147, March 2001.

19. Peter Suedfeld, "Extreme and Unusual Environments."

20. Peter Suedfeld and John Geiger, "The Sensed Presence as a Coping Resource in Extreme Environments."

21. Peter Suedfeld and Jane S.P. Mocellin, "The 'Sensed Presence' in Unusual Environments."

22. Ibid.

23. Peter Suedfeld, correspondence with John Geiger, May 28, 2007.

24. Peter Suedfeld and John Geiger, "The Sensed Presence as a Coping Resource in Extreme Environments."

25. Peter Suedfeld, "Extreme and Unusual Environments."

26. Peter Suedfeld and Jane S.P. Mocellin, "The 'Sensed Presence' in Unusual Environments."

27. Ibid.

28. Peter Suedfeld and John Geiger, "The Sensed Presence as a Coping Resource in Extreme Environments."

29. Peter Suedfeld, "Extreme and Unusual Environments."

30. Peter Suedfeld, correspondence with John Geiger, May 29, 2007.

31. J.N. Booth, S.A. Koren, and M.A. Persinger, "Increased Feelings of the Sensed Presence and Increased Geomagnetic Activity at the Time of the Experience During Exposures to Transcerebral Weak Complex Magnetic Fields," *International Journal of Neuroscience*, 115, 2005.

32. Walter Randall and Steffani Randall, "The Solar Wind and Hallucinations—A Possible Relation Due to Magnetic Disturbances," *Bioelectromagnetics*, 12, 1991.

33. M.A. Persinger and Katherine Makarec, "The Feeling of a Presence and Verbal Meaningfulness in Context of Temporal Lobe Function: Factor Analytic Verification of the Muses?" *Brain and Cognition*, 20, 1992.

34. L.S. St.-Pierre and M.A. Persinger, "Experimental Facilitation of the Sensed Presence Is Predicted by the Specific Patterns of the Applied Magnetic Fields, Not by Suggestibility: Re-Analyses of 19 Experiments," *International Journal of Neuroscience*, 116, 2006.

35. J.N. Booth, S.A. Koren, and M.A. Persinger, "Increased Feelings of the Sensed Presence …"

36. Jack Hitt, "This Is Your Brain on God," *Wired*, November 1999.

37. C.M. Cook and M.A. Persinger, "Experimental Induction of the

'Sensed Presence' in Normal Subjects and an Exceptional Subject," *Perceptional and Motor Skills*, 85, 1997.

38. L.S. St.-Pierre and M.A. Persinger, "Experimental Facilitation of the Sensed Presence."

39. Raj Persuad, "Holy Visions Elude Scientists," *Daily Telegraph*, March 20, 2003.

40. Pehr Granqvist, Mats Fredrikson, Patrik Unge, Andrea Hagenfeld, Sven Valind, Dan Larhammar, Marcus Larsson, "Sensed Presence and Mystical Experiences Are Predicted by Suggestibility, Not by the Application of Transcranial Weak Complex Magnetic Fields," *Neuroscience Letters*, 379, 2005.

41. Michael Persinger, "The Granqvist Group and Politics of the Sensed Presence, the Importance of Frequent InterLaboratory Communication," January 31, 2005, www.laurentian.ca.

42. John Horgan, *Rational Mysticism: Dispatches from the Border Between Science and Spirituality* (Boston: Houghton Mifflin, 2003).

43. "God and the Gap," *The Economist*, December 16, 2004.

44. Peter Suedfeld and Jane S.P. Mocellin, "The 'Sensed Presence' in Unusual Environments."

Chapter Ten

1. E.R. Dodds, *The Greeks and the Irrational* (Berkeley: University of California Press, 1971).

2. Shahar Arzy, Moshe Idel, Theodor Landis, Olaf Blanke, "Why Revelations Have Occurred on Mountains? Linking Mystical Experiences and Cognitive Neuroscience," *Medical Hypotheses*, 65, 2005.

3. Joe Simpson, *Storms of Silence* (Seattle: Mountaineers, 1996).

4. Shahar Arzy, Moshe Idel, Theodor Landis, Olaf Blanke, "Why Revelations Have Occurred on Mountains?"

5. Rob Taylor, *The Breach: Kilimanjaro and the Conquest of Self* (New York: Coward, McCann & Geoghegan, 1981).

6. Rob Taylor, interview with John Geiger, September 16, 2005.

7. Rob Taylor, *The Breach: Kilimanjaro and the Conquest of Self.*

8. Jim Wickwire, diary entry, 10:50 A.M., May 15, 1981. Courtesy Jim Wickwire. See also: Greg Child, "The Other Presence," *Backpacker*, January 1989.

9. Jim Wickwire and Dorthy Bullitt, *Addicted to Danger* (New York: Pocket Books, 1998).

10. Jim Wickwire, interview with John Geiger, August 15, 2005.

11. Walter Welsch, "Eine Besteigung des Fuji-san," *Der Bayerländer*, Mitteilungen der Sektion Bayerland des Deutschen Alpenvereins, 71. Heft, S. 54–56, Munich, 1985.

12. Walter Welsch, correspondence with John Geiger, September 29, 2005.

13. Paul Firth, correspondence with John Geiger, November 28, 2004.

14. Paul G. Firth and Hayrunnisa Bolay, "Transient High Altitude Neurological Dysfunction: An Origin in the Temporoparietal Cortex," *High Altitude Medicine & Biology*, vol. 5, no. 1, 2004.

15. Paul Firth, interview with John Geiger, November 24, 2005.

16. Paul Firth, "The Man Who Wasn't There," *The Guardian*, May 29, 2003.

17. Paul Firth, correspondence with John Geiger, November 29, 2004.

18. Paul Firth, interview with John Geiger, November 24, 2005.

19. http://www.sparknotes.com/psychology/abnormal/personality/terms.html.

20. R.R McCrae and P.T. Costa, "Conceptions and Correlates of Openness to Experience," in R. Hogan, J. Johnson, and S. Briggs (eds.), *Handbook of Personality Psychology* (Boston: Academic Press, 1997).

21. Corina Sas and Gregory O'Hare, "The Presence Equation: An Investigation into Cognitive Factors Underlying Presence," http://astro.temple.edu/~lombard/P2001/Sas.pdf.

22. Marianne Barabasz, Arreed F. Barabasz, and Charles S. Mullin, "Effects of Brief Antarctic Isolation on Absorption and Hypnotic Susceptibility—Preliminary Results and Recommendations: A Brief Communication," *International Journal of Clinical and Experimental Hypnosis*, vol. XXXI, no. 4, 1983.

23. M.A. Persinger and Katherine Makarec, "The Feeling of a Presence and Verbal Meaningfulness in Context of Temporal Lobe Function: Factor Analytic Verification of the Muses?" *Brain and Cognition*, 20, 1992.

24. Shahar Arzy, Moshe Idel, Theodor Landis, Olaf Blanke, "Why Revelations Have Occurred on Mountains?"

Chapter Eleven

1. Macdonald Critchley, *Shipwreck-Survivors: A Medical Study* (London: J.&A. Churchill, 1943).

2. E.C.B. Lee and Kenneth Lee, *Safety and Survival at Sea* (New York: W.W. Norton, 1980).

3. Macdonald Critchley, *Shipwreck-Survivors*.

4. Ibid.

5. E.C.B. Lee and Kenneth Lee, *Safety and Survival at Sea*.

6. Ruth Seifert and Charles Clarke, "The Third Man."

7. Kenneth Cooke, *What Cares the Sea?* (London: Hutchinson, 1960).

8. Ibid.

9. Ibid.

10. Adrian Hayter, *Sheila In The Wind*, (London: The Companion Book Club, 1959).

11. Ibid.

12. Rebecca Hayter, letter to John Geiger, Nov. 9, 2008.

13. Ensio Tiira, *Raft of Despair* (London: Hutchinson, 1954).

14. Ibid.

15. William Willis, *The Epic Voyage of the "Seven Little Sisters"* (London: Hutchinson, 1956).

16. Willis is one of a succession of people who set out to test the problem of survival at sea. Two years later, Hannes Lindemann, a German doctor, made a solo trans-Atlantic journey from the Canary Islands port of Las Palmas, in a five-metre folding boat. Lindemann was convinced that self-mastery, through prayer and concentration, would provide the key to survival at sea. Instead, one month into his journey, he found himself speaking to an unseen companion in the

form of a black youth. See Hannes Lindemann, *Alone at Sea* (New York: Random House, 1958). Another case involved Dr. David Lewis, who saw the 1960 Single-Handed Transatlantic Sailing Race, five thousand kilometers from Plymouth to New York, as an opportunity for medical research. As Lewis' 7.6-metre sloop, *Cardinal Vertue*, approached the Grand Banks, southeast of Newfoundland, in impenetrable fog, he too found that he was experiencing the "feeling that I am not alone." He had previously had the distinct feeling that "another person was at the helm." See David Lewis, *The Ship Would Not Travel Due West* (London: Temple Press, 1961).

17. Douglas Robertson, interview with John Geiger, January 28, 2004.

18. Ibid.

19. Dougal Robertson, *Survive the Savage Sea* (London: Elek, 1973). See also Douglas Robertson, *The Last Voyage of the* Lucette (Rendlesham, Suffolk: Seafarer Books, 2005).

20. William King, letter to John Geiger, October 28, 2004.

21. William King, letter to John Geiger, October 4, 2004.

22. William King, *Adventure in Depth* (New York: G.P. Putnam's Sons, 1975).

23. Ibid.

24. William King, letter to John Geiger, October 4, 2004.

25. Angus Matheson MacKinnon, *Atlantic Challenge* (Sydney, N.S.: Catalone Press, 1995).

28. Andrew Prossin, interview with John Geiger, May 4, 2006.

29. Ibid.

30. L. Lusne and W. Jones, *Anomalistic Psychology: A Study of Thirdordinary Phenomena of Behaviour and Experience* (New Jersey: Lawrench Erlbaum Associates, 1982).

31. Macdonald Critchley, *Shipwreck-Survivors*.

Chapter Twelve

1. Peter Brugger, Marianne Regard, and Theodor Landis, "Unilaterally Felt 'Presences': The Neuropsychiatry of One's Invisible

Doppelgänger," *Neuropsychiatry, Neuropsychology, and Behavioral Neurology*, vol. 9, no. 2.

2. Peter Brugger, "Phantomology: The Science of the Body in the Brain," www.artbrain.org/phantomlimb/brugger.html.

3. Jerzy Kukuczka, *My Vertical World* (Seattle: The Mountaineers, 1992).

4. Reinhold Messner, *The Crystal Horizon* (Marlborough: The Crowood Press, 1989).

5. Peter Brugger, "Phantomology…."

6. Steve Swenson, interview with John Geiger, October 10, 2005.

7. Michael Groom, *Sheer Will* (Sydney: Random House, 1997).

8. Nicholas Wollaston, *My Father, Sandy*.

9. Henry Bouiller, *Victor Ségalen* (Paris: Mercure de France, 1986).

10. Henry Bouiller (ed.), *Victor Ségalen: Oeuvres Complètes, Vol. 2 (Équipée)*, (Paris: Editions Robert Laffont, 1995).

11. Peter Brugger, Marianne Regard, and Theodor Landis, "Unilaterally Felt 'Presences.'"

12. J.A. Cheyne, "The Ominous Numinous: Sensed Presence and 'Other' Hallucinations," *Journal of Consciousness Studies*, vol. 8, no. 5–7, 2001

13. Ibid.

14. J. Allan Cheyne & Todd A. Girard, "Paranoid Delusions and Threatening Hallucinations: A Prospective Study of Sleep Paralysis Experiences," *Consciousness and Cognition*, vol. 16, 2007.

15. J. Allan Cheyne and Todd A. Girard, "The Nature and Varieties of Felt Presence Experiences: A Reply to Nielsen," *Consciousness and Cognition*, Vol. 16, 2007.

16. Justin L. Barrett, *Why Would Anyone Believe in God?* (Winter Creek, CA: AltaMira Press, 2004).

17. Tore Nielsen, "Felt Presence: Paranoid Delusion or Hallucinatory Social Imagery?" *Consciousness and Cognition*, vol. 16, 2007.

18. Ibid.

19. Ibid.

20. Sandra Blakeslee, "Out-of-Body Experience? Your Brain Is to Blame," *The New York Times*, October 3, 2006.

21. Shahar Arzy, Margitta Seek, Stephanie Ortigue, Laurent Spinelli, Olaf Blanke, "Induction of an Illusory Shadow Person," *Nature*, 443, September 21, 2006.

22. Ibid.

23. Ibid. Supplementary information, www.nature.com.

24. Anon. "A Mystical Union: Spiritual Neurology," *The Economist*, March 6, 2004.

25. Anne-Marie Landtblom, "The 'Sensed Presence': An Epileptic Aura with Religious Overtones," *Epilepsy & Behavior*, 9, 2006.

26. Paul Firth, "The Man Who Wasn't There."

27. Paul G. Firth and Hayrunnisa Bolay, "Transient High Altitude Neurological Dysfunction: An Origin in the Temporoparietal Cortex," *High Altitude Medicine & Biology*, vol. 5, no.1, 2004.

28. Olaf Blanke, "Out of Body Experiences and Their Neural Basis," *British Medical Journal*, 329, December 18, 2004.

29. Michael Hopkin, "Brain Electrodes Conjure Up Ghostly Visions," news@nature.com, September 20, 2006.

30. Ibid.

31. Olaf Blanke, correspondence with John Geiger, February 7, 2007.

32. Dennis Chan and Martin N. Rossor, "—But Who Is That on the Other Side of You? Extracampine Hallucinations Revisited," *The Lancet*, December 21, 2002.

Chapter Thirteen

1. Michael Murphy and Rhea A. White, *The Psychic Side of Sports* (Reading, Mass.: Addison-Wesley, 1978).

2. Greg Child, "The Other Presence," in Greg Child, *Mixed Emotions* (Seattle: The Mountaineers, 1993).

3. Stephen Venables, *Everest: Kangshung Face* (London: Hodder and Stoughton, 1989).

4. Stephen Venables, correspondence with John Geiger, December 22, 2005.

5. Kurt Diemberger, *The Endless Knot: K2, Mountain of Dreams and Destiny* (London: Grafton Books, 1991).

6. Reinhold Messner, interview with John Geiger, January 13, 2004.

7. Peter Hillary, interview with John Geiger, October 31, 2005.

8. Greg Child, correspondence with John Geiger, September 28, 2005.

9. Hilary Evans, *Visions, Apparitions, Alien Visitors* (Wellingborough, Northamptonshire: The Aquarian Press, 1984).

10. E.W. Anderson, "Abnormal Mental States in Survivors, with Special Reference to Collective Hallucinations," *Journal of the Royal Navy Medical Service*, No. 28, 1942.

11. Nicholas O'Connell, *Beyond Risk: Conversations with Climbers* (Seattle: The Mountaineers, 1993).

12. Lou Whittaker and Andrea Gabbard, *Lou Whittaker: Memoirs of a Mountain Guide* (Seattle: The Mountaineers, 1996).

13. Macdonald Critchley, *Shipwreck-Survivors*.

14. Nancy Lofholm, "Hiker Who Amputated His Own Arm Relives Ordeal," *Denver Post*, May 9, 2003. See also Aron Ralston, *Between a Rock and a Hard Place* (New York: Atria Books, 2004).

15. Airey Neave, *They Have Their Exits* (London: Hodder and Stoughton, 1953).

16. Avi Ohry, "The Idea of Presence, Etc.," unpublished article. See also: A. Ohry, "Extracampine hallucinations," *The Lancet*, vol. 361, no. 9367, 2003.

17. Avi Ohry, correspondence with John Geiger, January 2, 2004.

18. Jane Mocellin, correspondence with John Geiger, July 21, 2008. See also: Jane S.P. Mocellin, "Reintegrating Demobilized Militia and Former Combatants into Society: Lessons Learned from Somalia." In Mari Fitsduff and C. Stout, eds., *The Psychology of Resolving Global Conflicts: From War to Peace*, (Volume 3, Interventions) (West Port: Praeger Security International, 2006).

19. Peter Suedfeld, "Homo Invictus: The Indomitable Species," *Canadian Psychology*, vol. 35, no. 3, 1997.

20. Dennis Roberts, *I'll Climb Mount Everest Alone: The Story of Maurice Wilson* (London: Robert Hale, 1957).

21. Peter Suedfeld and Tara Weiszbeck, "The Impact of Outer Space on Inner Space," *Aviation, Space, and Environmental Medicine*, 75, July 2004.

22. Nick Kanas and Jennifer Ritsher, "Psychosocial Issues During a Mars Mission," 1st Space Exploration Conference; Continuing the Voyage of Discovery, January 30–February 1, 2005, Orlando, Florida.

23. Christine Gee, Garry Weare, and Margaret Gee (eds.), *Everest: Reflections from the Top* (London: Rider, 2003). During the 1975 ascent of Everest by a British team led by Sir Chris Bonington, the expedition's medical officer, Charles Clarke, reported that after a bivouac at high elevation two team members, Doug Scott and Dougal Haston, "told of a curious sensation that a third person had been sharing the snow hole during the night." (Charles Clarke, "On Surviving a Bivouac at High Altitude," *British Medical Journal*, January 10, 1976. See also Ruth Seifert and Charles Clarke, "The Third Man," *World Medicine*, December 1, 1979.) On the way down from the summit, Scott said he "also felt this presence, same sort of thing—replied to it—it to me. Seemed quite rational then … a bit queer now!" (C.J. Williamson, "The Everest Message," *Journal of the Society of Psychical Research*, No. 48, September 1976.) Scott told me that his experience with the Third Man had "been helpful, and given me confidence and advice … and at the time it never seemed out of place, it was not at all odd." (Doug Scott, interview with John Geiger, March 9, 2004.) Another expedition member, Nick Estcourt, had a sustained perception of a presence, reporting to Bonington he had been "followed by the appearance of a man." He said it was "definitely a human figure with arms and legs." C. Bonington, *Everest the Hard Way* (New York: Random House, 1976).

24. Wilfrid Noyce, *They Survived*.

25. Paul Firth, "The Man Who Wasn't There."

INDEX